TALES OF THE CRAZY

WHY MY EX EMBALMED HER UTERUS

TALES OF THE CRAZY

WHY MY EX EMBALMED HER UTERUS

An Unsuspecting Man's Journey of Marriage, Opioids, and Betrayal

Charles L. Cole

Copyright © 2017 by **Cole Media Productions LLC**
Authored by Charles L. Cole

All rights reserved. No part of this publication may be reproduced, transmitted, or stored in any form without permission in writing from Cole Media Productions LLC, except by a reviewer who wishes to quote brief passages in a review for inclusion in a magazine, newspaper, website, social media site, or broadcast.

To book the author to your live event or interview, contact Cole Media Productions LLC at media@ccole.org.

This book reflects the opinions of the author and does not represent all written events with complete accuracy. People's memories of the events described in this book may be different than the author's. This is the author's story and this book is not intended to harm or malign anyone. Some names, identities, locations, places, and physical descriptions of people have been changed to protect their privacy.

ISBN: 0999566709
ISBN: 9780999566701
Library of Congress Control Number: 2017917180
Cole Media Productions LLC, Ypsilanti, MI

CONTENTS

	Foreword by Herbert Cole, Charles's Father	vii
	Acknowledgments	ix
One	The Meet and Marriage	1
Two	Job Woes	15
Three	Fertility Problems and Debt	25
Four	The Pacific Ocean Is a Good Mother-in-Law Barrier	34
Five	Prescription Opioids Are Evil	45
Six	End of the Store	59
Seven	Spiritual Warfare	77
Eight	More Trouble Is Brewing	84
Nine	It Hits the Fan	95
Ten	From Bad to Worse	112
Eleven	Gathering Evidence and My Defense	127
Twelve	Phase Two of My Defense	149
Thirteen	Time to Eject	165
Fourteen	Lies and More Lies	184
Fifteen	She's Removed from the House!	216
Sixteen	The Embalmed Uterus	227
Seventeen	Finalizing the Divorce	244
Eighteen	The Problem with Modern Divorces	265
Nineteen	Tips for Single Men and Women Run Away from the Crazy	272
Twenty	What Attracts Us to the Opposite Sex	277
Twenty-One	Protecting Your Assets from a Business	284
Twenty-Two	Conclusion	287

FOREWORD BY HERBERT COLE, CHARLES'S FATHER

My son, a reflection of goodness:
You and your mother are people who give. You chose to stay away from people who were trouble. You stayed away from the high school burnouts. You never placed on me financial burdens or legal expenses. You paid your own way through college.

You handled with perfection the death of your mother and your spousal problems.

I am blessed to have a son who is a reflection of his mother's character.

I walked my son's bride down the aisle. I cried a little when we got to the altar and thought, *I lost my hunting partner*. Never thought that disaster was coming or that my son and I would come back together to overcome these issues.

I was in the courtroom and saw my son enter in handcuffs and leg shackles. He could only take short steps. He looked at me as he was led into the courtroom. The expression on his face was like a picture of Jesus being led to his crucifixion. His expression told me this was an injustice. I thought, *What did his wife say to the cops? How could this happen?* A year earlier, she'd said, "I love him so much. I can't imagine living without Chuck."

ACKNOWLEDGMENTS

My mother, Margaret Cole. She was the most caring and loving person I have ever known. I was truly blessed to have been raised by such a great woman of incredible character and great faith in God.

My father, Herbert Cole, and sister, Jane Cole, for their constant love and support throughout my ordeal.

The men of my theologizing group, which meets every Monday evening. This group of great men of caring and faith gave me endless counsel and was there when I needed to vent. Some of the regulars are Sean Egmon, Steve Hoover, Dan Meyer, Alan Morgan, Pastor Byron Schindel, Rick Wilson, Ryan Dorsey, Brian Holloway, and Phil Husak (our token Catholic, whom we jokingly refer to as the Vatican's representative).

I do wish to beg this group for forgiveness though: I subjected them to Laphroaig Quarter Cask scotch, and their howls of disgust and protest still ring in my ears. (But Sean needed it to shock him out of his severe Crown Royal affliction.)

Pastor Frank Pies and Pastor Christopher Thoma of Our Savior Evangelical Lutheran Church. Pastor Pies confirmed me when I was a teenager and gave the memorial sermon for my mother, Margaret Cole. Pastor Thoma gave my mother the last rites in the hospital. He also published three volumes of his book, *The Angels' Portion: A Clergyman's Whisky Narrative*.

Rick Darragh, an elder at St. Luke Lutheran Church. We met for meals many times to talk about my situation and how to handle the emotional trauma.

Don and Cathy Kersten and Esther McDonnell. They regularly sat next to me at church and always lent a sympathetic ear.

Christopher Bailey, a close and dear friend of mine. We have known each other for more than forty-six years and talked about my ordeal numerous times.

Alan Morgan, a close friend who helped me too many times to count. We used to meet every month at the Corner Brewery in Ypsilanti, Michigan, for beer release party, but that stopped when he went gluten free. I need to find a way to convince him that gluten in beer is a wonderful ingredient that he *must* ingest. Don Day should help me with this and get Alan back on track.

Steve and Katrina. Their willingness to do whatever it took to clear my name once they realized the betrayal we all had experienced was invaluable.

Michael Vincent, my criminal defense attorney. His pit bull–like tenacity and refusal to let an innocent man get convicted by a flawed legal system resulted in the dismissal of all my bogus criminal charges.

Ray Waldo, my divorce attorney. Without his wisdom and expertise in handling difficult cases, my situation would have turned out much worse.

Many more friends, aunts, uncles, cousins, and neighbors came to my aid. I'm an incredibly blessed man to have so many caring people in my life who supported me and knew I was not capable of all the horrific false accusations brought against me.

Loly Aristizabal is the cover model. Her contact e-mail for modeling projects is lolymen12@hotmail.com. Her husband will review all modeling requests and accompany her at photo shoots to weed out the cyber leg-humpers and ensure everything is legit.

The cover photo is courtesy of Crisandra Welch Photography. Her contact information for photography projects is crisandraphotography@gmail.com or crisandrawelch.zenfolio.com.

ONE

THE MEET AND MARRIAGE

I still remember the day I met Jess. (This is not her real name, which I'm hiding to protect her identity.) Seven months earlier, my six-month relationship with a woman named Lucette had ended very badly. I'd known Lucette a very long time, and our relationship was one of the few times I've ever gotten out of the friend zone with a beautiful woman. Unfortunately, during our time together, I found out she was cheating on me and lying about a great many things in her life. She was even manipulating facts and portraying another friend of mine, Cynthia, as psychologically disturbed—all so Lucette could cover up her own actions and claim anything Cynthia said about what was really going on was false. This really hurt Cynthia, and later, she and I had a few long talks about the damage Lucette had done to all the people around us.

I had bought Lucette an engagement ring before I learned the truth about everything. I showed it to her before I found out she was cheating, but she would not say anything. I loved her, and that breakup hurt me to my core. What also hurt was that some of my friends had known what Lucette was doing, but they'd said nothing. I felt an incredible sense of betrayal toward them. They justified not telling me by claiming they didn't want to stick their noses into other people's business. That was nothing but a cheap excuse—they simply didn't have the strength of character to get over being uncomfortable to help a friend. I stopped seeing those so-called friends who stood silent while this mess was going on. This experience reminded me of a saying that evil triumphs when good people do nothing.

I knew Lucette from St. Paul Lutheran Church in Ypsilanti, Michigan. At that time I'd been a member there for ten years. After Lucette, I didn't date much. I met some women and had a couple of casual dates, but nothing clicked. Not much was happening for me in the dating world either in or out of church.

I announced to my friends at church that I was making a radical change in my life and was leaving St. Paul for a while. At thirty-seven years old, I could not go on doing the same things that had resulted in not finding a woman I could love and spend my life with. There wasn't a faith crisis; I was feeling incomplete. I was happy and had plenty of friends and lots of support, but I wanted more.

I bounced around for a while, dated a bit, and went to different churches, but I didn't meet anyone with whom I felt a deep connection. One day I went to First Presbyterian Church after learning they had a very active singles ministry. That was the absolute worst day to go there. They were having a divorce-recovery workshop for women, and the place was full of spiteful and angry women. I left thinking I would not go there again.

A few months later, I went to the early Sunday service at a church up the road from me. As soon as I walked in, I had a strange feeling come over me and had to get out of there. It was bizarre to have this feeling in a Christian church, and I couldn't explain it. I thought that if I left now, I could make it to the service at First Presbyterian, so I hit the road.

I got there about ten minutes before the service, chatted a bit with a few people, and saw a couple of women surrounded by men. One of them, a very attractive Asian woman, was surrounded by a larger bunch of men. I went to a seat and was still standing while I talked with a guy in front of me, waiting for the service to start. I looked around a bit and then looked back, and there she was.

She was standing alone right behind me—the Asian woman. I said hi and couldn't help noticing how incredibly beautiful she was. She was tall, about five-foot eight, voluptuous, and she wore a snug but modest dress that showed every curve. I still remember the DKNY logo across her chest. I thought, *Look at her eyes; don't look down.* She introduced herself as Jess. The pupils of her eyes were green and absolutely stunning. Her hair was light brown and curly.

We chatted a bit, and then the service started with Jess still sitting behind me. I looked back a couple of times; she smiled, and I saw one empty seat next to her. I started to get up to move back and sit next to her, and then some old woman took the seat. Damn. That had always been my fault: losing opportunities with women by not acting fast enough.

After the service ended, we talked, and I found out that Jess was new to the area after moving from Chiang Mai, Thailand, and didn't know too many people here. She was staying with her stepdad's friend, John, in Livonia, Michigan, until she got a place of her own. I had to come up with a good activity she would like to do, so I told her that I usually had a party during spring at my house and that she was welcome to come and meet some people. I'd done this the last few years with friends, so this was not some pickup line I used on her. I gave her my name, phone number, and e-mail address. We both left, and I realized I hadn't asked for her number. What an idiot I was. I have to admit I was blown away by her smile and just went stupid. It was not the first time I had gone stupid in front of a woman.

The next day at work, I got an e-mail from her, and my heart jumped. She wrote, "Hello, Charles. I hope that you remembered me. This is my pager number, 734-8xx-xxxx, as I promised. It was nice meeting you, and have a pleasant week."

Of course I remembered her! How could any man not? I wrote her a quick reply, saying I'd give her a call that night.

A few days later, we went out for a very casual dinner and learned a bit more about each other. She was native Thai and grew up in Thailand, but her English was incredible with very little accent. Her biological father had died in a boat accident when she was a child. Her mother got married again a few years later to an American man traveling in Thailand. They spoke English frequently in their home in Chiang Mai, and that's why Jess's English was so good.

I had the party at my house the following weekend. Jess came over early, was the first to arrive, and helped fix the food. Coming a bit early impressed me, as most of the women I knew were always late. She was very impressed with my garden, saying that most men could not grow such a great garden. She was also an avid gardener, mostly with ornamentals, but she loved growing her own vegetables. She especially liked all the fresh herbs I had been growing and spoke about her family's garden in Thailand and all the different herbs they grew.

Jess really made the day, and her added touch to my cooking had everyone raving about how good the food was. The unique flavoring she added with different cooking techniques blended with mine made the food taste incredible. Her creative arrangement and presentation of all the dishes brought it up to an artistic level I didn't have the talent for. I gave all credit to her, and she beamed with happiness.

Jess really brought life to the party. I'm an introverted engineer, and she brought me out of my shell that day. A few of the women came up to me and asked what was going on with her. They said there was a real spark between us. All the guys were trying to get in a word with her, but she just came back to me. Some came up to me, asking if she was seeing anyone. I told them, "Too late. She's mine." I made absolutely sure that I kept all the other hound dogs away.

Late in the evening, everyone left except her and one of my longtime friends, Clyde. Jess was sitting on the couch, and I knew she wanted to talk and spend time with me alone. I gave Clyde a couple of subtle hints that it was time for him to leave, but he didn't get it and would not shut up or leave, even after I told him it was getting late. Finally I had to pull him aside and flat-out tell him it was time for him to go so I could spend time alone with Jess. He smiled and said he completely understood and wished me good luck.

Jess and I talked for a bit on my couch, and she explained why she came to the United States. After finishing high school in Thailand, she went to college in the U.S., and then got a job as an international marketing representative. When that job ended, she went back to Thailand for a couple of years. She had a business in Thailand, but it went under due to the economy. She was married in Thailand for a very short time, but this was only because her mother had pressured her to marry him. Jess said he was abusive and hit her, so she divorced him after six months of marriage and moved to the United States. She wanted to get a fresh start after all the bad experiences in Thailand.

She asked if I had ever been married. I said no, and then she asked if I had had any serious relationships. I told her a bit about the recent experience with Lucette, and she pressed for details. I spoke briefly about the pain it caused me. She moved in, took my hand while I was talking, leaned over, and gave me a very tender kiss. It was like a shock going through my entire body. She wiped her lipstick off my lips, and it felt like I was shocked again. We talked a bit more, closely holding each other, and then she left late at night.

Two days later we went out for dinner, and I told her I had been disappointed that the old woman sat next to her at church, preventing me from coming back. Jess laughed, saying she could tell. From that day, it was a whirlwind romance, and everything just clicked. We had similar conservative values. She was outgoing, bubbly, and the first woman I had dated who was a better cook than I was. Her being drop-dead gorgeous was a definite plus. Her body was absolutely incredible, and I really had to focus to keep my eyes from wandering. When we went out, I could see the eyes of other people following her. Both men and woman looked at her. Every once in a while, I noticed other women getting perturbed when they caught the guys they were with tracking Jess with their eyes. I've gone out with very attractive women before, but Jess was in a league of her own. We saw each other almost every day.

Jess and I started going together to St. Paul, since we didn't want any part of the singles crowd at First Presbyterian Church. I didn't agree with some of the Presbyterian theology anyway, since I'd been raised a very conservative Lutheran. When I was a child, my family attended Our Savior Evangelical Lutheran Church in Hartland, Michigan. Jess shared my Christian values even though she'd been raised in a Buddhist family. She became a member at St. Paul and was baptized.

I asked her how she had become Christian when all her family was Buddhist. When she was a child, she said, there was a Seventh-day Adventist church down the road from her house. She liked the music they played, which was very different from the traditional Thai Buddhist songs. It was at that church that she'd found her faith in Christ.

Fall arrived in Michigan, and for me, that's deer-hunting season. I went up north with my dad on September 29, 2000, to the family's property to do some bowhunting. Deer season using a bow and arrow starts on October 1. It was only my dad and me at hunt camp that year. I told Dad how well it was going with Jess but that I was going to take it slow. I got a deer the second day the season was open, but the weather was unseasonably warm. The deer would rot if it was hung in the warm weather, so I had to get it home and in the refrigerator right away. Dad and I talked about finding an old refrigerator in the future to keep in hunt camp, because this warmth had cut many previous hunting trips short, and a refrigerator would make it possible to save the meat. I left for home to butcher the deer and get it in the freezer. I called Jess on the way back and told her my plans for butchering the deer. She said she would come over and help.

What had I just heard? A woman wanted to come over and help butcher my deer? That was unheard of. Most women I had known over the years would have run away from this, the thought of butchering a deer gross to them. Some even thought I was savage for killing a deer, though they chowed down on other meats. That sure was hypocritical, and I never even considered dating those types.

Jess had a very tender heart and was a bit uncomfortable seeing the deer hanging with the hide on. It reminded her of Bambi. After I skinned and quartered it, she dived right in and helped cut up the quarters in the kitchen. I showed her what cuts were good for steak, stew meat, or burger, and she expertly helped carve up the meat. She was far more meticulous than I was and saved a lot for burger that normally would be discarded. She cut up all sorts of different internal organs for Thai food that I wouldn't have even considered saving.

Jess told me how her family would buy whole animals at the Thai market and butcher them at home. During her first trip to the United States, she was surprised to see there was no option to get a whole animal other than a chicken. There were only shrink-wrapped individual cuts of meat at the grocery store. She said that many good parts of an animal's internal organs, which gave foods the unique flavors they enjoyed in Thailand, were missing in the United States.

Many of the Thai dishes she made with venison had a vastly different flavor from anything I had tasted, but they were incredible. I was well-known for making great food for potluck dinners with friends, but when people experienced Jess's unique talent for blending Thai cuisine with my cooking, they were blown away at how good it was. Jess was surprised that people here bought the bland gunk at deli counters to share at others' homes. She would have been embarrassed to serve wretched stuff like that. When we passed the deli counter at grocery stores, she would comment on how horrible the containers of prepared food and party platters must taste.

There was a bad side to her Thai food that I always joked about with her. While Americans don't eat fish with a really strong fishy smell, many native Asians do. To most people in the United States, it's putrid-smelling stuff that can clear a room. Jess frequently bought fish called "preserved mud fish." I can only describe the smell as being what one would expect if someone set a carp out on a dirt road for a couple of hot summer days; let some cars dripping oil run over the fish while it rotted; and then put the rotted, smelly carcass in a jar of salty, spiced vinegar. It smelled that bad, but she loved it.

We were sitting on the couch when she cracked open a jar of mud fish for the first time. Foolishly, I leaned over to get a whiff of it before I knew what it was. I started having dry heaves and almost threw up. I was extremely concerned that it was not safe to eat due to the smell. To me, anything that smelled that bad was rotten and had to be thrown in the garbage. Jess gave me a what's-your-problem look and said I didn't know what I was missing. She dived right in. I could not understand how she could eat it, but mud fish was one of her go-to foods during PMS cravings. Sometimes she mixed it with hot sauce and lemon juice, which made the rotten smell even stronger.

Another food she loved to eat was durian. I discovered this new stench after we were married. Durian is truly awful and smells like rotten onions. It's so bad and strong smelling that many hotels in Asia have signs banning it. She agreed not to open it up in the house, as the stench would linger for hours. I tried to prove to her how bad it was by showing her a few episodes of *Bizarre Foods with Andrew Zimmern*. We saw some of the truly horrific stuff he ate, and she commented on how bad it must be. Then I showed her the episode of Andrew trying to eat durian. He had been able to stomach all that freaky, nasty stuff, but durian was his downfall. He was almost puking as he tried to eat it. Her response was that once you get past the smell, it tastes good. I just laughed. One time I gave some of it to my niece Victoria. She took a bite without knowing what it was, and the look on her face was pure disgust. It was hilarious—hey, that's what uncles do.

The day after Jess helped me butcher the deer, she came over to my house, and we talked about where our relationship was heading. We were both deeply in love, and as we talked of our future, the topic of marriage came up. We took the plunge right there and got engaged on October 4, 2000. It was completely unplanned on my part, and it was a mutual let's-do-it decision instead of a formal proposal. Just a few days earlier, I had told my dad we were taking it slow. We all laughed about that.

Later, during our marriage, I joked that any woman who would butcher my deer was a keeper and that's why we had gotten engaged the next day. Men were genuinely surprised she had done this, and they would look at their own wives, agreeing and laughing. But the women thought it was gross, gave their husbands the no-way look, and said they would never do such a thing.

The next day after we got engaged, we went to a funeral for the mother of my longtime friend, Janet. Janet and her mom were also members of our congregation. I hadn't had the chance to tell anyone at church about getting engaged, except for my family. We went up to pay our respects, and a woman I had dated seven years earlier, Betty, came up to us. I introduced Jess as my fiancée. Betty's face went blank; she was shocked and couldn't say much. I thought her reaction was funny, but Jess…not so much. Betty and I had dated for only two months, she dumped me, and I hadn't thought to tell Jess about her. After all, it had been seven years.

We went to greet others, and then Jess pulled me aside and gave me the look of a jealous woman. She asked, "Who was that?"

Her eyes were piercing into my soul. I was on the spot. It was very uncomfortable, and Jess knew from Betty's reaction that something was up. I told Jess about the two-month relationship that had happened seven years earlier. Jess said, "Seven years ago, and she reacted like that? She must still like you."

She asked if I had any feelings for Betty, and I said, "No, it's been over seven years."

That was the truth. I also told Jess that because she was in my hometown, she was bound to run into women I knew. I joked that it was not fair that I couldn't be in her hometown to run into her ex-boyfriends and make her uncomfortable. Jess smiled and said, "Good." We both laughed about the run-in with Betty and the look on her face for many years to come.

We came back to my house, and Jess left for the evening. I checked my e-mail, and there were a bunch of messages congratulating me on getting engaged. One person, Leo, wrote, "The bluebird of happiness told me the good news!" I was surprised how fast the news had spread in just a few hours. At church the next morning, almost everyone knew about the engagement. People were hugging both Jess and me, and everyone was extremely happy for us. It was a great day with such an outpouring of love. With Jess by my side, I had never felt such joy before.

We scheduled the wedding at St. Paul for next year in February. A few weeks later, I got a frantic call from Jess while I was at work. She was still staying at John's home in Livonia, and she had told him she was engaged. John got very angry, and she was scared and distraught and didn't know what to do. I thought John must have fallen for her, though he was in his late sixties. I told Jess there was no way she could stay there safely and that we had to find a place for her until we got married. This was in November, and the wedding was three months away. All the apartments wanted at least a six-month commitment. We didn't want to live together outside of marriage, so we scheduled a quick civil ceremony at the courthouse. Three days later we were married.

I asked Jess why she had waited a couple of weeks to tell John we were engaged, but she only gave excuses, saying that she did not want to tell him about me. I couldn't help but think, *Why would she not say anything?* This did not compute to me—I was overjoyed and wanted to tell everyone about this incredible woman with whom I planned to spend the rest of my life. I didn't push for an answer, thinking she must have a good reason and that it did not matter now.

Little did I know that her evasive pattern of withholding and hiding important information would become far worse. The things she withheld weren't minor; they were major issues, especially with finances. This behavior eventually became one of the reasons our marriage fell apart. She convinced herself that not telling me about issues was OK. Other times she thought it best to tell me only a partial truth, believing the whole truth was too bad to take in all at once. She rationalized that it was better for me not to know while she secretly tried to fix problems she had caused.

There are two types of lies: those of commission and those of omission. A lie of commission is an outright falsehood. It's like a child saying he didn't take a cookie out of the cookie jar when he really did. A lie of omission would be the child eating all the cookies but replying when asked where the cookies went that he'd had a few. That's true…but it's not the whole truth. Another type of omission would be if he heard his parents question his sister about the missing cookies, knew they thought she'd taken them, and stayed silent to hide the truth.

Lies of omission can be far more destructive in a close relationship, because the person is intentionally withholding information in an attempt to make the situation look better than it really is. It's scheming to keep a loved one unaware of serious problems, allowing a misconception to continue or even creating or strengthening a misconception. The person feels justified in creating this lie because it can be partly based on truth.

The next two months of preparing for the formal wedding at St. Paul were wonderful. We both were happy, but there was a little tension over the size of the wedding. We wanted a small wedding, maybe sixty people maximum, but then the mothers got involved. My mom wanted all her friends and relatives invited, but this made Jess very uncomfortable, because most of her family was in Thailand and could not come. Only her mother; sister; and longtime friend, Churai, were traveling from Thailand for the wedding, and about ten of her stepdad's relatives were coming. There was a huge disparity between my friends and family and hers, but Jess did not want to upset my mom, and we ended up with three hundred guests.

Jess was late for the prewedding dinner with family and the bridal party due to some last-minute stuff at the reception hall. She came in but didn't greet my sister, Jane. Jess had not met her before, because Jane had just arrived for the wedding from Kansas. I didn't know this happened, and my sister didn't tell me about it until a few years later. Jane said she felt snubbed and didn't know why Jess wouldn't say hi. Someone else had to introduce the two.

The wedding day finally arrived on February 17, 2001. My parents' wedding anniversary was on the eighteenth, so my anniversary would be easy to remember. Jess joked that I was responsible now for remembering two wedding anniversaries: the civil ceremony and the formal church wedding. She said it was "twice the joy."

Before the wedding started, I thought that because we were already married, this ceremony wouldn't make me too emotional. That's the logical engineer in me talking, and that guy would be proved wrong many, many times.

Everything was just fine and calm as I stood at the altar and watched the bridesmaids, the mothers, and finally the flower girls walk in. My father was going to walk Jess down the aisle because both of her dads had passed away.

Then I saw her on my dad's arm. My heart jumped, and I could feel and hear the pounding in my chest. I started getting tears in my eyes and had to tell myself to keep it together. I was shaking with emotion for this incredible woman whom I deeply loved. She joined me at the altar, and the service started.

Pastor Booth did the ceremony. Just a short while into the ceremony, I heard a loud bang followed by a couple of women screaming. My best man and best friend, Chris Bailey, had passed out and fallen face-first onto the steps of the altar. Chris had been very sick the past two days and still was not feeling well. Pastor Booth was incredibly calm and reassured everyone that everything was fine and Chris was being taken care of. Chris lay down on one of the pews for most of the service.

What's really funny is that in many of the wedding pictures, Chris's feet are sticking out from the pew into the center aisle. Some people think events like this are horrible during a wedding, but later on, it's these glitches and mistakes that everyone has fond memories of and laughs about. The screw-ups become the cherished highlights.

The reception was great, and everyone had a good time. We had a smoking ban inside the reception hall, but because it was February in Michigan, it was very cold, and some smokers complained about going outside. I thought it was funny watching them shiver outside just because they could not go for a few hours without a cigarette. The tobacco companies have them all by the short hairs.

The next morning, when I was sitting on the couch, Jess got down on her knees, bowed before me, and said, "You are my god." Wow, that took me by surprise. She said it was part of her culture to give respect to her husband.

I gently stopped her, saying that I understood the sentiment but must never be referred to as a god. I told her that there was only one God and that I was just a lowly, sinful man saved by the grace of Christ. I told her, "The farther up you put me on a pedestal, the farther I will fall." We talked a bit about growing in our faith together, the way that I viewed her as my equal, and that we were now one flesh before God as man and wife.

We waited a few weeks to go on our honeymoon, because her mother, sister, and Churai were still visiting from Thailand. They were staying at my parents' house. It had taken thirty-two hours for the women to reach Michigan. This was before Northwest Airlines built their international terminal at Detroit Metro Airport, so to get here from Thailand, they first had layovers in Tokyo and California. With the new terminal, the flight from Tokyo to Detroit is direct and cuts six hours from the trip.

Jess had told her mother not to pack sandals because there was a foot of snow on the ground. She said we would buy her some full-foot slippers for the house and warm boots to wear in the snow. This did not sink in with her, and she brought multiple pairs of sandals anyway. The weather she was accustomed to in Thailand was so warm that, during one of our trips there, I noticed that many cars didn't have a heater core to warm the inside of the vehicle or defrost the windshield. Because it doesn't get cold, drivers don't need heaters. I tell people that Thailand has two temperatures: hot and hotter. Jess's mother had never been in weather colder than sixty-five degrees before this trip, and the bitter cold of Michigan in February was a complete shock to her.

Jess's sister and Churai left in a few days, but her mother stayed for a few weeks. After her mother went home, we went to Disney World and Universal Studios in Orlando for our honeymoon. We had a blast, and she loved the extreme roller coasters and other rides, like I did.

At one point, as we walked around Universal Studios trying to decide which ride to take next, we saw a teenage girl being partially carried by two guys. She was completely freaked out from riding the roller coaster, and her legs wobbled and shook under her weight. Her eyes rolled at the horizon, unable to focus.

Jess saw her reaction, looked at me, and said, "This one must be really good; let's go!"

I looked at her and said, "I love you!"

Halfway through the honeymoon, Jess told me she felt that she might be pregnant. We'd been married almost four months since the civil marriage and were not using birth control. I was thirty-eight, and she was thirty-six. We both wanted children. I got her a pregnancy test kit from the drugstore, but the test was negative. She took another one the next day. It was also negative, but she still insisted that she might be pregnant. We avoided all the extreme rides for the rest of the honeymoon. I told her we'd already hit all the good ones anyway and could just relax and enjoy our trip.

For the rest of the trip, her behavior and eating were really out of control, and she was snapping at me for little things. When we got home, she had her period, so she was not pregnant. She went off on me for not caring enough and possibly hurting her pregnancy. That really took me by surprise, and it was completely unjustified and unfair. I tried talking with her and reminded her of all I had done after she thought she was pregnant, but nothing I said mattered. I was a target to vent her emotions on. Looking back all these years later, this was the first of many attacks where she claimed I didn't take care of her.

Other than the false-pregnancy incident, our marriage was great. We loved cooking new foods together. We grew many fresh Thai herbs at home, and it made the food taste much better than anything we got in restaurants. People at work were very envious of the Thai food I brought in for lunch, and when some asked me where to go for Thai food, I gave them my address. They gave me strange looks, and I replied, "My house." This was true though—Jess and I went to only two Thai restaurants together during our marriage. We were not impressed. Going out to eat was a very rare event, because we could usually make something far better at home.

I was eager to try creating different meals for Jess. I baked many different types of breads, and one day I came up with the idea of using garlic flowers from the garden in a soft pretzel. Our home was filled with the wonderful, soft smell of fresh-baked garlic bread. Jess was eager to try one of them. We each took a bite, but a harsh and bitter taste filled my mouth. It was absolutely horrible. The garlic flowers had ruined all the pretzels.

I was very disappointed, knowing something I had made for Jess had turned out so bad. Jess told me she loved it and kept eating it. I told her she didn't have to say that—I knew it was bad. She looked at me with those loving eyes and said, "Everything you make is wonderful."

I threw my pretzel in the trash and left the room to brush my teeth and get the nasty taste out of my mouth. I changed my mind, turned around, and headed back into the kitchen to toss the rest of the pretzels out. There was Jess, bending over the trash can, spitting out the rest of the pretzel! She was shocked and embarrassed that I'd caught her in the act. I laughed at her for not admitting it was that bad. This was a wonderful quality Jess had: she always wanted to make me happy, even when I messed up.

TWO

JOB WOES

Jess had a job at a paper-recycling trucking yard in Detroit, but that was not going well. I worked at Ford in Dearborn. Her office was close by, just inside the Detroit city limits, so we drove together to work.

As the weeks went by, her conflicts with people at her job increased. I noticed that she was easily offended and put off by situations, far more than most people. A few of her reasons for getting angry were justified, but most were not. She could not let comments go and took them to heart even if people didn't mean to offend her. I gave her the benefit of the doubt because this was a trucking company and she had to deal with some pretty rough truck drivers. Some of them were very crude. We talked a lot about dealing with them, and I tried to help her not get so easily offended. Nothing helped, and I chalked it up to the place being too unrefined for a very sensitive woman to tolerate.

There was one time I fully supported her in going to human resources over a coworker's exceptionally obscene comment. The guy said he had gone to Thailand once and noticed there were a lot of prostitutes there. Then he told Jess, "I think I met your mother." Jess was very upset when she came home and was crying. I was extremely pissed off, and my first reaction was to go over there and confront him. Jess and I talked for a while, and I told her she must go to HR and report him. No one should have to tolerate that type of behavior—even if he was joking.

One of her coworkers there, Shelly, didn't take crap from anyone. She would not hold back from getting in someone's face and telling him off with a string of f-bombs and other cursing. She and Jess got along well, and Jess told me many fond stories of how Shelly took care of situations and how everyone there knew not to mess with her. There were a few times we got together outside of work, and Shelly was a riot and fun to be around except for the cursing. Shelly also protected Jess quite a bit; she knew how sensitive Jess was. Jess asked me once if she should be more like Shelly, and I said, "Absolutely not." I asked her what I could do to help her not get so offended and hurt by what others said. But all she said was to listen to her, so I did.

Jess's job situation got worse; she was miserable working there, and then she stopped. I never did get a straight answer from her about whether she was laid off, was fired, or had quit. Had she been laid off, she could have received unemployment benefits for a while. I brought this up, but she dodged the question. It was better that she was not working there anymore, so I didn't press the issue.

Before we met, Jess had held a job at an automotive supplier, but that only lasted two months. She never told me why that didn't last longer.

One other thing about her job irked us both. Because her office was located one block inside the city limits of Detroit, the city deducted Detroit taxes from her paycheck. What a rip-off. Why should she have to pay for the hassle of working in that crime-ridden city? Ever since then, even after my divorce, I have avoided Detroit as much as possible out of principle. The amount of revenue that city has lost from me now far exceeds the amount of city taxes they took from her paycheck.

Jess sometimes told me stories of how she loved having her own business in Thailand. It was an import-export business for wine, but she claimed her business partner had run off with funds and stuck her with the bill when the Thai economy took a dive. She had also worked at a flower shop her family owned. She began to talk more about starting her own business but was unsure about what to do.

Jess didn't look or try much to get back to work. She enjoyed not having to go to work and tried to justify not looking for a job. She told me that keeping the house clean and cooking great meals to make me happy also made her happy. We had many talks about this, and I tried to make her understand that I was a simple guy, had lived on my own since I was eighteen, and didn't need anyone to take care of me. I only wanted to love her and be loved. In fact, having someone constantly fuss over me was irritating.

Jess wouldn't try to understand my needs. She had this idea in her head about how I should be treated, and that was it. She had convinced herself that taking care of me was better than getting a job or starting a business. It was also far easier to stay at home while I worked to pay the bills. Procrastination on her part was also responsible for her not looking for a job.

Eventually Jess got a job at a bookstore in Ann Arbor. That didn't last long. I began to wonder why Jess couldn't hold a job. She always gave some excuse about why other people caused problems and how she was the innocent victim.

A while later Jess told me she had contacted a woman who needed a helper to promote a fashion concept. The woman had health issues and could not work outside her home. Jess set up a meeting and wanted me to go along. The woman sent Jess instructions about what types of fabrics we could wear to her house and what soap to use when we showered. We had to start this ritual a few days before the meeting and were required to wash our clothes in special soap and in a certain way. This situation seemed very weird. Right away the alarm bells started going off in my head. Jess said the woman had severe allergies and could not have traces of chemicals in her home or she would get very sick.

We arrived at the woman's home, but before we came in, she questioned us about the procedures we had followed. Jess told her what we had done, but the woman was still unsure and eventually let us in after more interrogation. She started the conversation by telling us in extreme detail about what was wrong with her and how she had severe reactions to the modern world, which is full of toxic chemicals and artificial scents.

I looked around her house and saw a lot of furniture with commercial dyes, paints, lacquers, and polyurethane. I couldn't resist asking her about the types of finishes on wood she could tolerate, and she went into a rambling explanation about why the furniture she had was OK. It made no sense. I told her I did woodworking as a hobby and that shellac would be an ideal finish for her, as it's a natural excretion by the lac bug. The resin produced by the bug is dissolved in alcohol and applied to the wood, and then the alcohol evaporates, leaving no chemical traces. She looked at me in horror and said I was wrong, claiming that shellac was extremely toxic. Her statement confirmed my suspicions: she was just plain nuts. I knew this was a situation to keep far away from Jess and me.

Jess and the woman started talking about her fashion concept. It was a woman's sock with a zipper on it. She had grand plans that it would be the next fashion craze with teenage girls, but she needed someone else to do all the legwork for her because she could not leave her house. We reviewed her business terms and the compensation Jess would get for all her labor. The terms were completely unreasonable, with Jess doing all the traveling and meeting with clients. Jess would get very small commissions, which would not cover her expenses. Jess talked a bit with her to negotiate a better deal, but the sock lady wouldn't budge. When we were done, Jess asked to review the contract at home and propose changes. The woman was very hesitant but said she was going to e-mail Jess. I don't know if that ever happened.

We left, and while driving home, we laughed at just how unreal this woman's expectations were and how irrational her so-called reactions to chemicals were. Jess told me even she knew that shellac was a natural finish with no chemicals, and when the woman disagreed with me, Jess knew the woman had irrational issues. Jess named her the "crazy bubble lady," comparing her to the movie *Bubble Boy*. I said that dealing with this woman and her issues would not be worth the trouble. Jess talked with her a few more times, but nothing ever came from it. I thought the sock concept was silly anyway and was glad Jess didn't get involved with this. But then I know nothing about what teenage girls consider fashionable, and I don't care to learn.

Jess met a couple of Thai women in the Ann Arbor area and became friends with them. One of them was Preeda, who was married to a man named Jay. They were involved in a multilevel marketing phone company called Excel Communications, and Jess wanted to get involved. Oh, crap, I thought, not an MLM; those are pretty much all scams. I really tried to talk her out of this and showed her horror stories from other people sucked into MLMs, but she would not relent. Jay showed us marketing brochures about how they were the first MLM business model to be in telecommunication and how it would be very lucrative. Jess showed me the pyramid model's projections about how much she could make by all the downstream sales and was excited about this. Nothing I said could change her mind; this MLM had another victim, and it was my wife. Damn.

Jess signed up, paid for and took the required classes, paid other ridiculous fees, and then tried to get other people to sign up also. The problem was that it was a very feeble, halfhearted effort, and she stopped trying in a few weeks. Little did I know that this was a pattern in her life. She would get excited about and start something, but she didn't follow through or put in the required effort. If it was not fun, she stopped. We lost about $1,500 with this MLM scam.

Other than her job situation, our marriage was great, and we were deeply in love. She even laughed at all my stupid jokes. We acted like kids a lot at home and went into a phase of trying to scare each other. Jess would hide and try to sneak up and scare me. Usually it worked. She got me more often than I got her.

One time her attempt really backfired. I was in the shower and saw her shadow slowly creeping up on the shower curtain. I threw back the curtain and yelled, "Ha!" at her. It took her by such surprise that she actually leaped off the floor and came down huddled and shaking. She looked up at me like a scared little kitten as if it were my fault. We both laughed about that later in the evening. She said she'd felt like a cat in a cartoon that when scared, leaps up and clings to the ceiling.

One time I took the scaring routine a bit too far. It was close to Halloween, and the Red Cross was giving out glow-in-the-dark vampire teeth to people who donated blood. I donated, got my pair of fake teeth, and set the plan in motion to scare her.

That night, around two in the morning, she was sound asleep. I got the vampire teeth out, charged them up with a flashlight so they glowed, put them in my mouth, and then leaned over her. I shook her gently while saying "Honey" to wake her up. When her eyes opened, I let out a loud hiss, opening my mouth wide to bare the glowing teeth. She screamed, freaked out, and began violently shivering.

Her reaction and fear were incredibly extreme. I had crossed the line. It was more than simply crossing it; I had obliterated that line. I felt horrible. Because it was very early in our marriage, I had no idea how sensitive she was to this type of thing. Later in the month, we went to a haunted house, and she had to be taken out by the staff because she couldn't handle it. It wasn't because of the vampire-teeth incident; she couldn't handle anyone dressed up as ghosts or zombies jumping out at her. We never went to a haunted house together again. I told the vampire-teeth story to people and got very different reactions. Many men thought it was hilarious, but almost all women gave me a disparaging look and said something like, "You did what?"

Even though Jess was so sensitive to Halloween ghouls, ghosts, and zombies, she wanted to see the occasional horror movie. It was an emotional jolt that she enjoyed, but it usually ended up with her being very disturbed for the following few days. A couple of years later after the vampire-teeth incident, she wanted to see *Drag Me to Hell* at the dollar theater. I asked her if she really wanted to and if she knew that she would have sleepless nights and bad dreams afterward. Jess persisted, so we went.

Jess was sitting in the aisle seat; she didn't want to feel trapped in the middle of the row. About halfway through the movie, Jess started hitting and pulling on my arm. She was freaking out, her eyes wide. She pointed at the aisle and said to me, "Look! Look!"

An empty baby stroller had rolled down the aisle, and it stopped right next to Jess. My first thought was simply that someone's stroller got loose and rolled down. I also thought it was inappropriate to bring a baby or toddler to a movie like this. Jess didn't view the stroller as I did. She thought the stroller was possessed and had targeted her. A minute later a woman walked down and got her stroller, looked at Jess, and said sorry. The damage was done. Jess was a mess, but she still wanted to see the rest of the movie. After the movie, we met the couple with the baby stroller, and we talked briefly. I thought it was funny, but Jess remained shaken by the stroller. She calmed down a little bit after talking to the woman, but she had nightmares the next few nights.

After the Excel mess, Jess went into the same mode again of not trying to do anything with her life. She would make herself busy with unimportant activities that left her unfulfilled. She did some clothing alterations for people, and then a friend asked Jess if she could shorten the sleeves of a sweater. Sure, she could—Jess was incredibly talented at clothing design and alteration. After that, a few more people came to her, and she altered their sweaters too.

Jess came up with the idea of starting a company to alter sweaters since this type of alteration did not exist. I told her it might take off, but I'm a guy and am content with just rolling up my sleeves—I wouldn't pay for an alteration. She had this puzzled look and said, "But it doesn't look good." I didn't think there was much of a market for this, but I supported her anyway. Even if it didn't work, the investment was minimal, so the financial loss wasn't an issue. Knitting needles and yarn were cheap, and she would buy the yarn as needed to match sweaters. She would also unravel the existing yarn from the sweater's excess length to create a matching hem.

We worked together to come up with a name, Wool Creations. She registered the business name with Washtenaw County in August 2001. I set up a web server and created a website and e-mail accounts. She got a business license, contacted people, and sent out fliers and advertisements.

Her business didn't do much, and the excitement wore off within a few months. Just like Excel. She stopped trying, even though I spent a lot of time helping and encouraging her. The initial thrill had died, and it wasn't fun anymore. She continued with a few token efforts now and then, but she wasn't doing much of anything. I couldn't help but think, *What if I just quit my job because there were times it was not fun? What would we do financially?* I thought it was very irresponsible, especially with all the time I had spent on this for her, but I kept my opinion to myself. At least we hadn't lost much money.

Jess renewed her efforts with Wool Creations a year later. This time she wanted to start making custom wedding gowns and doing high-end alterations. Doing this from home didn't appear professional, and suppliers would not sell wedding gowns to someone without a commercial storefront. So she subleased a space in Ann Arbor for a while. Her business didn't do well—the space she'd leased was in an industrial complex, and no one went to that area for retail shopping. Jess then formed Formal Diva for designing and selling wedding gowns. In April 2003, she signed a mutual business agreement and sublease with Nellie's Wedding Shop in Romulus, Michigan.

The agreement between Jess and Nellie was a very strange one. Jess would make and sell custom-made garments through Wool Creations at Nellie's store, and Nellie would take a 12.5 percent commission on the Wool Creations garments. Nellie also was the sales representative for Formal Diva, and it was stipulated in the contract that Formal Diva was a "distributor, designer, and manufacturer of wedding gowns, formal and casual wear." I'm not sure what the difference was between Wool Creations and Formal Diva, except that Wool Creations was disappearing, and all the work Jess was doing was under Formal Diva. Then, in August 2003, something happened between the two of them, and Jess and Nellie signed a letter that stated, "No further advertising will include any mention of custom gowns, Formal Diva, or Wool Creations."

In September 2003, Nellie sent Jess a letter that terminated their shared-space agreement. Jess told me stories of how Nellie was being unreasonable and hard to work with. Once again Jess claimed that others caused the problem, not her.

This job situation with her didn't bother me much. We were happy, had a joyful time together, and were deeply in love. I gave thanks countless times as I lay in bed and watched this beautiful woman sleep. She really did adore me and was an extremely passionate woman. I felt blessed by having her in my life.

That summer, Jess wanted to go up to Frankenmuth, Michigan, for one of their "world-famous chicken dinners." We traveled up and went to eat at the Bavarian Inn. We both noticed that the World Expo of Beer, which offered more than a hundred different types of craft beer, was in Frankenmuth that weekend also.

Jess and I were sitting in the restaurant trying to decide what to eat. The menu didn't impress me, and I thought of it as higher-priced KFC chicken. Looking at what other people had on their plates didn't impress me either. The place was very crowded, loud, and cramped, and people kept bumping into us as they tried to get by. Knowing that Jess really wanted to be here, I kept my negative thoughts to myself. However, I kept thinking I'd rather be at the beer expo.

All of a sudden, after glancing over her menu, Jess looked at me and said, "Let's get out of here and go to the beer expo." I said she'd read my mind, and we got out of there. We headed to the beer expo and had a couple of grilled brats along with many samples of craft beer from different microbreweries. There was a live band playing too. Jess sat on my lap with a beer in one hand and a brat in the other as she bounced to the beat of the band, and I told her I loved her. She beamed with happiness. We had an awesome time.

A few weeks later, Jess began altering clothing for people at home. She came to me one day and said she wanted to open up her own bridal shop. I was very hesitant, given her history for not keeping projects going. I was very honest with her and expressed my concerns. She admitted she had failed in the other ventures, but what she had been doing was not her real passion. She had taken many courses in Thailand for fashion design, sewing, and patternmaking. She wanted to get back into that.

Jess is an extremely talented clothing designer, dressmaker, and seamstress. She could envision a design, create her own full-size paper patterns of the design, and make the dress. She was also a highly intelligent woman. I knew she was capable of doing great work, but I was worried about the finances and expenses of starting a bridal shop. Since I'm a white-collar electrical engineer with a bit of inner redneck going on, the fashion and wedding industry is completely foreign to me. There was little I could do to help her in this except for being the computer network nerd, web designer, and handyman.

We did a bit of research, and there were already multiple bridal shops in the area close to Ypsilanti, Michigan. We had many discussions about how she could compete and be profitable. None of the other shops did custom design work, and that's what Jess was very good at. I still was very concerned and knew failure would result in huge financial losses for us. I was not willing to commit to a lengthy and expensive commercial lease for her store with such competition and with neither of us having experience in running a bridal shop or marketing to attract clients.

A few weeks later, Jess came to me and said she had a solution for the finances. She'd found a dry cleaner close by in Saline who was using only a third of the space he was leasing. She had negotiated a deal with him for a sublease where she could use half the space—not only that, but the increased traffic would be good for his business. This was something I could agree to only if we were not committed to the sublease if her business failed. The cleaner agreed, and Jess started up Formal Diva with no other business partners.

If only I'd had a crystal ball to see how badly this would end up. Wow.

THREE

FERTILITY PROBLEMS AND DEBT

Two years had gone by since we were married, and we had not conceived yet. Jess was also experiencing pain in her lower abdomen. Her ob-gyn, Brad, was a member of our church, and he found some adhesions of scar tissue caused by a surgery she'd had in Thailand when she was eighteen. Brad removed the adhesions, and then he ran tests to see why she could not conceive. Jess told me one of her fallopian tubes had been detached in that old surgery. I asked her why she hadn't told me before but got only evasive answers from her. Brad's tests also showed that the other tube was blocked. It was medically impossible for us to conceive.

This was very emotionally difficult for Jess. She was very family oriented and was beating herself up for not being able to have a baby. She wanted to "give" me a child—this was how she put it. To her, it wasn't our problem; it was hers alone. We had many talks, and I tried to stress that it was about us having a child together as man and wife, not just her giving me a baby. However, I was the last hope of keeping the Cole name alive; the only other Cole male, my cousin Dave, had only girls. This fact about my grandfather's lineage ending bothered Jess greatly, and she heaped more guilt on herself. Nothing I said could soothe her feelings of being a failure as a woman for not being able to conceive.

We talked about options and adoption. She was dead set on only having a child who was our blood and didn't want to adopt. We looked into in vitro fertilization. Wow—it cost $20,000 and came with no guaranteed results, and our medical plan did not cover this procedure.

Jess had dual citizenship in the United States and Thailand, so she looked into having the procedure done in Bangkok instead. It was drastically cheaper at $3,000. We'd been planning to take a trip there anyway, and Jess was going to stay for two months to spend time with her family.

We arranged the procedure and booked the trip, and Jess left first. She had to take hormone medication that would make her reproductive system produce multiple eggs instead of the normal one per month. After that, I would stay for two weeks, and we would start the fertilization procedure. After her eggs were fertilized, three embryos were implanted. Doctors froze the other embryos just in case the procedure didn't work the first time. The frozen embryos could be thawed and implanted at a greatly reduced cost with fewer medications involved.

The procedure didn't take. Jess was absolutely devastated and sank into depression. It affected me, too, and I tried to reassure her that we would work this out together. I didn't tell Jess about my loss over this and feelings that I would probably never have children of my own. Expressing my feelings to her would only increase her guilt, so I had to bear them alone. We had countless talks about this, but Jess kept focusing on her own pain.

Her emotional state really sank to a low point one day when we were watching TV. The local news ran a story about the police arresting a prostitute addicted to crack. The woman had just had her sixth baby from a different father, and Jess started crying. She looked at me and said, "Am I so much worse than her that God will give her children and not me? Why is he punishing me?" It was shocking that she was comparing her self-worth to that of some prostitute on TV and felt that God was punishing her. That's how deeply she was tormenting herself.

My sister offered to try to carry an embryo to term since the first time with Jess did not work. Jess and I discussed this option, but she wanted to try it again herself. I joked with Jess that my inner redneck would be out there for all to see with my sister pregnant with my baby. Jess laughed about that, too, and it was wonderful to see her beautiful smile again.

A year later Jess was in Thailand by herself and had the embryos implanted. She flew back and continued the medications, hoping it would take this time.

The second in vitro procedure didn't work either. Jess was more prepared this time, and it didn't hit her as hard emotionally. We were both hurt by this news, but we talked it through. She wanted to go back for a third try, but her doctor here convinced her if it hadn't worked the first two times, the third most likely would not either and that all it would do was cause more emotional pain.

Jess would not let up. She began talking about trying again but this time using an egg from her sixteen-year-old niece, Phonphan. She really wanted a child from our family's bloodline, and if her egg and my sperm wouldn't work, Jess thought maybe she could carry to term an embryo created from an egg from her niece and my sperm.

This idea of hers was way out there, but I didn't tell Jess I thought it was crazy. I tried to put my reluctance in terms of it being too much of an emotional burden on a sixteen-year-old girl to do this. I also told Jess I didn't want to see her hurt again if the procedure failed. I asked her to wait until her new business started generating profit—this would be extremely expensive. Using Jess to carry the newly extracted fertilized eggs from another woman required months of each woman taking expensive hormone medications to synchronize their reproductive cycles. Jess agreed and focused on her work. A few years later, Jess required a hysterectomy due to pain caused by old scar tissue and other medical issues.

Her new business had been going on for a while, and she showed me promising financials. It seemed to be working out well, but the business was the beginning of severe problems in our marriage.

Communication with Jess was becoming increasingly difficult. She became short-tempered, irrational at times, and complained about how customers treated or insulted her. She frequently vented to me, and her stress led her to magnify all my imperfections. She had multiple clashes with the cleaner over little issues, and Jess would not relent. She was right, and he was wrong, and Jess refused to find middle ground on many issues. Jess also kept pushing the limits of what she could do. She was encroaching into space she was not entitled to per the sublease agreement. I tried to talk to her, saying I understood her motivation but that this was a legal agreement: she didn't have any right to use so much space. I was sucked in between them and had to be the level-headed mediator for Jess.

Jess began accusing me of never standing up for her and said I was taking the cleaner's side. I told her this was not fair and said she must know I wanted what was best for her and us, but everyone must adhere to the terms of the business contract. Jess refused to understand and still tried to push the limits on what she could do. The frequency of her accusations about my never taking her side and never listening to her increased dramatically.

After a couple of months, I noticed there was no improvement in the store's financials, and I couldn't get a straight answer out of her about what was really going on. There were no profits coming in, and her business drained all the money from my job. Finally, one day, she came clean: there was $20,000 in debt from her store. Damn.

I was very angry and didn't talk much to her for a few days. She had consistently fed me half-truths and had hidden the real story for all this time. A couple of days later, she wanted us to go to church so that we could talk about our marriage problems with Leo, the bluebird-of-happiness guy. Leo was the director of Christian education at our church, and we both held him in great regard. Jess trusted him completely, and this trust was well-founded. Leo was an all-around great guy, a man of incredible biblical knowledge, and he was highly respected by the congregation. He had great commonsense wisdom and wasn't one of those fake churchy, preaching types. If someone had a thing against Leo, it was most likely that person's fault, not Leo's.

We were talking about how we could reestablish good communication, strengthen our marriage, and get back to really enjoying each other. Jess began accusing me of not talking to her, not supporting her, and not taking her side. Leo had to stop her from these attacks and steered us toward moving on.

Then Jess looked at me and said, "I want to tell you something, but I am afraid you will be mad."

Leo looked at me and asked if I could try to listen to her with forgiveness, if I could accept that we are all very imperfect and listen to her. I said I would try but could not promise I wouldn't be angry. Leo asked Jess if she was OK with that since I was being fair and honest, and she said yes.

Jess said the debt was not $20,000; it was double that at $40,000. I went numb and didn't know what to say. She had lied to me again.

I didn't say much for the rest of the meeting with Leo. Jess did most of the talking. She tried to justify keeping the truth from me by saying she didn't want me to get mad and had kept trying to lower the debt for both of our futures, blah, blah. She even stated she had worked hard so that I could retire early. I started tuning her out at this point and didn't want to hear more excuses or her continual stream of blabbering justifications for lying to me.

One of Jess's greatest strengths as a salesperson was her ability to sell her point from all different angles. She was the best salesperson I had ever seen, and watching her convince a customer to buy something was truly a sight to see. I'm a typical engineer, who deals with facts, and have always worked with similar people. Jess was ignoring my need for truth and openness, and I was frustrated in dealing with her ability to completely ignore reality and justify actions with pure emotions. During the meeting with Leo, Jess was justifying her actions by coming in from all these well-practiced different angles.

After Leo stopped her from coming up with excuses, he asked us how we could move on. Jess promised to tell the whole truth in the future. She said she knew the huge mistakes she had made and how she had wronged me. She asked for forgiveness so that we could move on and be happy in our lives. She even had Leo convinced that she was turning over a new leaf.

When this talk occurred, we had been married four years. I still loved her greatly, and these problems did not seem to be a valid reason to consider divorce. We had many talks about her half-truths and the store's financials, and our goal was for us to work together and fix this situation.

A couple of weeks later at church, the pastor gave a talk about truth and the way people ignore real truth and substitute their own. He also spoke about lies of commission and lies of omission. This really affected

Jess, and she was very uncomfortable listening to this, due to her own guilt. I had forgiven her for the store situation, but she had not forgiven herself. Later in the day, she accused me of not forgiving her. This was due to her own guilt tearing her apart. She had so much guilt built up that she couldn't realize how others could forgive her.

One of Jess's ongoing issues that slowly got worse was her problem with forgiveness. She held things against people and did not truly forgive them. Her pride was so great that she could not let go. She demanded that people make reparations on her terms, or else she would not forgive them. She gave lip service about how she forgave, but deep down in her heart, she did not. Something within her prevented her from giving true forgiveness toward others.

She started holding my mistakes against me. I'm far from perfect and made plenty of mistakes in our marriage, but she could not forgive me as I forgave her. She also did this to herself. She accumulated so much guilt for what she had done in the past that it tore her up. We tried working on this together and took many classes, but nothing worked. She built up what I call a "hurt bank" and could justify holding a grudge against someone by pulling out the list of grievances she felt the other person had not corrected to her satisfaction.

We remortgaged the house to pay off the debt. It was either that or close the store, and we absorbed $40,000 in debt along with all the other investments in the store. She assured me there would be no more lies about finances and promised to show me everything, and we worked together to try and recover the losses. At this point in our marriage, I had accumulated $89,000 in equity in the house, which I had bought four years before we were married. The new mortgage was for $110,000 to pay off the existing mortgage, and the remaining funds went to her debt and for operating cash. What a mistake that turned out to be. I would have gladly accepted only $40,000 in losses had I known the extreme financial calamity that would later occur due to her lying again about the finances of her store.

A few months later, I got a frantic call at work from Jess. The dry cleaner had not been paying rent to the landlord, even though we had been paying him the sublease fees. Jess saw an eviction notice taped to the door. Her business was established and growing at that location, but now all that would be lost.

We had already suffered huge financial losses. We talked about this, and the only option to recover the $40,000 and all other expenses was to take over the lease of the whole space. Jess really pushed this and showed me promising financials. The store could become a full-fledged bridal shop, which would attract more customers. Looking back on this decision, I should have known better. At this time I still deeply loved and trusted her, believing we had worked out the past issues. I took my marriage vows very seriously, but seeds of doubt in her were in the back of my mind.

In addition to the store, Jess wanted to import and breed three Thai Ridgeback dogs from Thailand. I was completely opposed to this, but in her typical manner, she would not relent and pressured me for weeks. I caved, but it was with the understanding that I had no part of this and that it was 100 percent her responsibility. What a fool I was to agree to this, based on her history of failures to follow through. Part of the reason I relented was because I was tired of listening to her go on about how I didn't support her decisions.

The dog situation turned out to be a disaster and almost broke our marriage. Just like everything before, she utterly failed to follow through. She would not try to sell the eight puppies, and she would not train them. All the dogs were destroying our home. She responded to only a few people who came to us from ads I had to place. I pleaded with her to try harder to sell the dogs, but she didn't place a single ad. It really pissed me off that she did this and did nothing to correct the problem.

The stench of urine and feces hit me right in the face every day when I got home from work. I had to build gates to keep the dogs contained in the kitchen. I even put up a small fence around a small portion of the backyard. There was no more money available to fence in the entire yard. We started getting complaints from neighbors and the homeowners' association about running an unauthorized kennel.

Thai Ridgebacks are a very difficult breed to train and control. Jess tried at first to train the male, but she didn't follow through with the training. I even paid a dog handler to give Jess private lessons about how to train the dog, but she did not follow the trainer's recommendations. She would beg the dog to act correctly instead of being a pack leader. The trainer even told her she had to be trained to be a proper leader to the dog.

It was very bizarre watching Jess interact with all the dogs. She seemed to get an emotional fix when they greeted her. She was all smiles when the dogs were all over her, wagging their tails. All the other issues, the smell and destruction of our once-happy home, went away from her for a brief moment. Then she sank into her mode of being unhappy and ignored the reality of the situation. I had to place all additional ads since she did nothing, but only three of the eight puppies were sold.

Finally I'd had it. I took a couple of the dogs to the local shelter. They saw just how wild they were and how rare the breed was, and then they told me they would most likely euthanize them, as no one would adopt them due to the rareness of the breed. I brought them back to the house and told Jess about my visit to the shelter. I gave her an ultimatum. It was us or the dogs. They had to go—they were destroying our marriage and our home.

Jess knew deep in her heart that they had to go, but she completely shut down at this point and could not deal with the problem. She only wanted an emotional fix from dog kisses. She ignored the severe harm the dogs were doing to our relationship and home. I pleaded with her again to put in an effort to sell or give them away. I told her she had to do *something* or I would have no other option than to take them away.

Jess assured me she would act, but she did absolutely nothing. It was incredibly frustrating for me to know she had broken so many promises and was willing to let this horrible situation continue. I didn't feel valued in our marriage. I felt that I was secondary to all the things she was doing and the problems she caused.

Shortly before Christmas, I came home from work and was horrified. The dogs had clawed through the linoleum flooring in the kitchen and ripped portions of it up. One of the gates was broken down, and they had destroyed the living room furniture and other portions of the house. One dog had gone upstairs and chewed on my great-great-grandfather's mahogany bedroom set. That was my breaking point. I told Jess that the dogs must go, and I took them away.

Jess experienced extreme guilt for months, knowing that the dogs were euthanized due to her failing to act. She never admitted that it was her fault. She knew this had been her responsibility: she'd known she was supposed to take care of the situation and sell the puppies, and she'd known what would happen to the dogs if they were taken away, but she had done nothing. She redirected her guilt and shame toward me, making me out to be the evil guy, while she completely misrepresented the actual events and didn't tell people of her own failure to act on her promises.

For the first time, I considered divorcing her, but I stayed with her due to the vows I had taken. I still loved her, but I was very unhappy in our marriage with all the damage she had caused. I was tired of constantly having to bail us out of all the problems she created, only to be accused of not caring and not supporting her.

Four

The Pacific Ocean Is a Good Mother-in-Law Barrier

Jess's bridal and prom store was in full operation. She was very busy and had multiple employees. Her customer base and sales grew, but there was no profit. Jess was not paying herself a salary.

She needed more room for storage, so I paid a couple of kids from church to help me build a second story at the back of the store. I also built an office for her, ran all new electrical and network outlets, built dressing rooms for customers, and repainted the store. All my work at the store was in addition to my full-time job at Ford. My dad even came down and helped quite a bit. My mom was working there quite frequently to help with alterations.

The store looked great, but that didn't last long. Shortly after all my work, Jess began buying a huge amount of dresses and useless stuff. The store became extremely cluttered due to the huge amount of inventory. Both floors of the store were full. These dresses were not the current year's fashion; Jess was going to websites with bulk-clearance sales and buying excess inventory that other bridal or prom stores could not sell. She was on a buying spree, getting what she called "great deals," thinking she could resell the dresses at a profit. There was far more inventory coming in than she was selling. All her spending on the massive inventory that was not selling concerned me greatly.

I told Jess that the store no longer looked like a high-class bridal salon; it looked like a secondhand thrift store with all the mess and clutter. Jess didn't see it this way. She told me that many of the prom dresses were seasonal items and would not sell until prom season. She said that all the advertising would go out at the right times. She pretty much ignored all my concerns—I was just a guy with limited fashion sense. Jess assured me that she knew what she was doing.

Jess's emotional problems and conflicts with people got worse. She could not handle the jerks who came in every now and then. If they said anything negative, she took it very personally. She also couldn't handle people not liking her. Many times, when she got home, she would be crying about how others had treated her. My mom tried helping Jess with her issues, tried helping her to toughen up, but nothing worked. I tried telling Jess that these were not personal attacks on her; the people were just rude idiots. Jess knew she had to toughen up, but she would not change or help herself. She had this narrow view of how the world should be and how it should treat her. Nothing could change how she felt.

In a retail store, customers lie a lot. They will go to great lengths in trying to rip off the store. It goes way past normal behavior of haggling over prices. Some women will take two gowns into the dressing room and switch the tags. They'll attempt to remove markdown stickers from one dress and put them on another. They'll say one shop has a certain dress cheaper when it does not. When caught in a lie, they'll get indignant and start yelling. Whoever came up with the phrase "The customer is always right" clearly did not run a retail business. This abusive behavior took a huge toll on Jess's emotional well-being.

Many times when I got home from work and walked in the door, Jess would immediately go off on me, like a floodgate of emotions had opened. She frequently told me about the latest incident of how her character had been insulted. There were a few instances when I didn't even have a chance to get out of the car. She saw me pull into the driveway, came outside, and immediately started to rant while I was still sitting in the car. I asked her many times to please give me just a little while to decompress after I got home before hitting me with these issues, but as usual, she countered by accusing me of never wanting to talk to her. She let up a little for a while, but she soon resumed venting to me.

Internet websites selling bridal gowns increased dramatically, and the store's sales were not increasing. One of the ways bridal stores combat this is on alterations. When a person buys a gown at the store, a greatly reduced rate in alteration charges is given. Many times women complained that it was not fair that Jess was charging more on alterations for gowns they'd bought elsewhere. Jess was having a hard time managing these complaints and the stress and other issues of running the store.

Jess's pride had ramped up during the last few years, and customers falsely accusing her of lying further added to her stress and emotional issues. Jess could not adopt the attitude that they were simply idiots and that she shouldn't let them bother her. Due to her pride, she felt these incidents were a personal assault on her character, and these incidents damaged the very core of her being. There were also thefts in the store, so I installed a digital surveillance system with eight channels of video with audio. This system turned out to be invaluable.

It was prom season, and many mothers and daughters were coming in to get dresses. Jess was spending a lot of time dealing with one family with a morbidly obese daughter. Unfortunately for the girl, the mother and grandmother were trying to make her the perfect princess and dictate every aspect of the prom dress. They were extremely fussy and demanded that every stitch on the dress be perfect for them. It was only a $120 dress, but they loudly demanded all sorts of free alterations. Jess put her heart into this, as she really wanted the girl to have a nice prom. I saw their hateful and demanding behavior and warned Jess that they were nothing but trouble and that she should cut her losses and get out of this situation. Jess felt bad for the girl and continued trying to help. I made sure to archive the security video showing the interactions with these people just in case something happened.

The grandmother was being extremely unrealistic about the dress alterations. If she saw a small pucker in the fabric, she demanded free alteration work to make it near perfect. When someone is that obese, the fabric will pucker between the folds of fat. The grandmother even said, "I want to show off her curves." They were completely delusional, difficult, and abrasive. There was no way I would tolerate that horrible behavior if I were running a business.

Jess didn't want the mother and grandmother to ruin the girl's prom. With the large amount of alterations required, Jess got them to agree to half off the alterations. This was one of Jess's great gifts. She put her heart into someone and wanted to make that person happy, but it was also her greatest weakness, as she took this to the extreme. When someone didn't return the kindness in her store and instead took advantage of her, Jess was devastated.

After all the hours of tedious alterations Jess put into this girl's dress, it was finished, and the mother came in to pick it up. She came in, sat on the couch, refused to pay, and claimed it wasn't done on time. The dress was done, and these claims were an outright lie. Jess brought out the dress and set it on the couch next to her, but the mother refused to acknowledge it. The mother even called *her* mother and said the dress wasn't done and wasn't here. I saw and heard this on the video and couldn't believe she lied to her own mother. The daughter was not around for this. They had already paid for part of the alteration work and demanded a full refund. Jess refused.

A few weeks later, Jess got a small claims court summons. The women were suing her for the cost of the dress they'd never picked up and the alteration fees. They lied, claiming the dress had not been ready for prom and that they'd had to buy another from a different store.

Jess was devastated over this. Her emotional outrage was completely over the top and way outside any type of normal reaction. She wanted to express her anger in court about how her reputation and business had been harmed and how they had insulted her and caused her great pain. I tried to console her, saying they were despicable human beings and would have done the same thing to someone else.

Nothing I said mattered. We discussed how we would fight this lawsuit, and I spent hours trying to convince her that the court wanted facts, not just her describing how her pride was hurt or how she wanted revenge. I told her I would put together all the facts from the video to prove them wrong and that it would be a sure win for us. Jess would not relent. She was livid, beyond reason, and she wanted only to lash out, express her pain, and do whatever it took to get revenge. It took days, but finally Jess agreed to let me speak first in court to present the facts. Then she would speak about how this had hurt her.

I spent a few evenings transcribing the video and wrote up a document showing video screenshots with the dates, times, and what the mothers had said to Jess. I paid particular attention to placing screenshots of the video into my document that showed the dress sitting on the couch next to the mother. I also transcribed the mother's words from the audio with her claiming the dress was not there.

The great thing about small claims court is that you don't have to let the other side know what evidence you have. When the court appearance arrived, the mother and grandmother spoke first, and as I predicted, they lied about everything. They were very loud and hateful, and they expressed how their daughter had been hurt, claiming Jess had ruined her prom. It was all a con—after the hours of work Jess had put in, they had clearly changed their mind and decided to buy another dress somewhere else. I thought these despicable human beings were the ones who had hurt their own child, but they were being perpetual victims and liars. I smiled as I listened to them speak; I knew they were just digging their hole deeper and that I had all the evidence to prove them wrong. I calmly waited with great anticipation to destroy them.

Jess didn't see it this way. She was outraged and started interrupting to correct them. The magistrate, Charles Pope, had to tell Jess to let them speak. I whispered to Jess, "The more they lie, the more I'll destroy them." When the women finished their ridiculous and false story, I got up and spoke on Jess's behalf.

My testimony showing evidence and facts was brutal to them. I read part of the document I had prepared that showed screenshots of the video with their own words transcribed into text. All their false statements were obliterated with my facts. I also told the magistrate that I had a laptop with video evidence showing the completed dress if he wanted to see it.

He said yes, and then I played the video with the audio turned up for all to hear. I showed the portion with the dress sitting next to the mother as she lied into the phone and claimed the dress wasn't there. The women were shocked when they discovered it was all on video. It was glorious to see the look on their faces when they knew all their lies had been exposed. I took great pleasure in outing these despicable human beings in court for what they were. Jess still was not satisfied.

Jess began speaking. She couldn't contain herself and spoke only of her emotional pain. She went on and on. Then the magistrate had to stop her testimony. Luckily for us, I had already proved our case. After Jess finished talking, the mother had to get in the last word. The family was black, and the magistrate was white, and the mother had the pure audacity to say, "How do you know that is me? We all look alike." Charles Pope rolled his eyes in amazement at that outrageous statement of them pulling the race card with him.

Charles Pope wisely didn't issue the ruling in court. He said the court held retailers to a great level of integrity and must ensure all customers are treated fairly. The women smiled, thinking they had won. He would review the case and send out the ruling by mail. I knew Mr. Pope said this only to prevent their making a scene in the courtroom, but Jess was extremely worried. When we left, I tried to reassure her, saying this was a slam dunk for us, and I explained why Mr. Pope had said that. Jess could not be calmed.

A week later, the ruling arrived. We won! Not only that, but they had to pay Jess the balance of alterations due plus the dress's retail cost. When the balance was paid, the women could pick the dress up at the courthouse.

I showed the ruling to Jess and said, "This is great! Those evil bitches lost."

I was expecting Jess to be elated, but she showed a completely opposite reaction. She slumped over and complained how she was hurt. We talked at length, but she would not allow herself to feel any happiness in winning. This situation was all about her hurt pride, and she wanted to lash out and get her revenge. She wanted to make those women pay emotionally and wanted the world to see how she'd been hurt and empathize with her. She was in a depression for two months over this. Multiple people talked with her in an attempt to help, but because she hadn't claimed her vengeance by publicly humiliating these women and having the world sympathize with her emotional pain, Jess stayed depressed. Nothing mattered to her except her hurt pride.

Two years later, when we were waiting in line to vote in local elections, we unexpectedly met Charles Pope. He was running for judge. He recognized us, and we spoke briefly about the old small claims case. It was clear that he had been amused by the women's courtroom antics, and he told us the women had never paid the balance or picked up the dress; it was still at the courthouse. He also told us he felt sorry for the girl. Her mother and grandmother had caused all these problems, and the girl was the real victim in this case. The women's behavior had been so outrageous that this case stuck in his mind. We voted for him.

Jess's demands on me about the store were becoming unreasonable. One incident in particular was when Jess wanted me to go to a fashion expo. This wasn't a local bridal show where I was like a pack mule, helping her and the employees haul dresses, racks, and boxes; this was purely about women's fashion trends and all sorts of different things about women's clothing. It was definitely not my world.

I told her no way, but she said this would be fun for both of us. I looked at her and wondered what she was thinking. She knew I didn't like the fashion industry; she knew I didn't like being around all those dresses or listening to talk about fashion trends or other silly things. She knew I'd help her all I could with hauling boxes, moving racks of dresses, loading things up in our F-150 pickup, and doing the grunt work for bridal shows. Sitting around listening to designers yap about bridal fashion trends was the ultimate man hell for me.

I told her, "You know me; we agreed at the very start of this business that I was not going to be involved in fashion. I'm more comfortable in camo than designer clothes. I'd rather walk around with my bow and arrow in a swamp or in two feet of snow stalking animals. Why are you trying to get me to do something you know will make me miserable?" I also reminded her that I worked a full-time job.

Jess would not relent. She came at this from all different sorts of angles. She tried to tell me that this was something we could do to have fun together, that it would be great, and that we could have a nice trip together. She even said fashion was something I'd be good at.

What the hell? Me good at fashion? That was pure crazy talk. She knew without a doubt how silly and shallow I viewed the fashion industry, and she was only trying to manipulate me. At this point, with her unrelenting badgering, I was getting really irritated. She refused to stop or back down. It was very bizarre and another example of the fantasy she had built up in her head of how people were supposed to act with her. Anyone else who knew me would laugh if someone said I'd have fun going to a women's fashion show. My own wife, who was supposed to know me best, refused to accept this reality.

I'd had enough of it. I looked her straight in the eyes and said, "My balls don't belong in your purse."

She was shocked; she didn't like this comment at all. Then she said I was being unreasonable and crude. I have to admit that comment about my balls was a bit over the top. She then went into a tirade about how I never helped her, never supported her, and never listened to her, and she said I needed to understand her feelings. After all the times of working at her store after getting home from my full-time job, plus working there many weekends, and now she was trying to emotionally blackmail me.

I looked at her and sternly said, "No way in hell am I going to a woman's fashion show," and then I walked away without saying anything else. She packed up and left the next morning without speaking to me. I was OK with that.

The nation's economy took a downturn, and this turn for the worse greatly reduced sales in the store. I found out Jess was way behind on rent and had received an eviction notice. Damn, more money problems. Jess showed me financials that looked very good. She assured me there were no other outstanding debts, and I even saw a monthly credit card sales report that showed a very promising picture. She needed a bit of cash to make it through the economic downturn and hold her over until the next seasonal sale of dresses.

We took out a home equity loan to fund her store. This was on top of the mortgage. Jess assured me that $20,000 would see her through.

Jess's mother, Suda, came to visit from Thailand and was going to stay for three months. She wanted to help her daughter with the store since she was also an experienced seamstress. It went well for a short while, and then the extremely controlling aspect of her mother reared its ugly head. Suda would not follow Jess's directions about how a customer wanted a wedding gown or dress altered. Suda did it her way, which got customers upset, and then Jess had to redo the work. This added stress, and the worsening relationship with her mother really affected Jess. Suda ruled her with an iron fist. In Suda's world, she was the mother and knew best, and Jess had to do what she said. Jess would not stand up to her mother.

I spoke to Jess many times before getting involved between them and told her she couldn't let her mother control everything and put a guilt trip on her. I told Jess, "You are the boss of the store, and she must do what you tell her to satisfy the customers. This is our financial future at stake, not your mother's. If Suda has her way, she will ruin the store."

The next day Jess was an emotional wreck. She was extremely upset and could not work. She had the talk with her mom, and her mom reacted by putting the ultimate guilt trip on her. Suda told Jess, "When I die, you don't have to come to my grave, because I know you don't love me." It was a vicious and cruel thing to say. Jess did not have the strength to stand up to her mother, and this comment cut her deeply to the core.

Suda's control was not limited to the store. She stayed at our home and was trying to dictate to me how and when I should eat, whether we should keep certain doors in the home open or shut, how I needed to treat Jess, and many other things. I gave her a little slack because she was Jess's mom and there were some cultural differences, but that horrible comment about not having Jess come to her grave was way over the top and uncalled for in any culture. I had a talk with Suda and laid down the law. I told her I was not going to tolerate her treating my wife that way and would not allow her to run my home.

Suda went into a rage. It was a purely emotional reaction, simply because I would not put up with her control and submit to her. She cursed my character, told me I was a horrible husband, and said she was sorry Jess had married me. Just two weeks ago, she had told me I was the best man Jess could ever hope for, but now in her eyes, I was a horrible monster. The next day she accused me of having an affair with Leah, a sixteen-year-old girl who worked at the store. Leah was a girl whom both Jess and I had known for a long time, and our families were friends. Leah's mom even worked at the store sometimes. This horrible false accusation was the last straw.

I told Jess her mother was no longer welcome in our home and must leave. I went on to say I would not tolerate Suda causing such emotional harm to her and that I wouldn't tolerate Suda's false accusations and attempts to bring harm to our marriage. I was kicking her out, and Jess knew there was no bargaining with me about this. Jess was extremely upset, more so at her mother for saying those things to me, but a part of her appreciated me standing up to her mother and not letting her mom treat her that way. Jess wasn't all that upset with me; she was mainly upset with all the problems her mother's actions had caused.

Jess didn't want her to leave immediately and instead needed some time to heal their relationship. My mom and dad offered to have Suda stay at their home until she left, so Suda stayed there. My mom and Suda often came down to the store together to help Jess. Jess tried to explain away her mother's behavior to me, saying it was partly due to their culture, but I said no, not that type of behavior. Her actions were cruel, malicious, and unacceptable in any culture. Suda stayed another month and a half and wanted to extend her stay, but I told Jess that Suda couldn't intrude on my parents' lives anymore and that it was time for her to go home.

After Suda left, Jess remained upset about her mom's actions. Jess told me, "I wish my mother was more like yours." Jess loved and respected my mom a lot and sought out her counsel very frequently. One of the many reasons Jess held my mom in such high regard was that after we were married, my mom told Jess she would love her as if Jess were her own daughter. Jess was taken aback by this at first and couldn't understand how my mom could show such unconditional love. Jess asked me once how my mom did this, and I told Jess it was because of my mother's loving nature and values. I'm an incredibly blessed man to have been raised by such great parents.

A few years later, Suda developed Alzheimer's and Parkinson's diseases. She forgot the incident between us and thought of me as a good man. Weird how that worked out.

FIVE

Prescription Opioids Are Evil

It was 2006, and our marriage was getting worse. Jess's pride and sense of victimization had reached new heights. In addition to this, her perceived levels of pain over little things ramped up, and she seemed to slipping further into hypochondria. She told people incredible stories of extreme pain issues that didn't make sense to me, but when she told these stories, people gave her sympathy that Jess seemed to feed on.

We were in church one Sunday, and a man was asking about getting a suit altered. I told him Jess was an incredible seamstress and could do this type of work better than anyone around. Jess said in a stern voice, "I'm a designer, not a seamstress."

The intensity of her reaction really took me by surprise. We talked about this when we got home, and I tried to find out why Jess was so upset over what I'd said.

Jess asked me, "How would you feel if I called you a mechanic since you are an engineer?"

I said, "I'm a great mechanic, too, and it wouldn't bother me a bit. I know you would only be giving me a compliment."

Jess didn't see it this way, and she went into a rant about how I always cut her down in public and disagreed with her in front of other people. It was unbelievable how her pride had ramped up to such an out-of-control state that even when I gave her a compliment, she took it as an insult to her position and abilities.

One notable incident of her out-of-control pride happened with her trying to advertise with *Pageantry* magazine. Jess really enjoyed beauty pageants and was giddy when dealing with these women. I went to one local teenage beauty pageant with Jess just to see what it was like. Wow, what a strange world. It's a whole different subculture of behavior. Jess was a judge, and the other judges were hard-core pageant people. In my opinion, their votes didn't go to the teenage girl who had the best appearance or talent; the votes went to the girl who acted the best in this weird robot-like ritual of having the proper arm and hand wave, head tilt, contrived smile, and walking style. I thought the girl who won acted unnaturally, and her behavior was creepy.

I didn't find out about the situation with *Pageantry* magazine until Jess was ranting at home about her Christian values being insulted and their removing wording from her ad. She was livid over this. I asked what was wrong, and she showed me the ad in the magazine. Jess said they purposely had stripped out her mentioning that her faith was instrumental in helping the pageant girls. I started investigating to find out what had happened because, by Jess's description, it was completely unacceptable for a magazine to alter her ad wording.

What I found was shocking. Jess had missed multiple deadlines to submit her final ad copy for print. What she finally submitted was a total mess. It had looked like a child had written and formatted the ad, with multiple spelling and grammar errors. She had exceeded the space available, and the magazine had been forced to trim some of her wording. They actually did a very good job, considering the unprofessional mess Jess had submitted. I didn't dare tell Jess this. All I could do was to console her and offer my help in the future. This situation could have been avoided if Jess had done the work on time or asked for help. Instead of admitting her mistake and learning from it, she went into rage mode from feeling insulted and victimized by the magazine.

The situation at the store got worse. On top of all the clutter, Jess created an environment that was dangerous for her and the employees. There were sharp edges all over, with boxes on the floor and stairs. There was so much clutter in the alteration area that she was tripping over junk and getting hurt. Jess was getting bruises from falling or bumping into things. She claimed that she was accident-prone because of all the things that happened to her. Jess wasn't accident-prone; she was just careless. The teenage girls working there emulated her careless behavior and made it worse by adding to the clutter and creating more safety hazards.

I came there many times and had to get her to clean things up. I lost count of how many times I told her that if one of the girls got hurt falling down the stairs due to the junk piled on the steps, we would be sued and lose everything. Jess's attitude was frustrating. This was our future she was putting at risk due to her careless behavior. Jess would put trash in the doorway between rooms with the idea that the next person through would pick it up and take it to the Dumpster. She also piled things on the stairs with the same idea, but she and the girls just stepped over it, leaving the junk. She started doing this at home and almost fell down the stairs multiple times when she tripped on her crap. I put a stop to that at home, and she told me I was being unreasonable and controlling.

We scheduled a big cleanup at the store. There was so much piled-up clutter and useless stuff that we filled the Dumpster. I wasn't too happy about having to pay everyone to clear out the mess. It should have not been created in the first place, but the cleanup had to be done. Piles of junk were everywhere, making it difficult to work. When I was in the other room, I overheard Jess cutting me down in front of people about this. That didn't sit well with me, and I told Jess I didn't appreciate her remarks. She said I had misheard her—she would never say that.

The next weekend I came in to do more handyman work, and the piles of trash were back. Trash was on the floor, between doorways, on the steps. Trip hazards were everywhere. I was pissed. After all that work cleaning up, Jess was still doing it and had created another huge mess in just one week. She knew she was putting all the employees at risk, but she wouldn't stop her careless behavior. She would never survive in the corporate world and would have been fired over such repeated behavior.

I called everyone, including Jess, into the backroom and gave them all a harsh speech.

"Jess runs the store," I said, "but I will shut this place down and start firing anyone who creates these hazards. Do you people want me to review the security video now and start firing the people doing this? You all are responsible for each other's safety, and I won't ever tolerate any shit being put on the stairs or in the doorway. You are going to get someone seriously hurt or killed falling down the steps with this stupid behavior. Do you people understand?"

There was silence. They knew how serious I was. This speech finally got through to Jess and all of them, but I was very frustrated that I had to be the bad guy since Jess was complicit in causing this issue.

The next time I was at the store, one of the teenage girls came up to me and wanted an apology for my calling her stupid. The nerve of this silly teenager wanting me to appease her hurt feelings was unbelievable. I looked right at her and said, "I didn't call you stupid. I said everyone's behavior creating these hazards that will get people hurt is stupid. Are you being stupid, and should I review the security video to find out?"

She was speechless and walked away. I overheard her say to another girl, "Mr. Cole is mean."

Good, I thought. *Now this special little snowflake knows I won't tolerate her crap. She can't understand I care about her and everyone else's welfare. I'll gladly be the bad guy if that is what it takes to stop them from hurting themselves.*

Jess began a discussion with me about wanting to get a Yorkshire terrier. We still hadn't healed from that previous dog disaster, and after all the hell we'd gone through before, now she wanted to get another dog? No way. I told her it was too soon—we still needed some time, and I didn't want the hassle of a dog. There was too much hurt going around. Jess went into attack mode and started into more of her you-never-let-me-have-what-I-want routine. I stood my ground and said, "No way. We both have to agree on this." She said that this time it would be different and that she would take care of the dog.

A few days later, I saw a shoebox full of prescription pills from Thailand. There were painkillers, muscle relaxants, generic Prozac, and a bunch of other pills for mental disorders. What was this woman taking? Her behavior had become increasingly bizarre and out of control. Now I suspected why. She was self-medicating with pills without her doctor knowing what she was taking.

I asked Jess where she had gotten these pills, and she admitted her mother had given them to her. She said her mother had told her what to take and had said it would help with stress. I told her we needed to throw them away; they were dangerous and strong medications that should only be administered under the care of her doctor. Jess said she took the pills only when she needed them and did not want to have pills for mental disorders on her record. That was her pride talking again.

Nothing I said got through to her. I could have just tossed them all, but then she would have accused me of being controlling again. It was incredibly frustrating dealing with her.

A few days later, Jess called and told me she had bought a Yorkie and that it was at the store. Damn it. This was supposed to be a marriage where we agreed on things, but she did not care about my feelings. She did whatever she wanted without considering any consequences.

I was extremely angry and yelled into the phone, "How dare you do this? Don't you even think of bringing that damn animal into our home, or I'll cut its head off. Do you understand how serious I am? I want you to return it immediately."

I wouldn't have hurt the dog; I said that in anger, but it was wrong of me to say that. I wouldn't have let it in our house though—I had taken enough of this behavior from her.

I looked through her e-mails and found conversations with a Yorkie breeder. I called the breeder, gave her a history on Jess's behavior, and said we had not agreed to get a dog and there was no way I was letting it into our home. The breeder was angry, not at me but at Jess, for telling her a completely different story about how we both wanted a Yorkie.

Jess disappeared for most of the day. She came back to the house late in the afternoon and was completely out of it. She wasn't walking straight; she was confused and couldn't speak in complete sentences. I asked her to lie down, but she took off in the car. I was extremely worried for her in that mental state and called the police. I briefed them about her state of mind, and they put out a disturbed person report with a description of the car. Two hours later she came back home a little better but extremely agitated.

She started ranting using the same old false accusations about my not caring for her and controlling her and all sorts of other wild things. I couldn't understand much of what she said, as she was rambling and not making sense. I was extremely worried about her out-of-control mental state and called 911. I was talking to her and on my phone with the dispatcher during this exchange. Then she spiraled completely out of control. She got her .380 Kel-Tec semiauto pistol, held it in her hand, and said she was going to shoot herself.

The dispatcher sent someone out immediately and was asking me to get the gun from her. It took a while, but finally I got the gun. The police arrived, but Jess saw them. She ran upstairs and locked herself in the bathroom.

The police were going to bust down the door, but I told them I could open it. It's a typical interior door lock that can be opened from the outside with a small screwdriver. When I got the door open, the police tried talking to her, but she was in her own world and could not be reasoned with.

An ambulance arrived, and the police escorted her outside and strapped her down to a stretcher. They took her to the St. Joseph Hospital emergency room in Ann Arbor, Michigan. I took her box of pills and went to the hospital. I gave the nurses the pills, and they were shocked at how many there were. A couple of nurses began writing down a list of all the pills to show the doctors. A short while later, a couple of doctors talked with her, and then they brought in a psychiatrist. I didn't hear their conversations, but then they met with me alone.

They told me Jess was in severe distress, unstable, and very depressed. They recommended taking her to Providence Hospital for a three-day involuntary psych hold to evaluate her. I asked if this was necessary, and they said yes, especially because she had threatened to shoot herself. They told me either I could give my consent for her to be taken, or they would take the necessary steps to get her involuntarily committed for her own safety. I knew how bad she was and signed the commitment paperwork. This was a really, really horrible day.

Providence Hospital released Jess three days later but with the conditions that I had to show proof of arranging an appointment with a psychiatrist so that she could go through counseling. At first Jess was happy. She said nothing was wrong, and she believed she'd proved that to the staff at Providence Hospital. She said she had to help others there, because they were having a lot of issues. She was in complete denial about her own problems. A few days later, she turned her rage at me.

Jess accused me of lying to the police and making up everything, claiming it was my fault she'd been committed. She denied saying she was going to shoot herself. She demanded I get the 911 recording to hear what happened. I got the recording on a cassette tape in a few days after filing a Freedom of Information request with the Washtenaw County sheriff's office. I had to buy a cassette tape player because I didn't have one. Cassette tapes? Really? That's ancient tech, and it was very surprising they couldn't e-mail me the audio of the call or put the file on my flash drive.

Jess and I listened to it, and there it was, just as I said: she'd said she was going to shoot herself. Jess stayed in denial and accused me of not understanding her words because the tape was not clear. Listening to the tape only made her more hostile. She accused me of putting her in the hospital because I wanted her out of the house for some reason, and she said she'd find out why. Her ranting continued with her saying she would get me back for having her committed. In her mind, I had done this for some unknown malicious reason.

Over the next few weeks, we had many talks about this incident. After listening to the tape a few more times, Jess finally admitted that she had said she was going to shoot herself. She said it was still my fault for not understanding that she was being sarcastic, and she continued to blame me. For the next couple of months, this incident came up repeatedly, and Jess kept pressuring me to admit I was wrong. There was no way I was going to submit to her will, and she only ramped up the verbal attacks and kept accusing me of never talking to her about this. This began a habitual pattern with her: either I submitted to her, or she would not let up and would come after me with continuous false accusations to get her way. She began calling me the controller in our marriage.

Our relationship settled down a bit, but she was still having many issues. The stress at the store only added to her problems. One day Jess called me at work and said she had hurt herself. She was at home standing on a table in the basement and had stepped backward and fallen off the table. I asked if she was OK or if she needed to go to the hospital. She wasn't sure about going to the hospital, but she wasn't dizzy and was seeing clearly. I asked if she wanted me to come home right away to take her to the doctor. She said no.

Little did we know that she had done more damage than we thought. She started having neck pain, and the doctors thought it was from whiplash. In addition to this, they said arthritis had set in from the damage to the C4 and C5 vertebrae. They didn't know if a previous injury had added to the issue. The doctors started Jess on Vicodin and other pain meds.

Once she started on those pills, her physical and mental health went downhill. Jess always was extremely physically sensitive and felt pain at a much higher level than most. Her mental issues were not being taken care of, and she began having panic and anxiety attacks multiple times a week.

Jess started seeing a psychiatrist on a regular basis. The first one was Dr. Mendell. He was a very kind elderly man, but there was very little progress with improving her behavior. In August 2007, Jess asked what things I would like the doctor to help her with. Jess finally realized she had many problems, so it was a positive sign that she asked me. She asked me to put together a list of my concerns. I told her I would write up my thoughts and send her an e-mail that she could bring to the doctor if she wanted. She also asked if I wanted to go with her for a session with Mendell.

I replied, "Of course I'll go." Jess started crying and went upstairs to soak in the bathtub.

I spent the next few days putting together a list of issues that I thought were major issues Jess needed help with. This is an excerpt of the e-mail I sent her:

Worry
She is an extremely sensitive person and the little problems in life severely affect her well being. Even when these problems are solved, she holds on to the worry and emotional pain it caused her for months or years. She will not let go of the past problems of her life and the multitude of problems and worry builds up.

Taking things personally
If someone at the store or other places does something wrong, tries to rip her off, or is dishonest, Jess takes it extremely personally. She also can be very offended at what others will say, or how she perceives people thing about her. She will put herself into a very depressed state and ask why did they do this to her. I have tried to explain to her that some people are just jerks and that this is what they do. They will do this to the next store, situation, or person just because they are not a decent moral person and they will do anything to get an advantage or money. I tell her that these situations have nothing to do with who she is, but she cannot stop being hurt and holding on to the hurt for months.

Planning.
She is a very poor planner, does not keep a consistent schedule for herself, and is habitually late in both her personal and professional life. She forgets appointments and things she has to do. She will write things down on loose scraps of paper, but loses them. I have tried to get her to keep one book where she writes all things down, but she still resorts to the loose scraps of paper and loses them. She also will not keep one notebook of things that she wants me to do for the store. I have asked repeatedly for this, but she just keeps on with her way and still hits me with requests at odd times during the day when she has the impulse or idea.

Self image and guilt.
She feels bad about herself. Many times when I look at her she immediately looks down at herself and says I am looking at her

because she is fat. She automatically assumes and accuses me of looking at her in a negative way because she is feeling guilty about herself some way. This can be about her weight, hair, not doing something right, or the many other faults she thinks she has. She also asks me many times if she is a bad person. Often she feels that people treat her bad because of something she might have done.

Trying to please everyone.
She tries to help and make everyone happy. This in itself is not wrong, but when people are not happy, she feels bad that she did something wrong.

Treating her employees as her close friends.
She treats her employees as her friends, then takes it personally and gets hurt when they do something wrong. She will call them and say, " hello dear" and be overly sweet to them. I try to get her to separate herself from this and explain that the employees are there for the business, not for her personal friendships. She knows this, but will not stop trying to make them all her friends. The result is that she gets hurt often.

Eating right.
She has a terrible diet and does not eat balanced meals unless I prepare them for her or remind her. If left to herself, she will eat just meat, rice, or junk food. She is a snacker and will eat what she "feels" instead of a decent meal. She will binge on junk food like KFC, and then gets upset if I say something when her health is being affected and declines.

She does not take the time to eat right in the morning or during the day. She does not get up early enough to eat breakfast. She gets busy (or says she forgot to eat) at the store and does not eat properly during the day. She has collapsed three times in the past 4 years and was taken to the hospital via ambulance twice due to poor diet. When she does not eat during the day, at night she gets very hungry and eats sweets or fruit late at night. This causes her to gain weight and she feels worse about herself. She knows what she has to do, but refuses to do it and comes up with multiple excuses to justify her bad habits. She will resort to blaming me when she is feeling very guilty about herself and accuses me of watching her eating and that I cause her to eat poorly.

Her mood gets depressed and she gets headaches when she drinks diet soda with aspartame. She will still drink it and gives the excuse "I like it." She will buy it by the case and it causes her great harm but she still will not stop.

Taking sleeping medication.
She knows that she has to stop at night and take the sleeping medication in bed and not do anything else. She repeatedly will not do this and will not stop even though she is tired. I have gotten with her a number of times because of this and get frustrated because she will not do what is right for herself. I have asked, and even pleaded with her probably 20 plus times on this one issue, but she will not do what she knows is right for her.

Exaggeration of what I do.
When she is mad, she uses terms like, "always" "every time" for my behavior. She feels that I really do this and can't admit that she is wrong. If I present the facts, she becomes very angry and defensive and says it was my fault for misunderstanding her or not doing what she wanted.

After I sent this to her in an e-mail, she made no mention of it again.

We went to see Dr. Mendell together. During this session, Jess talked, and he only asked her how she was sleeping, if she was staying asleep, or if she felt anxious or upset. He wrote several prescriptions based on what Jess told him. There was no counseling and no attempt to address her behaviors or issues. The guy only gave her pills. I wasn't happy about this at all and told Jess that handing out pills like candy without counseling is not the answer. I asked if she would see a different psychiatrist and see a therapist, but she refused.

Jess continued to see Mendell. Her issues went unresolved. Her anger ramped up, her pride increased, and her victim mentality got worse. She also became very jealous. Jess even cut Lucette's picture out of the church directory. I had to refrain from mentioning female coworkers, or I could expect an interrogation from her. She was OK with only one woman at my work, Anna. Jess had met her a few years earlier.

Anna was an incredibly brilliant woman. She was also a rabid atheist and a far-left liberal. People had thought we would battle it out due my being a conservative Christian, but I never pushed my faith on Anna and tried to live according to my faith. Anna respected that. Anna was single, and I had met her when I was single. But Jess had no jealous thoughts of her because of the first time she had met Anna, shortly after we were married.

A few years earlier, when Jess had met Anna, Anna had been building a barn for her horses. She had ordered a bunch of rough sawn oak boards for the stalls. I added some wood on to her order since woodworking was a hobby of mine. The wood was delivered, and Jess and I went over to help Anna unload and to pick mine up. This was a working horse ranch on ten acres, so you had to dress accordingly: Carhartt jackets, gloves, boots, and other gear. It had rained the previous day, so the soil was muddy.

Jess said hi to Anna. They chatted a bit during this first meeting, and then we got to work. The oak planks were freshly cut and very heavy from being wet. They were twelve feet long, ten inches wide, and an inch and a quarter thick. Jess and Anna could handle a board together; I carried one at a time. Then Anna told us about Phil, the new guy she had met online. He was an optometrist and was coming over to her house today. It was their first face-to-face meeting. There was one problem: Anna hadn't told Phil he was going to be put to work to haul lumber for her new horse stalls.

Phil showed up in his cute little Volvo. He was wearing a trendy Eddie Bauer fleece vest with clogs on his feet. Just from the first impression I had of Phil, I knew a dating relationship was not going to last with him and Anna. Anna immediately put him to work. We had to carry these boards across a muddy corral with scattered piles of horse manure into the barn. I felt sorry for Phil. He seemed the type who hadn't done any hard physical labor in his life, and even though he was six inches taller and bigger than me, he really struggled carrying the heavy boards.

His pretty clogs were useless for trudging through mud and horse manure. I lost count of how many times the clogs got pulled off his feet. I still remember the sucking sound they made when Phil had to balance on one foot, slip the other foot back into the clog, and pull it out of the mud. It was hilarious watching a pampered yuppie in this foreign and harsh environment as he tried to look competent for Anna. His soft fleece vest was shredded from the rough oak planks and looked like a pincushion filled with splinters.

Then the day got even more intriguing with drama. (This is pretty much a given with Anna.) Earlier in the day, Anna thought we might need more help, so she called her ex-boyfriend to come over to lend a hand. He still had feelings for Anna and came over with high hopes of getting back together. It was hilarious watching this interaction between the two guys. Here were the ex-boyfriend and the new boyfriend working together for Anna, hauling planks through mud and horse manure. We finished unloading the planks, and Anna ordered pizza for lunch. Phil said he couldn't stay and left. You don't have to be a rocket scientist to understand why he left.

Jess had no idea why this drama had unfolded before her and could not understand why the two men were acting very weird toward each other. She also didn't understand why Phil had been dressed like that, so I briefed her on this bizarre situation.

Jess's eyes opened in amazement, and she said, "That was Phil's first date with Anna?"

"Yes, dear," I said with a laugh.

"Did Phil know what we would be doing?"

"No, dear."

"She invited over her ex, too?"

"Yes, dear."

"Why would she do that?"

"That's just Anna, dear."

We burst out laughing. I asked Jess what would have happened if I had had her haul lumber on our first date. She looked at me and said, "There would not be a second."

It was due to this experience that Jess never felt any jealousy toward Anna, even if I went over to her place alone to help with the barn. Jess knew I would never have any romantic attraction toward Anna.

When the previous situation with Jess being put in the psych ward calmed down, she brought up the subject of getting some Yorkies again. I was more open to this now and agreed, but I had her sign an agreement that the dogs would be spayed and that she was completely responsible for their care and training. Even my mom said that a little dog might help Jess, as she needed more love in her life since we could not have children. We got two Yorkie puppies, and Jess named them both. The first one was Diva, and we picked her up in January of 2007. Then we got the second one, Sasi, a few months later. Jess took them both to the store with her, and almost all the women and girls who came in loved to see the two Yorkies with bows in their hair.

I have to admit that Diva stole my heart—she was a real daddy's girl. She had a rough-and-tumble personality and was not the typical fragile little lapdog. Jess was a bit jealous about how Diva bonded to me. It's because Diva loved to play rough, but Jess wanted Diva to calmly stay on her lap. It was not in Diva's character to stay calm on a lap, but it was Sasi's, and Sasi always stayed right next to Jess.

However, if Diva got hurt or was feeling sick, she would go to Jess over me. There was one incident when Diva and I were running around playing. I ran out of the room, and Diva chased me. Diva collided with a door and let out a little yelp. She immediately ran back to Jess, jumped on her lap for comfort, and looked back at me with a dirty look.

Jess petted Diva, laughed at me, and said, "What did Daddy do to you?"

We remembered and laughed about this incident for many years.

SIX

END OF THE STORE

I spent a lot of time building a website for the business, but working with Jess on this was extremely frustrating. She wanted to control everything but knew nothing about website programming. We spent many hours together going over fonts, colors, and format for the site, and I designed it with a style Jess really liked.

The day it was supposed to go live on the Internet, Jess changed her mind about how it was going to look. These last-minute major changes she wanted were out of the question. I told her no—we had agreed on this and couldn't make these major changes now. We could make tweaks to it while the website was up, but the website had to go up ASAP to generate business for the store.

Jess still would not relent. She asked me to teach her how to change it, and I tried to convince her to let me be the nerd. I explained to her that as the store owner and manager, it wasn't her job to get into the inner workings of website programming and that she did not have the time to learn this. Jess would not relent and then demanded I give her the base code so that she could modify it. This request was completely unreasonable, and I told her no. Jess had no clue how the website worked or about the HTML coding required.

She was not happy with my refusal. She called me a control freak and said I wouldn't even let her try. I tried to explain to her that she could not do everything and had to trust others, especially with a job like this, where she had no fundamental understanding of coding. Jess still wanted to try, but I would not give in to her, knowing that she would completely screw things up and cause me more aggravation in fixing what she broke.

With the website up, both Jess and I wanted to get the entire inventory online to sell, but this was going to be a huge task. There were over eight hundred dresses to sell, and each dress needed five pictures: ones to show the front, back, and sides and a close-up. I told Jess I would do the research to see what we needed for camera equipment and lights to take pictures. I also set up a shopping cart system on the website. With all these dresses, we needed at least four thousand pictures to populate the online catalog. Efficiency was key to getting this done with minimal color correction of each picture.

There was no way we had the time to individually edit more than four thousand pictures to ensure the dress color people saw online matched what they bought. After a long time asking questions on different Internet forums and consulting photographers, I had a consensus about how to do this in the cheapest and fastest way with great results. What we needed was a dedicated room using lighting not affected by natural sunlight. We would take a few pictures and then adjust the light position and color settings on the camera to get reasonable and repeatable results good enough for all the pictures we had to take. The pros said never to use natural sunlight, as the light colors changed with different times of day and weather conditions.

Jess agreed this was the way to go, so I bought the equipment. All we needed was a dedicated room. Jess was going to clear out a space for this, but she didn't. I asked her multiple times over a couple of weeks. She promised me many times and told me the employees were going to rearrange stuff to make space, but she never got it done.

Instead of clearing out a room, Jess had a new idea to take pictures at the front of the store by the large windows because there was space there. This was a huge problem, since it was the area used for window displays; we would have to tear everything down to take pictures and then put the displays back up every time. The natural sunlight would also screw up the colors, and every photo would need color correction.

It would be a nearly impossible task to do this every day, and I told Jess it couldn't work. We needed a dedicated room, as we had agreed. Jess argued that her way would work if she could just show me, but I explained to her the magnitude of repetitive work required. She would not listen, wanted to do it her way, and said I wouldn't even let her try, just like with the website. I showed Jess again what the pros had said and tried to convince her to rely on their judgment. She still would not listen. Her stubbornness and unwillingness to listen to people who did this for a living was unbelievable. Jess dug her heels in and refused to listen to anyone.

I finally told Jess, "Go ahead and take pictures your way, but I refuse to waste my time in direct contradiction to what we agreed on and what the pros said."

I reminded her I had a full-time job and couldn't spend all these hours working on her store doing things only her way. Jess didn't budge. Not only that, but she took only a few pictures doing it her way and then stopped. I tried multiple times to get the pictures taken, but Jess sabotaged my best efforts. The result of Jess's stubbornness and not following through was that we could not sell anything online. The potential of another revenue stream was lost.

The last year her store was open, 2007 to 2008, the business was not going well. I attempted to find out what the financial situation was, but she accused me of not trusting her and trying to control her. She revealed some debt but hid how bad it really was. When creditors started coming after me, the situation could not be hidden anymore, and the business collapsed in March 2008. Jess was served with an eviction notice due to being three months behind in rent.

I looked at the daily sales and tried to come up with a solution. We could have paid the back rent to stay awhile longer and have a complete going-out-of-business sale to minimize the debt, but at this point, Jess was unwilling to try and said the money coming in wouldn't justify it. There was nothing I could do. Jess would not continue, so the store had to close.

We had a weeklong going-out-of-business sale, but that didn't generate as much cash as I had expected. The huge inventory Jess had accumulated was not selling, and she did not advertise as she said she would. I was able to sell some of the furniture and fixtures on Craigslist and other Internet sites, but all that cash went to the costs of closing the business.

I looked around town to find a short-term lease for about three months so we could sell the rest of the inventory. I would have to take charge and do all the advertising and marketing; Jess was a mess and not able to do it. No one was willing to give us a short-term lease; they all wanted a multiyear commitment.

The staff, Jess, and I boxed up the entire inventory. There were 135 two-foot-square boxes in total containing close to nine hundred dresses. We put all this in our 1,550-square-foot home, along with the clothing racks, fixtures, fabric, sewing equipment, and everything else from the store. Our house was packed full. The next day there was a major incident with a customer at our house. The woman had paid for her wedding dress, and alterations had been completed. Jess said the dress had been shipped to her via FedEx. The woman had not received it, so Jess told her to come to our house.

I'm not exactly sure of all the details, but there was a huge blowup between Jess and the woman. I tried to help, but Jess was completely out of it and irrational. I asked Jess if she had the FedEx receipt to show the woman the dress had been shipped, but there was no receipt. The woman was very upset and knew Jess was irrational. She made multiple angry comments that Jess had serious issues and was not right.

Jess retreated into the house, started slamming things around, and then smashed an expensive camera on the floor. I went outside and told the woman I'd find out what happened and would ensure the dress was delivered to her. It turned out the dress had not been shipped, but Jess's pride would not allow her to admit this. Jess claimed the store manager was supposed to ship it. I never found out why the package had not been shipped, but I made sure the woman got her dress. Jess accused me again of controlling her.

A week after all the inventory was moved in our house, I told Jess I wanted to leave the past behind and move on, but Jess would not forgive herself or other people she felt had wronged her. She tore herself apart with feelings of failure, anger, and low self-esteem, and she couldn't move on. She accused me of not being able to move on. Jess would not stop accusing others and me of not caring about her. We had many talks about moving forward and not bringing up our past mistakes, but she still was controlled by her emotions and lashed out at those around her, using my past mistakes as a weapon to justify her anger and pride. Even though we had talked at length about the same issues over and over, she still accused me of "never" talking, not understanding her, and "never" putting her first. Her false accusations against me were becoming unbearable.

Jess started telling me she was afraid I would hurt her, because she'd been beaten by her ex-husband. Based on her history of habitual lying with a wild victim mentality, I had doubts about this alleged abuse. I asked her if I had ever shoved her, hit her, raised a hand to her, or thrown things at her. She said, "Of course not," and then I asked why she thought I might. She said only that it might happen, and I asked her if I was anything like her ex. She said no. I said I didn't get into conflicts with other people, because I wanted peace, and then she accused me of being too passive and letting people walk all over me.

A few months passed, but Jess was completely unmotivated to do anything about the inventory in our home. She talked about selling dresses out of the house, but it was just talk. I asked her many times to try and do something, but she refused. I even put a couple of ads on Craigslist and eBay to try and sell everything as bulk lots, but she would not follow up on any of the ads. It was very frustrating. She ignored the problem with our home, which now looked like it belonged on one of those hoarder shows on TV. Store stuff was everywhere, and I was constantly shifting boxes around to try to make space. We stopped having people over due to the huge mess. It was embarrassing.

The mess in our home was very difficult to take. I lost count of how many times I came back to my once happy, clean home and thought, *Why has my life come to this?* Being a slightly nerdy and tidy engineer now surrounded by all this crap packed into almost every room in my home was very frustrating. This frustration was compounded by my having to work hard to pay off the second mortgage and home equity loan, while Jess did nothing to help with the finances. She avoided the problem by going shopping instead of trying to help. I asked every couple of weeks if she had tried to sell the inventory or do something, but she always came up with a lame excuse, like she'd had a busy day.

It took quite a while for her to start doing something about the inventory in our home. Mom had many talks with her and was a big help in motivating Jess. Jess got a teenager to help her move things around and relied on word of mouth to sell dresses. She called a bunch of her prior customers to tell them she was selling dresses below cost. She sold only a few.

One of my concerns, I told her, was that now we were opening up our home to strangers and potential criminals. I was worried for her safety—someone might think we had a lot of money stashed in the home from dress sales. Jess said her customers were nice people and would never do that, but I thought the problem was that their friends could be potential criminals. They might come over to rob and harm her while I was at work. I repeatedly asked her to look into selling everything off as bulk lots for her own safety. I didn't tell Jess that her efforts were not working—anything negative would further demotivate her.

After only a few weeks, Jess stopped doing anything about the dresses. I asked her to look for a job to keep herself occupied and to help with all our expenses. One of my reasons for asking her to do this was that her depression and victim mentality were getting worse. She was not doing anything with her life, and sitting around watching TV all day was destroying her. The pure trash on daytime TV seemed to be geared toward people with no careers or aspirations. The commercials for ambulance-chasing attorneys telling people they are all victims were a constant bombardment. It was negatively affecting her outlook on life.

Instead of getting a job she was talented at, she took a part-time position as a receptionist at St. Paul. I was glad and told her it was good that she was working again and was surrounded by good people. Part of me wasn't too happy with this menial job, but at least it was something. Jess was an incredible salesperson, dress designer, and seamstress, but all her natural gifts and talents were being wasted. She took the easy route instead of starting her career back up. I kept my mouth shut about my thoughts on her not trying to do better, for her own sake.

Creditors continued calling Jess and me on a regular basis and sending mail demanding payment. A few creditors served her with papers to appear in court, and Jess began the paperwork to declare chapter 7 bankruptcy to keep them at bay. Before she could file, she was required to go through credit counseling and take a class. We had to submit our household income and expenses and tally all the known creditors with their debt.

Jess did an exceptional job with this. She knew how important it was and spent weeks digging through all the files and getting the totals. The debt was huge. She declared $293,000 owed to creditors, but there was $551,000 of total debt. This included what we owed from remortgaging our home, the additional home equity loan, and taxes to the IRS and Michigan Department of Treasury she had not paid. The bankruptcy didn't cover the costs of the second mortgage and home equity loan used to fund her store, and I was stuck paying those.

Chapter 7 bankruptcy does not eliminate tax debt. Jess had $74,300 combined tax debt between the IRS and the Michigan Treasury. I was numb at this point. Jess had hidden this from me also. Even with all the talks we'd had about lies of omission, she had still done it again.

It was also bad for my parents. Jess had convinced my mom to give her an initial $30,000 loan without telling me. Jess had an incredible gift for manipulating facts and coming up with stories to make people do things they would not normally do. This loan was another example of how she could bend people to her will. The loan wasn't all the money she took from my mom. Jess also manipulated her into signing up for credit cards with my mom as the account holder and then getting additional cards issued in Jess's name for the store. Jess convinced Mom that I would be extremely angry if I found out about these credit cards, so this was hidden from me also. Near the end of the store's closing, Jess racked up an additional $43,800 in credit card debt in my mom's name. My parents were out $73,800 in total.

A while after the store closed, my dad told me my mom had been crying at their home before everything collapsed. She had told Jess to stop charging on the cards, but Jess didn't stop. My mom had to cancel all the cards and pay all the credit card debt.

I was shocked the total debt was this much. I'd known it was bad... but not *this* bad. My parents were also included in the bankruptcy, so they lost their $73,800. Jess promised they would get as much back as possible when she sold the inventory. Jess gave my mom a very expensive ruby ring, appraised for around $8,000, from Thailand out of guilt since my mom had lost all her money.

Before the bankruptcy was filed, Dearborn Federal Credit Union (DFCU) filed a lawsuit both "Jointly and Severally" against Jess and me in early 2009. Jess had accumulated $42,800 of debt on DFCU credit cards used for her store. They couldn't get any money out of her with previous debt-collection notices, but because Jess had credit cards issued in my name, they also came after me.

DFCU's case stood on their alleging that Jess had bought personal items on these business cards, and DFCU tried to argue that I had bought personal items and so was also responsible for her debt. All the credit card statements I provided proved that I had not bought any personal items. The court ruled in my favor in July 2009, after I proved the business was in Jess's name only and I had cards only to buy supplies for her store. In the court order releasing me from all DFCU's claims, I was the only one released; Jess still could be taken to court again for this debt. It cost me $2,580 in legal fees to get this cleared up.

Jess filed for bankruptcy in October 2009. When we went to court to get the ruling, the only people who appeared in the courtroom to protest the bankruptcy were two attorneys from DFCU. The court approved the bankruptcy anyway. In the bankruptcy, all creditors were given time to collect assets from the store, but they never contacted us. The entire inventory remained in our home, and Jess stopped doing anything about it. About once a month, I would ask her about what progress she had made. This only angered her, and she gave lame excuses for why she had done nothing.

One excuse she gave for not selling the inventory was that she had an emotional block and needed time. I never told her I thought this was just a feeble excuse. I couldn't help but think that she was leeching off me. I was paying for everything, and she wouldn't lift a finger to help with the financial disaster she had caused. What if I decided to quit my job and not do anything, using the "emotional block" excuse? We would lose everything and be homeless.

To make the financial situation worse, I intercepted a home equity loan statement in the mail before Jess got it and discovered that the principle balance had not gone down; it had risen. When we took this loan out, Jess had assured me that she needed only $20,000 out of $60,000 available in our home's equity. It turned out that Jess had used up all the equity, and the balance of the loan was now $70,000. This was really bad.

I went through boxes trying to find out information on the home equity loan taken out a couple of years earlier and was shocked when I found the paperwork. In addition to the loan, Jess had apparently signed up for insurance on the loan, which cost half of the monthly payments I was making. My signature had been forged on the paperwork. This explained why the balance had increased to $70,000—the payments I'd been making minus insurance payments were not enough to lower the principle. Damn. After all we had gone through, yet again she'd hidden information from me.

I was pissed and lost it. I started yelling at her and punched her curio cabinet. I broke the glass and bloodied my fist. This was the only time in our entire marriage that I hit anything in anger. Later on Jess denied that she had signed up for the insurance and claimed the bank must have done it. I did not believe her. I could not trust her at all now.

After all this bankruptcy mess, Jess started staying out very late, not returning calls, and making up stories of where she was. She drove home drunk once that I know of. I discovered she had bought a second cell phone and was hiding it from me. One evening she told me she was out with a female friend of hers. I called the woman, and she had no idea what Jess was talking about.

Suspicions and thoughts of her cheating on me were going through my head. Jess would not give me straight answers, and I knew her well enough to recognize patterns when she was hiding something. I installed a key logger on our computer to find out what was going on. I even got a GPS tracker and kept it in the trunk of our car. I knew she was hiding what was going on, and I had to resort to this to find out the truth. Jess told me multiple stories of where she was, but the GPS tracker proved she was lying.

Jess was up until two in the morning on the computer on October 15, 2009. The next day she came up with a shallow excuse about what she had been doing, but I could tell she was not telling the truth. I intercepted a chat conversation with the key logger, and my worst fears came true. I found out she was seeing another man, Tony B., whom she had met at the gym. We all went to Bally by Briarwood Mall in Ann Arbor, but I had never met Tony.

In their chat conversation starting at midnight, Tony wrote that he was at the hospital taking care of his daughter, Lorena. Jess and Tony were going back and forth on many things about their relationship, and Jess was playing around with him. Tony wrote, "I know u don't do planned events regarding love/sex." Jess wrote in response, "love can't be planned, on the other hand, sex can." Later on in the chat log, Jess wrote, "it doesn't matter h much I like you, the matter is you never answered my question of how you feel about me." She also wrote, "I oftenly think of the first moment that I was undertoxicationed. I threw myself at you, and you rejected me."

I have no clear understanding of what Jess meant by writing "undertoxicationed."

They went back and forth for a while, and near the end of the session, at 2:20 a.m., Tony wrote, "if I say "I love you" would believe me?" Jess did not reply to this, and the chat session ended. It was really hard for me to read this, and I was furious. I thought of Jess as nothing but a lying, cheating slut.

This was the proverbial straw that broke the camel's back. I had had it, and it was time to eject myself from the marriage. I met with a divorce attorney in Ypsilanti. But he was a smarmy little man, and I had a dark feeling about him. I began looking for a different attorney.

A few days later, I confronted Jess about Tony. She countered by claiming there had been no sex; there was just talking, and he had kissed her. She said he was only a friend and that things had gone too far. I didn't tell her I knew what they'd typed on the chat log and knew she was lying. But in her own words on the chat log, it was clear she was the one who had sexually offered herself, but there was no evidence of sex actually happening. She tried to convince me that she wanted to end it but was afraid he would blackmail her—she claimed she was the victim. That was pure bullshit. She also blamed this on me, saying she just had needed someone to talk to since I wasn't there for her. That pissed me off, and I told her there was never a valid excuse for cheating on your spouse. If you wanted to see someone else, the marriage had to be over. I didn't believe any of her excuses, especially her tired victim routine where she blamed me.

Jess begged me to talk with one of the pastors at St. Paul with her. Hearing my marriage-had-to-over statement really shook her up. I agreed to go, but I still felt the marriage was over, and I planned to file for divorce. I had put up with too much for too long.

The pastor talked with us, and I said my intentions were to end the marriage. Jess didn't want this and still claimed there had been no sex; she was just depressed, scared, and lost. She still loved me and didn't want to lose me. The thing is, part of me still loved Jess, even after all the crap she had pulled throughout our marriage. We talked more, and the pastor convinced me to stay in the marriage. He asked us both to agree that Bally was off-limits forever for both of us; we needed to find a different gym. We both agreed.

It was only due to my Christian faith and the vows I had taken that I stayed with her. Jess had many issues, but vows also include staying together in sickness and health. Staying with Jess was another bad decision on my part. Sickness with mental issues is one thing, but Jess's habitual pattern of deceit was unacceptable. A marriage will not last if only one person is honoring his or her vows of honor, truthfulness, and faithfulness.

Our marriage wasn't good; it was barely OK. I had lost a lot of love for Jess due to all these past events. We were in a holding pattern, with both of us trying to come to terms with all these issues. Compounding the issues were Jess's pain levels with her old neck injury. She ramped up taking narcotics for pain plus other pills for depression, anxiety, and panic attacks. Jess also further descended into being a hypochondriac. Her pain levels were directly tied to her emotional state. When she was happy, there was little pain. When she was sad, her entire body hurt, and she dumped all her issues on me and described how all the parts of her body hurt.

Other issues at home that really caused tension for me were her hoarding and her refusal to try to sell any of the inventory from her store. The contents of her bridal shop had been in our home, packed from floor to ceiling, for more than two years since the store had closed. I placed some ads for her, but she found excuses not to act or follow through and instead criticized how I worded the ads. She responded to my ads only after I reminded her multiple times. She accused me of controlling how she wanted to deal with the inventory, but she did not act and talked only about what she was planning to do.

One time she had the idea of taking the inventory to a friend's house. This friend of hers was an accountant who had done some of our taxes. Jess's plan was to work at his house to take pictures of the dresses for advertising, but it was a two-hour drive to his house each way. Others and I tried to tell her this could not be done, due to the distance, and that spending at least four total hours on the road each day was too hard. Jess would not accept others' opinions. This idea was firmly entrenched in her mind, and that was it. She responded by accusing me of trying to control her and not letting her do what she wanted, even though any reasonable person would know her plan was ridiculous.

Jess's inability to get rid of junk in the house started before the store closed, but now it had reached new levels. If I attempted to throw away useless stuff, she reacted in anger, accusing me of throwing away her important things. These were *not* important things of value, but her hoarding mentality had caused her to assign a bizarre emotional value to the useless things piling up. I was embarrassed to have people at our house because of the mess and had not invited anyone over for a while because of it. I tried to make an effort to clean things out, but she prevented my efforts to clean up the house. She also felt guilty when I cleaned and she did nothing. I resorted to purposely breaking useless stuff so that she could not find some excuse to keep it.

Her usual excuses for keeping things were so that she could donate, sell, or use them, but she did not act. The stuff always ended up shifted into another pile. I could not even throw away my old, worn shirts or socks without her protests. There had been only one or two times in the past two years when she'd taken a bag out of the house to donate it. When I reached a point in the clutter and mess that I would not tolerate, I threw things away. This enraged her.

I've seen shows on TV about hoarding, and I've seen how some people completely submit to their spouses who hoard because they don't want to create conflicts or get their spouses mad at them. They just take it and let their spouses ruin their homes and lives. Not me.

There were a few major incidents due to my frustration with all this stuff packed in our house. I tried to get Jess to start clearing stuff out, but she refused to act and instead avoided the problem. I even tried bargaining with her, saying I would do all the cooking, cleaning, and housework after I got home from work. She still wouldn't act and came up with creative excuses why she wouldn't or how she was too busy, even though she had not had a real job since 2008, when she was running her store. Twice, over arguments with her about this, I told her to either start doing something about it or get out. I followed up with e-mails on this also and later apologized for talking harshly with her.

I wrote this in July 2010 about her hoarding:

My Dearest Love,

I love you so much, but I just can't live like this in this clutter and mess anymore.

Yes, I throw things away when I'm angry. I can't take looking at all this mess and clutter anymore. You know this. This morning I told you I was sorry for throwing away the mango pits, the mango peelings, and the cherry pits/stems. For the first time in our marriage this morning, I said I was sorry when I was not. I lied, and for that I am truly sorry. In the future, I will not tell you something I don't feel again and will do my best to be honest with you. You deserve that. But please, look at this mango and cherry stuff. What need was there to leave it out for months and to keep such a large pile? Why so many? Why not just dry and store a few properly so they could be germinated the right way? Why keep the piles out to have more stuff and clutter out to see every day? Can't you see how excessive this is and how it makes our home look?

Please start an honest effort in throwing away all this clutter you have accumulated. I haven't been asking much over the years; just one hour of progress a day. All the other household stuff I'll take care of. I'll work 10 hours a day, then come home, cook and clean, do the garden and all the outside stuff. All you have to do is just one hour a day in throwing things out and making an effort getting rid of the store inventory. That's it. That's all I'm asking of you.

Please be able to choose us and get rid of the stuff in the house stuff instead of coming up with reasons to keep it. Keeping this stuff is not making our lives better; it is ruining it, it has destroyed our home, it's destroying our marriage, and destroying me. When you see something you want to keep, please ask yourself how it will make "US" happy, and then decide to throw it away.

Leah is coming over this weekend. Let's get a start and fill up the truck so I can take it to the dump. I'll help. Please don't come up with more excuses or reasons to hold it so you can take it somewhere. It needs to go now.

I have pleaded with you, I have begged you. You have seen how angry I get over how full of clutter this house is. You have seen me lose it many times because of all this stuff, but you still continue to do nothing but give me excuses. You make reasons to keep and collect stuff because you want to do something with it. It's just not a little bit; the collection is on a huge scale, far above what can ever be done with it. The problem is that you don't follow through with your plans or do anything with it and it creates another pile of junk in the house that has to be stored. When I finally do throw it out, you get angry because you say you had plans for it or you assign it with some value. Why don't you follow through with your plans and just create another pile? Can't you see how this cycle is creating massive problems?

I see how you continually come up with excuse after excuse and not do the one thing about the store inventory and clutter that I have been asking the past 2 1/2 years. You say you want to make me happy, yet you won't. I don't care about all the other stuff you come up with to fool yourself that you are making me happy. It is not. There is only one main thing that will relieve my tension and make me happy. It's clearing out this house.

I can't be continually reminding and asking you to do this. Nearly every week I tell you trash day is coming up and I plead with you to throw something out; but you don't. You say you will, but then don't act. There has been only one time recently when you threw something out for trash day. This was the noodles in the attic. Thank you for getting rid of the 40 or more old boxes of noodles. That was a start and I was very happy you did not come up with a reason to keep them longer.

Please make us happy and do something. Please just don't shift things around to find a more creative way of storing stuff.

I posted the Craig's list ad for the inventory a couple of times because you won't do it. I even had to remind you to follow up on the people that replied to the ad because you would not do it. I need you to post in other sites like eBay and start calling and emailing bridal shops. I'll help you with the wording of the emails so it looks professional. Please cc me on the emails you send out.

You need to make a choice. You can choose us and our marriage, or you can choose to continue collecting stuff and do nothing on cleaning out this mess. I want to be able to have friends over and not be embarrassed by our home. I want to fix up the house for us, but it can't be done with all this stuff covering every room. Please, please choose us. I love you and truly want you to choose us so we can be together and happy.

After I sent this, she still did nothing. Eleven days later I asked that we take a load of junk to the dump. Jess went completely ballistic and stormed out of the house. Dealing with her about this mess was impossible.

We both joined the gym at the Washtenaw Community College fitness center. Jess really liked it, because it had a sauna and hot tub in the women's locker room and she did not have to worry about guys hitting on her. Jess went there a lot while I was at work and liked to stay in the sauna. Soon after we joined, she started telling me stories of how difficult and rude other people were. She got into an altercation with another woman in the sauna, and Jess claimed that the woman had grabbed and twisted her wrist to stop Jess from putting water on the hot rocks. There were a few more incidents where Jess claimed she was the victim.

One incident with her at the gym was extremely troubling. I got home from work, and Jess was livid with rage. As soon as I walked in the door, she dumped all her problems from the gym on me. She'd had an argument with a female staff member who told her she had to wear shoes on the workout floor. Jess was yelling about how the woman had no right to interrupt her workout. Jess also claimed the woman had insulted her in front of everyone else. Jess was completely unhinged and out of control.

I was numb as I listened to Jess rage on about such a silly thing, getting so upset over not wearing shoes. This over-the-top reaction was something no normal person would have. I wouldn't have believed this type of extreme reaction over something so petty unless I had seen it with my own eyes.

The rules of the gym were clear. Everyone on the gym floor was required to wear shoes, but this didn't matter to Jess. She was going to do what she wanted and demanded they submit to her will. When they didn't, she blew up. It was a very surreal moment watching this out-of-control rage. I thought, *What has this woman become?* I literally felt my love for her drain out of me while I watched her rage and bitterly complain about her confrontation with the staff over a stupid thing like shoes.

Shortly after this, in August 2010, the gym kicked Jess out. I'm not sure of all that happened. But Jess talked with the director, Greg, on the phone over another conflict she had, and he terminated her membership. After talking with her, Greg mailed her a letter to our home. The letter said Jess had been in "two documented occurrences resulting in conflict over shared services with other members."

He also wrote, "During both episodes (and the subsequent staff conversations that followed) your observed communication with other members and staff was noted to be argumentative and witnesses on November 22, 2009 reported hearing profanity. These interactions have caused distress and concerns to members and staff alike. This argumentative communication and failure to share services in a cooperative manner violate the basic rules of proper conduct and member etiquette which are outlined in our member handbook."

Jess blew up again, and then she claimed that she was the victim, and the other people had lied. This pattern of hers was like a broken record, repeating the same thing over and over. I told her I would have a talk with Greg and see if he would reinstate her. I met with him the next day, but he wouldn't budge. It was clear that the staff had enough of her nonsense. I would have done the same thing if I had been in his position, but I didn't dare tell Jess this. Jess demanded that I immediately end my membership there, as my staying would be an insult to her. I told her I would, but I didn't. I had made more than enough sacrifices, and her bizarre and unreasonable behavior was not going to control what I wanted to do in my life.

A few months later, we both joined Planet Fitness with a one-year promotional special, and I stopped my membership at the Washtenaw Community College fitness center. We went there a couple of times, but Planet Fitness wasn't a good place to work out. It also didn't have the nice amenities we were used to, such as a sauna and a hot tub. Jess asked to go back to Bally, and I immediately reminded her of our agreement with the pastor that Bally was forever off-limits. I expected that she would keep our promise. Jess accused me of not understanding her feelings and said I was not being fair. I walked away without discussing it any further. No way in hell was Bally an option. Two weeks later I found a Life Time gym that was not too far out of the way from work. It was a very nice gym and had all the equipment and saunas that Jess liked. We went there for the next few years.

Jess could work out for three hours straight at the gym. I was surprised and very impressed she could do this. She became stronger and fit and lost weight but still refused to get a job, using the tired excuse that she hurt too much and was not physically capable. I brought up how hard she could exercise and asked why she could not work at a job. Her only reply was that working was different. Even though she was in excellent physical shape, she still had great levels of pain and emotional issues with no clear purpose in her life. Our home life was not good.

Reflecting on all this, I was not happy with how my life had turned out. My finances were a mess, my home was a mess, and my wife was the one who had caused all this. Trying to recover, I was working hard to pay off debts. Jess was not helping; she was doing the opposite by creating more problems that I had to take care of. Then one day she came up to me with a ridiculous request: "I want a sports car."

Un-freaking-believable. After this crippling financial disaster she had caused, now this woman wanted me to buy her a sports car. No way in hell was that going to happen. I flat-out told her that we couldn't afford it and that wanting me to buy her a sports car was unreasonable. I asked, "Why won't you help pay off this debt?"

She only responded that I could stop or reduce my 401(k) contributions to pay for the car. No way was that going to happen. I told her I wanted to retire at a normal age so we could travel together and have a great life. I had to do what was best for us in our marriage, and for me, not saving was not an option. She got angry and began accusing me of never doing what she wanted and thinking only of myself. That was it. I'd had enough of her shit. I told her that if she wanted a car, she should stop being lazy, get off her ass, get a job, and buy her own damn car. Then I stormed off. She never brought up wanting a sports car again while we were married.

SEVEN

Spiritual Warfare

During the time of the problems with the gym in August 2010, Jess's emotional state was a mess. She was hostile and argumentative and could not get along with people. Going to psychiatrists and counselors was not helping. Jess was convinced that everyone else was the problem and she was the victim. I spoke to different people at St. Paul, and they suggested we see the prayer team together. I was sure that deep down Jess knew she had issues, but her overpowering pride and stubbornness prevented her from admitting fault in herself. We talked numerous times about seeing the prayer team together to help with both our issues, and then Jess finally agreed. I had to frame it by saying "our" issues and claiming I needed help with my issues also before Jess would agree.

We had two sessions with Arlo and others on the prayer team for healing with her physical pain and both our individual issues, but then she refused to see them anymore. Jess said she would allow Arlo to pray over her only for physical healing and nothing else. She accused the prayer team of judging her and said they were wrong. She also accused them of not listening to her, not sympathizing with her, and not understanding her. I told Jess I didn't feel they were judging her; they truly cared for her, were sympathetic, and were only trying to help. This was true, but I couldn't convince Jess.

During our second and last session with the prayer team on August 23, 2010, Arlo told her they were there to help and not harm her, but she was arguing with them. He also told us both that in order for physical healing to take place, there had to be spiritual renewal, forgiveness, and letting go of anger. Instead of believing him, she battled with him and said that he was wrong and that I was the one with issues. She claimed I was the one with anger, the one who was arguing, and the one who was wrong. When we got back home, she said she'd felt ambushed; she said they didn't "know what they are talking about," and she didn't "want to hear their opinion." She also said we only went there to help with my issues, not hers. When I asked her about this later on, she claimed she'd never said this and accused me of wanting to make her look bad so that I could look good.

When I called Arlo later, he said he believed Jess had been under a spiritual attack combined with severe psychological problems.

Because Jess would not accept help from the prayer team anymore, Jess asked to meet with her previous ob-gyn, Brad, and his wife, Abby, who used to be members of our church. They also had a ministry helping people. When we met with them, we both spoke briefly, and then Abby wanted to pray over Jess.

Jess refused at first and then said, "When we talk with someone, why are people always focusing on me? He is the one with issues; he is angry, and he is wrong."

Abby persuaded Jess to let her pray over her first because she had called them, and Jess finally relented. For the first time in years, Jess accepted that we both had to work out our issues for healing to take place and that it was not all my fault. This was due to the deep trust Jess had in Brad.

The prayer session slowly turned into a deliverance session once they felt some dark spiritual influence was involved with Jess. Both Brad and Abby told us they felt a strong "inheritance of anger" from Jess's family's pagan past and an "evil spirit of a high priestess." This seemed like a bit out there to me at first and was more like a line from *The Exorcist*.

During the deliverance prayer, Jess started seeing images of a round white object with a black dot in the center. She said it was an evil eye and was staring at her and was angry. Further into the deliverance prayer, something within Jess screamed, "No!" very loudly when Brad and Abby were praying to drive out any evil spirits in the name of Christ. The force of this scream shocked us all. I was quite skeptical when this all started, but suspected something very dark and not of God was within Jess.

During this deliverance, Jess also said that the focus of the eye had shifted from her to Abby and that it was now looking at Abby in anger. She said the image slowly transformed into an old woman standing over her, who was trying to control her. Jess began shaking in fear and was greatly troubled. Both Brad and Abby were commanding the "high priestess" to leave in the name of Christ. Jess wanted to push their hands away from her. Everything that went on during this session involved deeply troubling spiritual issues, according to Brad. They thought a strong demonic influence was involved, and Jess was in great fear. There was much Jess did not remember, including screaming.

The next day, during Sunday service at St. Paul, Jess took notes on the sermon. At one point she drew multiple boxes over one another around the word *God* printed in the order of service pamphlet. After taking communion, she was very upset and troubled. When we got home, I asked her about this and tried to coax an answer out of her about why she had done this. She avoided this and tried to justify her feelings by bringing up examples of her past conduct and how she had previously taken notes during sermons. I attempted to have her to accept what caused her feelings and look into her heart. I told her I thought whatever was in her was attempting to put God in a box and separate her from Christ so that it could remain. I also said that her being upset with taking communion was not her; it was something else reacting to the Body and Blood of Christ, and this thing was in fear now that it had been identified and was being commanded out.

Jess asked if I was going to use her notes on the sermon against her. I told her that this thing within her was in great fear and was causing these feelings. It was not her, and I would never use anything against her. But I would use anything I could against any evil that was causing harm to her. She also told me not to tell anyone about what had happened with Brad and Abby and that she would do it in her own time. This session with Brad and Abby was the first big breakthrough. Jess saw some calm afterward, but she made no effort to follow up with them again.

Jess made no progress afterward, and her conflicts and arguing did not stop. I asked her a few times if she had called them to set up another session, but I only got excuses about why she had not. Jess now started saying that no one here cared about her or knew her. She wanted to drive to Missouri and talk with Leo. Jess said he was the only one she trusted.

During all the time that had passed since we were married, Leo had gone to seminary to become a pastor and now had his own congregation. Jess talked with him on the phone. I didn't know what she said, and she did not go see him. I sent Pastor Leo Sturly an e-mail telling him what was going on and what had happened with the prayer team at St. Paul and with Brad and Abby. Pastor Sturly encouraged Jess and me to continue seeing Brad and asked Jess to see someone with me at St. Paul for marriage counseling.

In October 2010, we started seeing Pastor Timor every Monday evening at our church, because according to Jess, I was the main problem. One of the things that came up was her hoarding. Jess still refused to throw things out and continued to collect useless items. She was unstoppable. Jess would buy large quantities of stuff purely because it was a good deal. She also had the idea she could sell this stuff at a profit, but she never did. During one session with Pastor Timor, we agreed that we would both throw some things out, but Jess did not and refused to talk about it. After two months, pretty much the same results happened as before when we had talked with people over our issues: Jess said Pastor Timor was wrong and did not understand her. Jess refused to see him anymore, and we stopped.

Jess started finding different people to tell about how poorly the others and her doctors treated her. Instead of taking charge and making positive changes in her life, she sought out new people who would sympathize with her and reinforce her belief that she was the victim.

Jess began accusing me of "never" wanting to go to counseling with her, even after we had met with several groups of people together to talk about problems. She started telling other people that I refused to see anyone with her. She also began telling me I needed to see a counselor for my issues. When others found out what was really happening and started asking her questions, she got argumentative, accused them of not knowing what they were talking about, said they were taking my side, and felt they were insulting her. This cycle happened again and again.

Jess further descended into feeling that people were not helping her and were judging her, insulting her pride, and ruining her reputation. Her extremely low self-esteem with feelings of failure and guilt worsened. Many times she said she was sorry for insignificant things she felt may have upset others or me. I told her there was nothing to be sorry about and that these things didn't matter, but she still beat herself up and couldn't let go. It got very bad over the last few years with her not being able to handle the little problems in everyday life due to her feeling that people were personally attacking her. She was not able to forgive herself and others or to let go of her feelings of persecution and anger, but then she accused me of not letting go of issues.

Since I didn't share her extreme outrage or believe that people were insulting and refusing to help her, I was accused of not standing by her, not helping her, not listening to her, not putting her first, and being wrong. Lately I had become numb to hearing her stories of how another person or group had insulted her, and I had to walk away—I didn't want to hear more of it. A couple of times, I slammed the door and walked out in frustration after pleading with her to stop her verbal attacks. Now, in her eyes, I was violent and destructive and wouldn't talk with her. There was no way to have a reasonable talk with Jess. What she wanted was to unload on me and expected me to take it, submit to her, and agree that she was right and I was wrong.

Many times, when she got into bed, she accused me of looking at her because I thought she was fat. Jess had gained about thirty pounds, but she was still a very beautiful woman. She had caused the weight gain through poor eating habits. She would eat a lot of sweets or junk food close to bedtime and had started trying to give this junk to me also. I asked her to stop giving junk food to me, but her response was that she was only trying to make me happy. She still wanted to feed me junk even though I told her it didn't make me happy. When I told her it would make me happy if she gave me healthy food, she still would not relent. She was trying to emotionally justify her out-of-control eating by having me join her. When I didn't join in, she ramped up her attack by starting accusing me of having a fat phobia; she claimed I had a bad psychological condition and then further accused me of hating fat people.

I had been diagnosed with type 2 diabetes a few years earlier and kept a very strict low-carb diet. I had always been very lean, eaten right, and exercised, but genetics got me. It was very frustrating that my wife was willing to cause me harm by wanting me to eat junk food so that she could justify her own bad habits. We had many talks about this and my special dietary needs, but she would not relent. I even told her that as my wife, she was supposed to be my best advocate for watching my health. One time Jess took it way too far and accused me of wanting to look good for other women, claiming I enjoyed admiring myself. I didn't take too kindly to those remarks.

In late December 2010, we met with a team of surgeons who specialized in TMJ. Jess did have TMJ, and the doctors suspected it was causing her to have severe headaches. They had her try to open her mouth as wide as possible, but she could only open it about twenty-one millimeters. She should have been able to do double that amount. The doctors then injected her jaw muscle on one side to numb it. They had her open her mouth again, and she went right up to forty millimeters. The doctors told her that the jaw muscle tightening up and pulling on the jawbone and her head was the cause of the headaches. Surgery would not help the problem. Still, Jess argued with them and insisted that she needed surgery.

They told Jess she had to stretch her mouth open at least ten times a day for the next month to get the muscle back to normal in order to stop the pain. They gave her a bunch of tongue depressors to stick in her mouth to hold it open, but these were too bulky. I made her a small, light wooden device she could use, and she really appreciated this. However, she did not make a good effort to use it enough. I had to remind her very often, but after three days, she gave up. She tried telling me that I just did not see her use it. She later said the doctors were wrong; they were misdiagnosing and refusing to properly treat her by giving her the surgery she needed. Jess said she would take Vicodin for the pain. She then accused me of having to be right all the time because I asked her to try to follow the doctors' advice. About two weeks later, she collapsed at church. I thought she was having another anxiety attack, but I found out it was a reaction to taking too much Vicodin and other drugs.

December 27, 2010, was a horrible day. Jess had another anxiety attack at home, but this one was far worse than most. She insisted that she was having a heart attack and would not think otherwise. I took her blood pressure and pulse twice, showed her nothing was wrong, and tried to calm her down. She would not relent and kept working herself up, making the anxiety worse. She demanded I look up heart attack symptoms so that I could see she was having a heart attack. I did, and then I showed her that these symptoms were caused by anxiety attacks and said we had been through this many times before.

She demanded I call the emergency room at the hospital and talk to the nurse. I tried explaining that they didn't know her history with anxiety and didn't know she'd had multiple heart tests that found nothing wrong, but she would not relent. I asked her to trust me and let me help, but she started verbally attacking me, accusing me of not helping her, not caring for her, and wanting her to die. She was vicious, and I'd had enough of it.

I yelled, "Here is your damn phone! Call the nurse yourself!"

Then I stormed out of the house. I shouldn't have done this, but at that point, the frustration from all her attacks over the last few months was too much for me to put up with, and I had to get away.

EIGHT

More Trouble Is Brewing

In early 2011, our marriage was in a holding pattern for the next three years. It got a little better, and Jess's emotional issues subsided a bit. The narcotics she took for pain were not working, and I was convinced this was partly due to her emotional state. She started getting steroid injections in her neck for pain management. These injections would last a few weeks, and then she would go back for another injection. Jess also had bunions removed from both feet, and she started getting steroid injections in her feet when the doctors thought her tarsal tunnel was causing foot pain. All these issues were a great stress on Jess, and she could find no relief from pain.

In 2011, we went to Thailand together and had a blast. Jess left a few weeks before I did in July so that she could take care of her mother, Suda. I stayed for two weeks, but Jess planned to stay until September. She ended up extending her trip until the end of November.

Normally Jess complained that her feet hurt constantly, and she walked more slowly than my seventy-six-year-old mother, who'd had one hip replaced and needed to replace the other. It was painfully slow to take a walk with Jess. I wondered if this was an unconscious attempt to exert control by forcing everyone to be at her pace.

When I was with her in Thailand, Jess's pain levels were extremely low. She didn't walk slowly, as she normally did. She walked around quickly, and I had a hard time keeping up with her as she wove through the crowds. She was a completely different person: happy, content, and driven. It was absolutely wonderful to see, and it gave me renewed hope for our marriage. Jess had acquired several properties she claimed were from her mother, and she had a lot to do to get the paperwork done. She sold one vacant property to help pay for her mother's medical costs.

We went on a couple of day trips, including a zip-line tour of the rain forest. It was a blast. Jess showed no fear of heights and absolutely loved traveling down the cables. She didn't have a care in the world and had an incredible sense of freedom zipping through the forest. She didn't even hold on to her harness and instead swam through the air as she sped down the cable. I don't have a great fear of heights, but I always kept a firm grip on the cable attachment and inspected all the cables and mounting hardware before taking off on the line.

After I left Thailand, I found out that Jess bought her mom a new Ford Fiesta from the sale of one of her properties. Why? Her mom couldn't even drive. Jess said the car would be only for her mother and that members of the family would use it to take her places. I thought this was an incredibly foolish financial decision to make, and I told her we both had to talk and agree about major purchases like this. Jess ignored me and started complaining about buttons on the dashboard that did nothing and asked me to look into it since I worked at Ford.

Since Jess stayed in Thailand for a few extra months after I left, I did a lot of cleaning in the house with her gone. For the next couple of weeks, I maxed out the trash containers with junk she had hoarded over the years. Other than the store inventory, the house looked better than it had in years. I knew she would be extremely pissed off that I had thrown out her precious trash, but all this useless junk had to go. My mission was to take the house back from her hoarding and get it tidy and clean.

A few months later, on the day she came back from Thailand, she was shocked when she walked through the front door. Her reaction took me by complete surprise. I had expected that she would blow up again, because so much of the stuff she had hoarded was gone, but I didn't care if she got mad. She looked around and exclaimed that the house looked very nice and that I had done a lot of work. This was weird. She had been very angry before when I had thrown out only piles of mango and cherry pits, but now, with such a massive amount gone, she was happy. It made no rational sense. This proved to me you couldn't rationalize or bargain with hoarders. You had to find a time to act, and then maybe, just maybe, when they didn't experience the emotions of seeing their precious bits of trash being thrown away one at a time, they would realize how much better the home was when the trash was gone.

With Jess recently back from Thailand, her pain levels were greatly reduced for a while. She was happy and back to her old self…especially with a clean home. I believe it was due to her mother and family needing her during the trip. Now at home, she soon fell into the same trap of not doing anything that gave her fulfillment. Instead of using her gifts and being active, she withdrew into herself and became depressed again. The sadder she became, the higher her pain levels were. I tried my best to motivate her to do something. Loving her and showing compassion were not enough. Jess had to make the choice to get off her butt, do something, and get meaning into her life, but she wouldn't try.

On this latest trip, Jess brought some cash back from the sale of one of her properties. This cash also paid for our trip. She wanted me to use part of it to get a motorcycle. I'd always wanted to get one, but Jess had been dead set against it. Her close friend had died in a motorcycle accident when she was only ten years old, and ever since then, she'd had a fear of them. She was especially fearful of me riding one. It had taken more than ten years, but she was finally OK with it. I found a great deal on a used 2008 Suzuki V-Strom DL650 and bought it for $4,400. I took the Motorcycle Safety Foundation (MSF) course at Washtenaw Community College and got a cycle endorsement on my driver's license.

I really enjoyed riding the motorcycle and commuted to work on it, and I rode with a couple of different groups on the weekends. On one of the weekend rides, a Harley guy made a couple of negative remarks about my "Jap" bike. Then I pointed at his running engine, which was shaking and vibrating the entire bike. I said, "I think your bike has Parkinson's." He didn't appreciate that remark, but I and the others thought it was really funny.

Jess saw how much I liked riding the bike and wanted to join me, so she got over her fears and took the MSF course the following year. We spent a lot of time going over the materials together to prep her for the final exam. She aced it, and I was really proud of her. Jess even got a better score than I had during the riding evaluation. With Jess being so tiny, she needed a small motorcycle but was capable of cruising on the highway. She bought a used Honda Shadow VT600 for $3,000. Jess was not very sure of herself and wouldn't devote time to practice. The following year she dumped the motorcycle three different times at intersections. Even with me trying to encourage her to practice, she wouldn't. After this, she never rode again, and the motorcycle sat unused.

Just as before, Jess soon fell into the same ways of not doing anything with her life, and her mood sank. She started talking of getting a job at a florist shop, since she had done that for a while in Thailand before we had met. She bought all the supplies and took a class on flower arranging to get certified as a florist at Washtenaw Community College. Jess really excelled and did amazing arrangements. I told her many times that she had an incredible talent for this and that a florist shop would be lucky to hire her. After she finished the classwork, she had to take only the final certification exam but never did. The exam that her class was taking was during the next Thailand trip she had scheduled, but she didn't try to take the next certification test. It was one excuse after another about why she didn't take the test or didn't look for work at a florist after taking this class.

One of the members at our church owned a florist shop and offered Jess a job at ten dollars an hour. Instead of her feeling good that someone wanted to hire her, Jess's pride took over again, and she felt greatly insulted that they did not offer her a higher starting salary. I tried to put a positive spin on this and told her that she had an opportunity to show just how good she was and that she could ask for a much higher salary once she proved herself. I even told her that with her talent, she could end up being the manager of the store in a short time. Nothing I said gave her encouragement, since her outrageous pride had taken hold. She just sat around the house feeling depressed instead of making positive changes with her life.

In 2012, Jess went back to Thailand, again by herself, from January to February to take care of more issues with her mom. Suda's Alzheimer's and Parkinson's disease worsened, and she could no longer live by herself without help. Suda wanted to stay in her home, but we knew that other arrangements eventually had to be made for her long-term care.

After this trip, Jess's emotional and physical health were dramatically better. She had a purpose in Thailand, and it was to help her mom. Just like her last trip, her pain levels were much lower since she had a sense of direction in her life. Now she started talking about selling the inventory, saying she had got over her emotional block. Finally!

Jess came up with a new idea of wanting to buy a foreclosed property to start up a new store. She even tried talking me into buying a house that was zoned for commercial use, saying we could sell our home to pay for it. Her proposal was for us to live in the upstairs with her business on the lower floor. No way was I going to do this.

The thing was, Jess hadn't learned from the past; she still kept repeating the same old mistakes, didn't follow through, and another disaster would surely happen if she opened up another store. In addition to all this, I still had serious trust issues with her. I suggested starting up an online discount website so that she could sell the inventory without the cost of a storefront. This would not require any large financial investments on our part. The cost of a website was minimal, since I could do all the website work. Jess thought this was a good idea.

I registered a number of domain names for her that she wanted and did all I could to get her to start. Just like so many times before, she lost interest and did nothing. She only talked about what she was going to do for a while. Sure was glad I hadn't agreed to sell our home to fund another store.

Shortly after this, Jess had the idea she wanted to make jewelry, so she took a jewelry making class. She wanted me to help get her tools, so I helped her get a bunch of specialized hand tools along with an acetylene tank, regulator, and jeweler's torch. After she finished the class, she did nothing with all these tools, and they sat unused. I thought that Jess would never make anything of herself and would never have a meaningful career. She had the talent and incredible potential, but no drive. She was just lazy, and for her, it was too easy sitting back and having me take care of and pay for everything.

Jess's new idea to help with her neck pain was to buy a neck brace. I only saw her wear it twice at home. She wore it to church a few time, and the interactions she had with people were very bizarre. She seemed to feed on their sympathy. I saw the expression on her face when people asked what had happened, and she truly loved the attention. Instead of being a loving, caring woman who helped others and gave of herself, Jess became the opposite and took from the good intentions and emotions of others. People soon learned not to ask her how she was doing, because Jess would go into a long diatribe on her health issues.

I asked Jess why she wore the brace at church but not at home, and she angrily replied, "You don't see me wearing it since you are at work." Her anger ramped up more, and she accused me of not understanding.

Jess also began to develop some very strange germ phobias. There was one bizarre incident after I got home from work. I went upstairs to change clothes and set my shirt and pants on the bed before putting them in the laundry hamper. Jess asked me not to do this because of germs. What? This seemed nuts.

I asked her why she thought this, and she said it was because I'd been in contact with all sorts of stuff out of the home and now I was bringing all the germs to the bed where we sleep. I asked her about Diva and Sasi walking through all the stuff in the yard, sometimes rolling in animal poop, and why it was OK for them to sleep in the bed.

Jess said that was different.

"Different?" I asked.

I asked her, "What's worse: my clothes on the bed or Sasi sleeping on your pillow all night with her butt against your face? Her fur is still holding all the nasty stuff picked up on her walks, and she has not been bathed in two weeks."

Jess was frustrated at not being able to give me a reasonable reply and did not bring up the subject of my clothes on the bed again.

In late August 2012, I got a couple of bounced check notices and notifications that automatic payments did not have sufficient funds from my checking account. What? I always had more than enough to cover bills. After going online and looking at my checking account, I saw that there was a levy from the Michigan Department of Treasury for $3,207 and an additional garnishment fee from the bank for $125. I had no idea what this was and hadn't received any notices from the bank.

I asked Jess if she had received any notices, and she said no. I talked with the bank, but they were of little help. The only thing they could tell me was that it was an authorized garnishment. They did tell me that multiple notices had been mailed to Jess. I asked why, considering I was the primary account holder and Jess was only a joint user. Notices hadn't been sent to me.

They said the levy was in Jess's name, so notices were mailed to her only. I searched the house looking for letters from the bank, and then I found a very large pile of unopened mail mixed in with a box of Jess's stuff and found four letters from the bank. Jess hadn't opened any of the mail, and the garnishment notices were there. Damn. Once again I was taking hits due to her ignoring issues and not following up. Jess claimed she hadn't seen the letters.

The only reason Michigan garnished my account for her tax debt was due to Jess's name being listed on my account. She also had another account at the same bank. Notices of the levy had been delivered to her for this account also, but the balance was only about twenty dollars.

Jess and I tried to get the funds returned, and the people at the Department of Treasury told us that if I proved that all funds were from my job and nothing came from Jess, they would return the funds. I gathered up all the statements showing that all deposits were from my job, but they went back on their word and refused to return the money. I spoke with an attorney about this and was told I would probably win this case due to the fact that what the state had done was technically illegal, but it would cost almost $3,000 in legal fees to fight this in court. That's why the state wouldn't return my money—they knew that the amount of legal fees it would take to fight this would be close to the amount of the levy. The people I spoke to in the Michigan Department of Treasury had lied to me, and there was not a damned thing I could do about it. The money was gone. Laws apply only to peasants.

With Jess in the same mode of not doing anything, her mood fell, and her pain levels increased. Narcotics had little effect on the pain. Jess asked me to come with her to a visit with her primary-care physician, and I agreed. Jess told her doctor about all her pain, and then the doctor asked her what she was doing with her life. Jess didn't say much. The doctor told her that by sitting around with no purpose in life, she was focusing on what was wrong and pain instead of what she could do.

The doctor said, "If I did nothing with my life and sat around all day, I'd start feeling pain also."

She asked Jess to get involved in a small charitable project as a start. I said that we both went to St. Paul and that there were many opportunities there available. Jess agreed that seeing what was available at St. Paul would be a start. After this visit to the doctor, Jess still did nothing.

Jess's doctor finally gave her a referral to go down to the Cleveland Pain Clinic to see if they could help Jess.

The doctor at the clinic ran some tests on Jess while I was in the room and when I was out. He also had an hour-long conversation with her alone and then talked with me alone. He called us both in after writing up a report with a course of suggested treatment. He said that Jess's nervous system was hypersensitive. Over the years, she had trained her body to feel pain. Much of the pain should not be there, but it was due to her current psychological condition that she felt this phantom pain.

He told us this was common with people with chronic pain issues who rely on narcotics. Jess's treatment plan was for her to stay there at the clinic by herself for six weeks. Every Friday the family would come down, and we would talk together in a group counseling session. The plan also was to get her off narcotics, as her body had built up a tolerance to them. There would also be extensive physical therapy and psychological work done to remap her nervous system to get her back to feeling normal pain levels and not the exaggerated levels she was experiencing. It was going to be a very long road ahead.

We went back home, and her primary care physician submitted the paperwork for the stay at the Cleveland Clinic to our health care insurer, HAP, which denied the request. They approved only four separate visits, not the full treatment plan. We made a second request appealing to their board, but HAP denied the appeal. Without health insurance covering this, it was impossible to pay for Jess's treatment with all the past financial disasters. Instead of the six-week stay at the Cleveland Clinic, HAP enrolled Jess in the pain clinic at University of Michigan. Jess made no progress there. It was more of the same she had already done: seeing counselors, getting dosed on narcotics, and getting neck and feet steroid injections. I saw no improvement with Jess.

In addition to getting neck and foot injections, Jess began demanding to get wrist injections. She began wearing braces on both wrists and claimed that she had pain due to carpal tunnel syndrome, but I didn't see any confirmation of this on her medical reports. She told me the doctors did not know why she was feeling pain in her wrists. There were times when she hardly left the bedroom from being depressed and feeling all this pain.

One Sunday when Jess and I were at church, there was a prayer list displayed on the projector screen of people requesting for prayers for various problems. No names were shown, only the first initial of their name. There was one person with the initial of J asking for prayers and guidance due to trouble he or she was in because of committing a crime.

I didn't think anything of this, but Jess was extremely agitated. After the service, she spoke to a couple of people, expressing her outrage over J being shown to everyone. Because Jess's nickname was only the first letter of her name, she tried to convince the staff that everyone in St. Paul now thought that person was her and that she was a criminal. Any reasonable person would know this was not the case. But Jess's pride had skyrocketed to incredible levels, and she was not being reasonable.

Jess even went to the pastor and demanded that he inform the congregation at all services that this person with the J initial was not her. The pastor tried to calm her down and told her that bringing this up would only raise more questions. Jess still was not satisfied. She even went back to the staff and told them if there was a period after the J and all other initials in the prayer list, she would not be confused with the initials on the prayer list. It was an incredibly stupid argument. Jess wanted me to talk to people about this, but I tried to assure her that no one assumed that she was this person and that the pastor was correct in letting this go. She was very angry at me and once again accused me of never standing up for her.

To compound Jess's medical issues, there was a large fungal infection outbreak in 2012, with many people dying from contaminated steroids. Eight hundred people got fungal infections, and sixty-four died. One of the steroid lots Jess was injected with in her ankle was identified as possibly contaminated. Jess looked at the symptoms others had and was sure she had a fungal infection. During the course of diagnosing this, Jess had two spinal taps, which showed no signs of infection. Getting these spinal taps was horrible for Jess with her needle phobia.

She also had multiple MRIs of her ankles and neck, but these were inconclusive. The doctors thought that they saw a mass in her ankle but were not sure if it actually was a fungal infection. Jess insisted she had the infection by telling the doctors that her symptoms were the same as other people who had it. At one time one of her ankles was swollen and looked bruised, but the doctors had doubts that this was caused by a fungal infection because all other tests were negative.

With Jess describing all the symptoms she had of the infection in detail, the doctors didn't want to take a chance and instead admitted her to St. Joseph Hospital in October 2012. An entire floor was dedicated to treating this fungal infection, due to the large number of people in Michigan affected by these steroid injections. The doctor put Jess on an IV drip of Itraconazole for a week. She was there for about ten days and then released. To this day, I doubt that Jess had a fungal infection, but I could be wrong.

In late 2012, Jess joined in on the class-action lawsuit against the New England Compounding Center. They were responsible for the extremely unsanitary conditions that caused this disaster.

In 2013, Jess started seeing a neurologist. Jess had been Googling medical symptoms and browsing medical websites, and she was convinced that she had fibromyalgia. She thought that her symptoms mimicked others with fibromyalgia. I didn't believe this latest claim of hers. How could one person have so many problems? Over the next few months, Jess had numerous doctor visits to diagnose this. She didn't talk about much else and was happy seeing many new doctors. Some doctors said she had it; others did not.

It was very tiresome for me to hear more tales of her newfound disease and medical procedures. I'd heard enough stories of medical misery from Jess to last multiple lifetimes. It had been an unrelenting, constant barrage of issues, and I'd been driven to the point of not wanting to hear about medical problems from anyone else.

NINE

IT HITS THE FAN

In May 2014, Mom and Jess went to Kansas for my niece Elizabeth's graduation from high school and to help my other niece Victoria move back to Jane's house from college. There was a big blowup between Jess and my sister. Jess called me and claimed that Jane had threatened and assaulted her, but according to Mom and Jane, that did not happen.

The series of events that led to this blowup was complicated, but both Mom and Jane said that Jess was interfering with Jane's family and trying to manipulate people to make herself look good and Jane look bad. Jess told Jane that she needed to treat Mom better and to stop Mom from cleaning the garage. Jane told Jess that she did not need to be told how to treat her own mother and that Mom was an independent woman and knew her limits. Jane also told Jess that Mom was very smart and knew what she was capable of doing. Mom was only helping to get things ready for the graduation party by cleaning the garage with a Shop-Vac and had done some sweeping.

Mom told Jess, "I don't want to be taken care of."

After Mom said this, according to Jane, Jess walked over to the couch with a dazed look; she was smiling as if she were in a daydream. She was completely disconnected from everyone else and reality.

A few days before Jess called me about being assaulted, she sat on an exercise ball and fell off and hurt her neck. She claimed that she had wanted to do some sit-ups on the ball. This was not true. The truth was that she had been holding Elizabeth's baby while bouncing on the ball to get him to sleep and had fallen. Jane told me they used the ball regularly to bounce the baby to get him to sleep, and Jess was doing the same thing. After Jess fell off, she demanded to be taken to the emergency room, but the ER staff didn't see anything wrong and released her. Jess called me and said she needed her neck brace, so I mailed it to my sister's house via next-day air. Jess claimed that her injury was Jane's fault because the ball was too soft and that Jane was negligent by not keeping it properly inflated. She was demanding that Jane pay the costs of the ER visit.

To add more fuel to the fire, according to Mom and Jane, Jess was disrupting plans to help Victoria move home from college by calling Jane's ex-husband to get involved. Jane had asked Jess not to get involved with the ex-husband and Victoria and said they could handle the move. Jess started yelling at Jane, accusing Jane of always jumping on her, and then Jane had enough.

She told Jess that she was not jumping on her and that, ever since Jess had arrived in Kansas, she had caused nothing but problems with the family. Jane let loose on Jess with anger from dealing with Jess over the years, and this latest crap was the catalyst that pushed Jane over the edge. She told Jess exactly what she thought of her and even said that Mom didn't want to travel with Jess, due to her issues. Mom was horrified at what Jane said, but it was all true. Mom would never have said those things aloud even though she thought them.

That was the breaking point that started the shouting match between Jess and Jane. According to both Jane and Mom, Mom was between Jane and Jess, trying to calm Jess down, but Jess kept on. Jess was the aggressor, reaching over Mom's shoulder and poking her finger at Jane while yelling profanities. Jane pushed Jess's finger aside, sidestepped her, and told her to stop, and then Jess hit Jane in her chest with the palm of her hand. It was only a light thump.

Jane said, "Stop. Do not hit me. Back off."

Jess swore at Jane and said she could hit her, and then Jane replied, "Don't touch me. I can take you down with my pinky."

Jane had been taking martial arts for a number of years and could have wiped the floor with Jess, but Jane held back.

Jess said, "You can take your pinky and shove it up your ass."

Jane had had enough of Jess and told her, "This is the last time you are coming to my house. You are never coming here again after this trip with Mom."

Jess claimed that Jane kicked her out, but this was not true.

Jess called a cab and stayed the night in a hotel. This was when she called me and said that Jane had caused all the trouble. She claimed that Jane had assaulted and threatened to hurt her. Jess wanted to file charges for assault and sue Jane and was rambling on about other issues, but she was so upset that I could not understand it all. I wasn't going to try and sort things out over the phone, so I asked Jess if she wanted to come home right away. She said yes. The fastest way was to take the train, so she booked the next one out and got home the next day. I called Jane and talked to her and Mom and got the real story about what had happened. Once again it was all Jess's fault, but she believed she had done no wrong.

When I picked Jess up at the train station in Ann Arbor, she was extremely agitated and claimed that everyone down there wanted to hurt her, no one had stood up for her, and no one loved her. Jess wanted me to call Jane and have her send us the money spent for the emergency room trip. Jess then started tearing into me even though I was not even there when all this happened.

I had had enough of it and told her to stop. It was the same story I had heard over and over. She had caused trouble by her own controlling and manipulative behavior. Her pride got hurt, and then she claimed someone else was at fault. Thinking back on this incident, if I really wanted our marriage to work, I should have shown her more sympathy. But these types of incidents with Jess causing problems with others were too frequent, and I had had enough of listening to her habitual victim routine. I did not love her anymore.

Jess was very upset and angry with me for not taking her description of the events as the unadulterated truth and not defending her against everyone else there. She was also very upset that Mom had not taken her side. Jess accused me of "never" standing up for her. I had heard this too many times to count. It was extremely tense at the home for the next two months. I was walking on eggshells, and Jess would not let up on wanting to sue Jane. Jess had been having multiple anxiety and panic attacks per week ever since the Kansas trip.

During these two months, Jess's obsession with and hatred of Jane did not subside. In fact, her hatred and lust for vengeance grew worse. One incident that occurred at home was when I had our Verizon phone account up on the PC. Jess went into the account and deleted Jane's number from the friends and family list. I asked her why, and she replied that she wanted no one to have any contact with Jane again and that I was not to contact her. I said this was unreasonable and that she was being vindictive. I also told her that she couldn't order me to cut off all contact with my sister and that I wouldn't ask her permission to call Jane.

Jess blew up. She began yelling that I never took her side, and then she went upstairs. She came down a bit later and said, "You'd better watch yourself and what you say."

The hateful look in her eyes was really dark and evil. The normal olive-colored glow of her face was replaced by an ashen shade of gray, and her lips were in an unnatural contorted expression of hate. I asked her what she meant by this, but she did not reply. This entire situation with Jane had consumed her. I had a flashback to the deliverance session with Brad and Abby and thought, *Something is seriously wrong with her. This is not the woman I married.*

Jess continued not letting up on wanting to sue Jane for damages from falling off the exercise ball at Jane's house, and she repeated it was Jane's fault because the ball was underinflated. She still wanted to sue for emergency room costs, along with payment for her pain and suffering. I asked once if she had checked the ball and why she had still used it if it was low, but that only enraged her more. She accused me again of not taking her side. Asking her that question was a mistake by the logical engineer in me.

In order to help keep the peace between her and Mom, I didn't tell Jess what Mom had said. Jess was still very upset at Mom. She thought that Mom should have taken her side and should have apologized for not coming to her defense. Mom and I had multiple talks about this incident. She told me that Jess was trying to manipulate both my nieces, Victoria and Elizabeth, to make Jess look good and make Jane look bad, but Jane would not put up with it. That was another thing that had set off the fight between them. Mom remained steadfast that Jess had caused all the trouble.

During Jess's and my many talks about this incident, every third or fourth day since, she could not let go and tried to get me to believe she was the victim. She kept bringing this up, trying to convince me she had done no wrong. I asked her why she got into so many conflicts with people when I did not. She accused me of being too passive, saying I let people walk over me. She said she was the one who had to defend her family. She stated that everything she did was "out of love and to protect us from others who want to harm our marriage." I had no reply for this; I knew nothing I said would get through to her.

This was it. The woman was out of her mind with rage and hate. I'd put up with her hateful nonsense for far too long and knew I had to divorce her, not just for my sake but for my family's as well. I didn't want to be around her. I didn't like her, and I had lost all love for her. When I looked at her, I saw only a obsessed, hateful woman, who was completely out of control. I had tried for too long to sustain our marriage, but now there was no option but to get out of this before she destroyed my life. She had already destroyed hers and almost all her friendships.

A few days later, on July 29, we went to bed around nine at night, and then she started in again on how Jane had assaulted her and how we needed to sue her for assault. Jess repeated her prior demands about suing for the cost of the ER visit, her pain and suffering, and other damages for falling off the exercise ball. It was pure psychotic and uncontrolled hate. She would not stop this obsession and hatred of Jane. It had been over two months of hell putting up with her insane behavior. Her ranting had been almost nonstop.

I tried again to calm her, saying to her that there was no case since there were only different accounts of what people said that would make it impossible to put a case together. Nothing good could ever come of it, and it would not even make it to court with no hard evidence. Jess was relentless. She again accused me of not believing her and not standing up for her, and she said that everyone was lying except for her. I asked her to stop, but she would not and instead upped the verbal attack on me, saying I never did anything for her.

I yelled, "Stop it!" and threw the TV remote on the floor and left the bedroom to get away from her. I slept on the couch downstairs. The next morning I got ready for work and left without speaking to her.

After work, I stopped and bought groceries. I picked up some Rainier cherries for her; I knew they were her favorite, and I hoped she would appreciate the effort. When I got home, I set the groceries on the kitchen counter, and Jess immediately went into attack mode. She yelled at me and said I had crushed her plant on the counter. It was only a damn mint stem. The counters were a mess and full of junk. The sink was full of dishes, and there was only a small area for me to set groceries on. I left without saying anything to her and turned down the loud music that was on.

She went off on me again, yelling that I had to ask her first before turning down her music. I said, "Is this what I have to do now? Ask you permission before doing things in our own home?" She replied that it was her music and I had to ask first.

I really had to put in effort to remain calm and defuse this. I started putting groceries away and held out the cherries to her, saying I had bought them for her.

Jess yelled, "What?"

I yelled right back at her, saying I had tried to do something nice for her and all she could do was yell at me. I slammed the cherries back down on the counter and then threw them in the trash. Screw her and her damn cherries. I went upstairs to the bedroom and slammed the door shut to get away from her. Diva was on the bed, shaking because of the anger and tension in the house, and I was petting her, trying to calm her. Jess came upstairs, slammed open the bedroom door to confront me again, and began another verbal attack. I asked her to be calm because Diva was scared and shaking.

She yelled at me, "It's all your fault!"

She left the room. I slammed the door shut and then yelled, "Keep away from me! I've had enough of you."

Her cell phone was in the bedroom, and it started blaring when one of her alarms went off. I tossed the phone in a container in the hallway. She yelled at me for that. I stayed in the bedroom, and she left the house. *Good*, I thought. She was being insanely vicious, and with her gone, I could get some peace. I was firm in my resolve to call a divorce attorney tomorrow.

An hour and a half later, there was knocking at the front door. I left the bedroom and opened the door, and two cops were there. They tried to push into the house, saying they had to come in. I said, "We can talk outside," so I came out and shut the door behind me.

That ticked them off, and then they threatened me, saying, "We can do this the easy way, or it will go very bad for you."

I was thinking, *What the hell is going on?*

The cops took out handcuffs and said they had to cuff me. I put my hands in front. They grabbed my arm, pulled it back, and yelled for me to put my hands behind my back. They said I was being arrested for domestic violence. No Miranda rights were given. I was dumbfounded at this point and could not believe this was happening. They asked me what had happened, and I told them what had happened that day. I even told them of Jess's psychological problems, the multiple narcotics and antidepressants she was on, and her previous involuntary commitment. They asked if there were any firearms in the home. I said yes, and then they pushed into the home without permission and demanded I show them where the firearms were. I complied, and they took them.

They said Jess had claimed I was throwing things across the room and had thrown cherries at her. I denied this, told them nothing was thrown, and then told them the only thing that had happened was that I had slammed the cherries back on the counter and thrown them in the trash. I even showed them that the cherries were still intact in the Ziploc bag in the garbage to prove I hadn't thrown them. They took me to the police car and put me in the back seat. They left me there and went back into the house, where they rummaged around some more. I was sitting in the back of the cruiser alone for what seemed like a half hour.

I was able to get my cell phone out of my pocket with my hands cuffed behind my back in order to call my dad and tell him what had happened. He was extremely upset, and I told him I had had enough of Jess. I was filing for divorce when this mess was over, but for now, I had to be nice to her. I thought for sure that the charges would be dropped when the court found out nothing had happened, but that was very naïve of me.

Travis, a neighbor who is a Washtenaw County deputy, was driving back when we were about to leave, and they talked with him for about fifteen minutes. I couldn't hear what they talked about, but I assumed it was about this situation.

The police drove me to the Washtenaw County jail, where they booked me in and kept me in the jail's common area overnight. It was just a large room with chairs for everyone. Some people were kept in individual cells. During the night, some were put in the cells for causing problems.

When the cops brought me in, they immediately took everything I had in my pockets and removed my belt and shoelaces. The next stop was to see the nurse. I told the nurse that I was diabetic and needed my Metformin to control my blood sugar. I also told her that I needed low-carb food and had not had anything to eat or taken my Metformin since lunch. She took my blood sugar, and it had shot up to 270. They made no effort to get anything to keep my blood sugar under control. All this stress had affected my sugar levels—they normally did not go that high.

After the booking was done, I got my one free call. I called my dad and told him where I was and that I would call him back when I knew when the arraignment would be. The problem with calling him back was that the police had a moneymaking scam going on with their phone system. A person could call anyone from the phone in the jail, but the people answering on the other end had to register and pay for a prepaid service with a pin number to answer. It was extremely overpriced, about five dollars a minute. There was no other option, though, and you were forced to pay for it. There was no privacy with these calls either, as they occurred out in the open next to the cop's desk.

After I found out the court appearance would be at 9:00 a.m. the next morning, July 31, at the 14b court in Ypsilanti, I called Dad and told him where to be to pick me up. I also gave him the password to my Gmail account so that he and Mom could get my boss's phone number to tell him what had happened and that I would not be in to work tomorrow.

Jail was a very bad experience. Here I was, a white, clean-cut engineer in my casual clothes stuck in with a bunch of really rough and crude people. There were about thirty people in the common area, and 90 percent were black. Knowing that I was very out of place, some of them came up to me and asked what I was in for. I told them a false DV charge. They asked if I had ever been arrested before, and I told them no; I'd never even been questioned about a crime. This was the wrong thing to say, and they immediately took a hostile attitude to me, thinking I had white privilege because I had not been hassled by the police before. A couple of guys told me what the process was and said I would probably get released with a PR the next morning since I had never been arrested before.

"PR" is short for personal recognizance. It's when the court releases someone during the arraignment as long as the person promises to show up for the next court date. I wouldn't have to pay any bail. There was one guy who was very experienced from being arrested multiple times; he knew all the ins and outs of the process. I asked him if the judge would throw it out and not go through the long court process if he or she knew I was innocent.

He laughed and said, "This is Washtenaw County. You are fucked."

A few more guys came over and told me about all the different places they had been arrested. They said this place was the worst. They said the judges and prosecutors only wanted successful prosecutions on their record and didn't give a damn about people's rights. I didn't give the other inmates much credibility, but all their statements gave me a really bad feeling about what would happen next.

A couple of people came up to me and asked right away how much money I made. This was very odd behavior. Most men I interact with would ask another guy what he did for a living, but they wouldn't ask what someone was paid—it's not proper social conduct. These guys in jail were very different. I overheard many conversations about how much money they pulled in one night or over the weekend, and that was their sole focus. It didn't matter how they got the money; only the amount was important. Many had no sense of ethical behavior and were devoid of feeling good about themselves from their own accomplishments. They got a perverse pleasure about how much they could take and bragged about it.

One guy asked me what I did for a living, and I told him I was an engineer at Ford. He immediately said, "You must be rich." The other guys also started saying I was rich.

I thought, *Just freaking wonderful. This will only be worse now with them thinking I'm rich and with white privilege. I'm a middle-class working guy, definitely not rich, but that's not what they think or want to believe.*

I kept pretty much to myself the rest of the night. I didn't sleep at all. During the night, a group of three men constantly raised their voices, bullshitting with one another. The cops repeatedly told them to keep their voices down. The three did tone it down, but the one guy who was the ringleader would consistently start back up again and not shut up. The other two were sucked into his conversation, and it was repeated over and over again with the cops telling them to be quiet. Others would eventually join in, too, and it soon became very loud with everyone trying to out bullshit and talk over the next guy.

One cop lost his temper over these three idiots' behavior. He ordered everyone to go from the common area and into in the separate cells, which held five people each. It was very clear to me these three were the troublemakers; if they were put in a cell and isolated from others, the noise problem would be taken care of. The cop was an idiot and didn't realize that isolating these three would stop the problem. The cops released us all from the cells about two hours later, and we returned to the common area.

The next morning I was transported in a fifteen-passenger van, restrained in handcuffs, leg shackles, and chains to the 14b court, with a bunch of other people. They chained us up together in groups of three. Being in chains was way over the top, and I couldn't believe this was happening to me. The whole concept of being innocent before you're proven guilty is pure bullshit in today's system. They treated me like a violent convicted criminal.

During the ride to the court, the guy I was chained up next to told the story of how he and his buddy had decided during a drug and alcohol fueled rage to set something on fire. They torched a couple of construction vehicles, including a crane, because it was fun to watch. He was laughing about it while describing what they had done. The other guys laughed also. I was shocked at his attitude; he could not understand how screwed-up this behavior was or how it affected others who had to work to support their families.

There was a complete absence of decency or any shame for what he had done. I knew this guy would be in and out of the legal system for the rest of his life if he didn't straighten out. He had to go through mandatory drug testing when released, but he bragged to us how he had hidden a joint and lighter in a plastic bag under a boulder next to the Washtenaw jail. His plan was to celebrate his short-lived freedom by getting high when released. What a fool.

When we arrived at the court, the cops led us into jail cells that held six people each. They unchained us but kept the handcuffs and leg shackles on.

At nine thirty, it was my turn to be arraigned. A cop led me into the courtroom; I was still wearing the prison jacket, handcuffs, and leg shackles. My parents watched me from the back of the courtroom when I was brought in. My mom was crying, and my dad was very upset. Being led out in chains to court in front of my parents was very hard to take, but at this point, I was emotionally drained and numb. I had tried to do the right thing by staying true to my marriage vows to God and not ending the marriage; being thrown in jail was the consequence of not divorcing her sooner. Keeping my marriage vows had done nothing but cause misery to me and my family due to her unrepentant lying and out-of-control behavior.

The arraignment was very brief and took only five minutes. Jess was there, standing next to the prosecutor. She argued with the prosecutor that this was all wrong and I should not have been put in jail. The court ordered her to be quiet. There was absolutely no consideration from the court that I could be innocent. The judge, Charles Pope, scheduled another court appearance for August 11 and set a $5,000 bail, but 10 percent paid would release me immediately. I also got a no-contact order with Jess and was banned from my home. I had to submit to a drug test. Dad paid the $500 bail right away. I thought I would be released right then, but I was transported back to the jail in chains with the same group I had been brought in with.

Judge Pope was the magistrate who had ruled on the old small claims case with Jess's store. I wondered if he recognized Jess and me.

When I was taken out of the chains and put back in the jail's common area, a bunch of people surrounded me and wanted to know if I had gotten off with a PR or not. It was clear that they were expecting me to get off with the PR or even be released with no charges because I was white. Their hostile attitude toward me was very evident. I held up the arraignment paperwork showing a $5,000 bail, which also showed that I had to take a mandatory drug test within a week as a condition to continue being out of jail on bail.

They were shocked. One guy, who seemed to be the loudest ringleader of the group, yelled, "What the fuck!" He pointed at me and then addressed the rest of the people in jail and said, "This nigger right here—never been arrested, never done anything wrong in his life, but these motherfuckers just want his money just because he is rich." He pointed at the cops behind the counter when he made the money comment.

Many others came up to me to say things like, "We got your back, nigger; those assholes are just fucking with you." This was the first time I had ever been called a "nigger" by black men or anyone else in my life. The situation went from them being hostile, thinking I was going to get preferential treatment because I was white and rich, to them thinking I was being screwed by the system because I had money the county could take. My situation reinforced their belief that there was no justice. It was a very surreal experience. The guy who had torched the construction vehicles got off with a PR, even with a previous arrest record. He was unemployed with no income. This was unreal, and there was a lot of truth in what the other guys said that I got screwed only because I had the means to pay.

After being transported back to the jail, I was supposed to be released. That didn't happen until eight hours later. The court sent my release paperwork to the jail within an hour of the arraignment, and I saw my folder containing the release order on the counter. The cops did nothing, and the paperwork just sat there. They knew my seventy-nine-year-old parents were waiting there to pick me up, but they refused to do anything about it. I asked what the holdup was, and the only response I got was, "I don't know."

Another four hours went by, I asked again and reminded them that my seventy-nine-year-old parents had been waiting all this time, but they still did nothing. Other inmates were also getting angry because they were supposed to be released too. A couple of them were so outraged about my situation, since they knew I was being "fucked" by the court and the cops, that they even told the cops I should have been released by now. The real reason was that the cops waited for the next shift to take care of it. My view of the police really went downhill, and I thought of them as a bunch of lazy assholes.

It was clear that they didn't care about following the court order to release me. They were ordered to release me, but they held me in jail in violation of the court order. I fully understood a reasonable wait period to process paperwork, but eight hours was pure negligence on their part. After experiencing all these events, I understood the other inmates' hatred of cops.

At 6:00 p.m., they finally released me. I hadn't been given anything to eat that I could have for twenty-four hours. I had only a carton of milk and an apple the whole time. Earlier, I had told the sergeant in charge that I couldn't eat all the sugary food, rice, and starch they gave everyone due to my high blood sugar, but nothing was done. I even asked if I could get some peanut butter, but he ignored me. Asshole.

I asked my parents if they knew why the cops had held me so long. Dad said they had asked the cops multiple times. The cops had given them same lame excuse, saying, "I don't know." This further reinforced my thoughts of them as assholes—this time lying and lazy assholes. I was definitely not in a good mood.

Because the court had banned me from my own home and given me a no-contact order, Dad had gone to the house earlier to get clothes and personal items and to drive my pickup to the jail so I could stay at their home. My parents told Jess about the no-contact order, but she drove up to the jail anyway with other things she thought I might need. I was sitting in Mom's Ford Escape in the parking lot at the jail while Dad got the stuff Jess had put in her car for me.

Jess was crying and came up to my window. She said, "This isn't my fault."

Still sitting in the passenger seat of the Escape, I held up the no-contact order and said that I had been ordered to have no contact and she couldn't be here. She replied it was not fair and again said this was not her fault. I felt nothing but contempt for her, due to all the problems she had caused for my family and me. Her tears meant nothing. Her words were just the same thing I had heard repeatedly throughout the years from her: "It's not my fault." The thing was, it *was* her fault; it always had been, but she would never change and would always play the victim card.

Being out of jail was a relief, but I had a lot of stress knowing there was a long, hard road ahead. I was not sure of my future. If this DV charge didn't go away, I could lose my job—I could lose *everything*. I had to plan my next course of action very carefully. I went to work the next day, Friday, and told people what had happened. They could not believe this could happen to someone like me. I was worried some might ask if I had ever been violent to Jess. But everyone told me there was no way I could be capable of this, and they all believed I had gotten caught up in the system because of Jess. Some women came up to me over the next few weeks and said that, even though they had met her only once or twice, they felt something was wrong with Jess.

After work, I called for a civil standby at our house. This is when a police officer must be present for a person to come near another person when there is a no-contact order. I had to get my computer, clothes, and other personal items for a long stay away from the house. Jess wanted to give me a hug after I packed my things, but the cop said no and told her she had to keep her distance. Jess knew I was very upset and pissed off, so she didn't say much. She tried again to explain that this was not her fault. She told me she had left the house only to talk with Laura, Travis's wife, and had been very angry that I wouldn't talk to her the night I was arrested. Jess claimed that Laura had called the police, and it was because her husband, Travis, was a cop that I was arrested. Jess claimed she hadn't said anything that would get me arrested.

I got my stuff packed in my F-150, and when I left, Jess said we would work this out and she was on my side. Part of me wanted to tell her that

I didn't believe a word she said, but I had to play it cool until this DV mess was over. I had to keep her on my side for now to get the charges dropped. I told Jess we would work this out together and I'd be home soon.

I spent the weekend trying to come to terms with what had happened. I went to church on Sunday. Jess was not there. Good. I didn't want to see her anyway. I told a couple of people what had happened, and they were shocked. One person walked up mid-conversation and asked, "What did Jess do now?"

I got nothing but support, and they all knew Jess had caused this. It was a great relief knowing I had so many people who knew my character and had no doubt that I had done nothing wrong. I asked if they knew any good attorneys and got some recommendations. One man at church, Stan, was an attorney, and I asked him about this situation. Stan confidently said he could take care of this. He also said this was not about guilt or innocence; it was all about the amount of money the county could take from me and about the prosecutor getting another successful prosecution on her record. More successful DV prosecutions would get more federal dollars coming in. I told Stan, "Let's do this," and he took on the case as my defense attorney.

Back at my parents' house, I started writing a detailed diary on my PC, beginning with the Kansas incident. I had to keep a detailed and accurate time line of what had happened to use as part of my defense. Mom wrote a letter describing what had happened in Kansas as an example of Jess's out-of-control behavior and the way she started conflicts. This last situation with Jane was what had sent Jess off the deep end. Mom told me Jess was claiming it was Jane's fault I'd been put in jail. What the hell was this woman thinking to justify this line of reasoning? It was crazy, and Jess was in complete denial of what she had done.

Both Mom and Dad were talking on the phone to Jess, trying to get information for me. They said Jess was blaming everyone else for this situation. Mom was very worried for me and upset at Jess for whatever lies she had told that got me arrested. We didn't know what Jess had said to the cops yet, but I expected the worst from her. Mom said Jess would not fess up to what she had told the cops, and then Mom told me not to believe a word Jess said. We all agreed that if Jess had told the truth and acted sane, this arrest would not have happened. Mom was still upset at Jess for not apologizing for her out-of-control behavior, yelling profanities and obscenities at Jane in Kansas, and putting her between Jess and Jane. Jane did apologize to Mom and said she should have handled it better.

The dangerous fact now was that I believed Jess had convinced herself that her fantasies and lies were the truth. She was not capable of seeing reality at this point and was in a full-blown victim mentality, hating anyone who did not believe her.

Before all this mess, Mom really had tried to be a counselor to Jess, and she had kept a lot to herself because she wanted my marriage to work. With Mom being raised Catholic and then becoming a very conservative Lutheran, she never wanted me to divorce Jess, but at this point, even she knew it had to end or my life would be destroyed. Mom and I spoke at length about how I had honored my vows, but Jess had not.

Mom showed me an e-mail Jess had sent to Stan on Friday, August 1, the day after I was released on bail. Jess had forwarded this e-mail to Mom, trying to prove she was trying to help me. I had no idea Jess had been talking with Stan about this DV case. Her rambling e-mail was pure madness. She started off with four different links to articles about diabetes and mood swings. She also wrote this:

3. Prosecutor just called, she is really out to get him…she didn't not listen to me at all. She said that she only listening to the police report which I asked her for a copy, but she refused to give it to me before the hearing day. She said something about he broke my neck… he never done such a thing. That was on a police report.
4. Is there any way that I can get the police report, because it sounded like police exaggerated the report.
5. I asked them to talk to my husband, not arrested him. The police lied to me that I can drop the charge, but I've never signed any paper. They tricked me in some questions.

In the last paragraph of her e-mail, Jess claimed I had an illness and needed help. She thought she had not done anything wrong. She seemed completely delusional and incapable of realizing she was the cause of this mess.

She wrote in the last paragraph, "My ex-husband whom was very abusive...I married him for a wrong reason. I ran away before I married him and ran away during the time I was married to him. The time that we actually spent together was less than a year. If you asked me why I stay with my husband for 13 years, because there were so many good years and many good days. I am looking for the day that he is aware of his illness and get help, so we can have many more good years."

TEN

From Bad to Worse

The drive back and forth to work in Dearborn from my parents' house in Hartland was horrible. By leaving at 5:30 a.m., I could get to work in an hour, but coming home in traffic took an hour and thirty minutes. It sucked. It was forty-five miles one way, and driving my F-150 in city traffic was a lot more expensive with fuel costs. I was considering selling the truck and getting another Focus to save money. I normally commuted to work in our 2003 Focus. It was a great vehicle, got good fuel economy, and had no major mechanical issues.

I sent Pastor Dannor at St. Paul an e-mail wanting to get in touch with him and talk about everything that had happened. He did a lot of marriage counseling at church.

Mom had laser surgery on her throat on Monday, August 4. She had a tracheotomy tube put in so that she could breathe while healing. Thirty years earlier, she'd had thyroid cancer, and scar tissue built up in her throat after she had surgery to remove the thyroid gland. She'd had a laser procedure done fifteen years ago to remove this scar tissue, but it had come back again. I was really worried that the severe stress she was under with my DV case would create complications.

I was at work when Dad took her home two days later in the morning. Later in the afternoon, my dad called me. He was hysterical and crying.

Something had come up from her lungs, lodged in her throat, and blocked her airway. Her heart had stopped, and the paramedics were rushing her to St. Joseph Hospital. I left work immediately to head to the hospital. The weight of this, combined with the past few days of dealing with my false arrest, hit me hard, and I was crying during the drive to the hospital. The thought of losing my mom was horrible.

When I arrived at the hospital, I found out what had happened. A hard mass of mucus had blocked her airway below the tracheotomy opening, and the suction machine my dad and mom had for her throat had not been able to remove it. She had collapsed from lack of oxygen, and my dad had immediately called 911. Her heart had stopped, but the paramedics were able to restart it. The paramedics had a difficult time getting the throat clear to get air in her lungs, and it was possible that she had been without oxygen for up to twenty minutes. Her brain shut down during transport to the hospital due to lack of oxygen.

When she arrived at St. Joseph, they immediately cooled her down to ninety degrees to help prevent further brain damage and to aid healing. At this temperature, brain function is minimized, and brain healing will best occur. The nurses carefully monitored her vital signs, and they administered medications to prevent shivering. The plan was to keep her at this cool temperature for twenty-four hours, and then the warming process would begin on Thursday, August 7, to bring her up to her normal body temperature. This warming procedure would take eighteen hours, and then they would perform preliminary exams to determine the extent of her brain damage.

I called Jane and told her what had happened. I'll never forget her starting to cry over the phone with her repeating, "Oh no, Mom…" I told her it didn't look good and that she needed to get here right away. An hour later she called me back and told me she was driving up from Kansas and would leave in the middle of the night. Elizabeth, her daughter, would not give a straight answer about whether she was coming with her. Jane wasn't going to go back and forth with Elizabeth trying to get an answer, so she was leaving without her to come up and be with Mom.

There was nothing else my dad could have done without specialized medical equipment. The paramedics and doctor told him he had done everything right, but my dad was torturing himself with guilt, thinking he should have done something more. I just held him, and we cried in each other's arms. Jane arrived, and we spent the next two days in the hospital with Mom. Jane and I went back to their house at night, but Dad stayed by Mom's side at the hospital.

Jess wanted to come and see Mom, but with the no-contact order, she couldn't be there when I was around. Dad and Jane didn't want her there, but they knew they had to arrange to let Jess see Mom or she might go into vengeance mode and purposely worsen my legal troubles. I didn't want Jess there either. We arranged a couple of times when I would leave for a while so that Jess could see Mom. Jess loved Mom a great deal and was heartbroken over what had happened. She considered Mom more than just her mother-in-law; Mom was her best friend.

The doctor performed preliminary exams on Friday, August 8. Mom was completely unresponsive. They were to do another round of tests on the tenth, but the doctors told us that in cases like this, there was very little chance of recovery. We had to come to terms that Mom would never recover, and it was emotionally devastating for all of us. Mom was gone; only her body remained functioning on life support. Dad was an absolute wreck. The next day Jane and I spoke about getting Elizabeth up here to see Mom before we had to disconnect life support. Jane didn't want Elizabeth to feel that it was Jane's fault for not bringing her up to see Mom before life support was disconnected. I booked a flight for Elizabeth to come up the next day, and I told Jane I'd pay for it.

During all this, I was calling our family and close friends to tell them what had happened. It was emotionally nerve-racking to tell the series of events over and over again to each person, but it had to be done. I was completely drained and had little physical strength.

The weight of all this in my life happening at once was crushing, and I was an emotional mess. My thoughts of Jess were only, *That lying, psycho bitch.* I hated her and had nothing but contempt for her. As a Christian man, I knew I had to forgive, but I was not capable of giving her any forgiveness at this point. Fueling my contempt was the knowledge that Jess had created Mom's stress by getting me arrested. It was very possible that this stress had contributed to Mom's complications with the surgery. One of the last memories I have of Mom alive is her crying at my arraignment after seeing me in chains. All because of that lying psycho.

I have been a Christian all my life, have regularly gone to church, and have heard countless people giving their testimonies of miracles, being brought to faith in Christ, being relieved of addictions, and having no more desire to commit previous wicked acts. I lived a pretty decent life and had no great testimonies to give, as I didn't have any great tales of misery or being lost. I am far from perfect and have had my fair share of moments and mistakes, but I never had any relapses with my faith. Christ was always in my heart, and this was partly due to my being incredibly blessed with wonderful, loving parents who had a deep faith in God.

For the past few days, I had been praying to be helped with this burden of the DV charge and for Mom's healing. I wondered if my inability to forgive Jess would affect any of my prayers for Mom's healing and for help with these charges. Countless other friends and family told me they had been praying too. They were shocked at all these events and were extremely concerned about my welfare and whether I could handle all this stress without self-destructing. Many of them also expressed their hatred of Jess for all the problems she had caused the family over the years and especially my arrest. I had to tell them not to say anything to Jess—I needed her on my side until I could beat these charges.

Friday night I couldn't go to sleep and was curled up in a fetal position. My heart was racing, and my breathing was labored and erratic. I was nauseated, and it felt like a huge weight was pressing down on my lungs. I dozed off around 1:00 a.m. but woke up an hour later crying uncontrollably.

All of a sudden, I started to feel joy. I couldn't understand why. Then I felt the presence of Christ. It was a very real, tangible, physical presence that I felt, and it was pure love. I felt all the hate, pain, and fear literally being pulled out of me. It was an incredible experience I couldn't fully comprehend, but I was at complete peace. The tears of pain were replaced by tears of joy. I didn't understand why at first, but then it was clear. I was loved and was given grace and peace. I gave thanks to God for this miraculous gift. This heavy burden was lifted, and I forgave Jess. It wasn't just lip service; it was a genuine forgiveness I felt, and there was no more anger for her.

Forgiving Jess was not my doing, and I could not forgive her by myself. Only through the grace of Christ was I able to do this.

Even though I forgave her, I knew there was no future for us unless there was a radical shift in her actions. Still, there was a huge difference between forgiveness and trust, and I knew a massive shift in her personality probably would never happen.

I had another revelation that night. I was able to spend five days with Mom before she went to be with the Lord. I gave thanks for this also. Somehow, in all these twisted events, time was given to me to spend with her. I was amazed by what had happened, but I didn't realize it before, due to my all-consuming contempt for Jess. I didn't know if this really was Mom's time to be with the Lord or was just another accident due to our imperfections; all I knew was that being able to spend this time with her was an incredible gift. I slept soundly through the rest of the night and woke up Saturday completely refreshed.

Jane, Dad, and I talked and laughed on Saturday, recounting all the good times and love we'd had with Mom. I recalled and told the story about a really crude joke I had told Dad twenty years ago. Mom had overheard this joke, given us a condescending look, and said, "That's bad." A month later, a high-school friend of mine, Liz, was over at the house after she, Mom, and a few other women had gone bowling.

Liz said, "I couldn't believe the dirty joke your mom told us at the bowling alley!"

I asked Liz what was it about, and when she told me, I said, "That was my joke I told Dad!" We looked over at Mom. This extremely pious and reserved woman had a little grin on her face, knowing she was so busted.

When Dad heard this story in the hospital room, he started laughing. It was a deep belly laugh. It was a truly joyful moment seeing Dad laugh after all the sadness we had experienced. We also cried. But those were tears of love for her, and we were secure in our faith that Mom was with the Lord. Her unwavering faith throughout her entire life assured her of salvation. There was no doubt that she was with the Lord now. It made the decisions we had to make over the next few days much easier.

I went to church Sunday to help clear my mind and saw Jess in church by the coffee station. We met briefly. I told her that by meeting her, I was in violation of the no-contact order, but I wanted to give her comfort and had to tell her about my experience with God the past Friday and the way He had taken all the pain, sorrow, and hurt I felt and given me joy. I told her I felt no anger toward her and forgave her. I also told her that somehow, through this horrible situation with the DV charge, I had been able to spend the last few days with my mom while she was alive, and I gave thanks to God for this. To be clear, I forgave her, but there was no way I trusted her. It wasn't *if* Jess would flip out again; it was *when* and *how bad* it would be.

Jess stared at me with a blank look on her face and could not understand what I'd said. Her eyes were empty, and she seemed to be just a shell of a person with no depth or soul. She replied only that she was still angry about being committed in the psych hospital. She was completely incapable of letting go of all the past hurt in her life, and that was all she saw and felt. She couldn't recognize her own horrible actions, accept forgiveness, or forgive herself. I walked away from her without saying anything more and left church for the hospital to see Mom.

The neurologist performed some tests on Mom. There were no signs of any higher brain function, and she was still completely unresponsive. He said that in his experience, people never recovered from this when higher brain function was not detected. He also said that after watching for brain function to improve for a couple of days, there was no progress, nothing had improved, and there was little hope that any recovery would be possible.

Dad, Jane, and I made the decision to stop life support. We knew Mom was gone. This was not hard to do, because we all knew that her salvation was assured and that Mom never would have wanted to be kept alive with machines. There were no second thoughts on this. We even said we all felt the same and didn't want to be kept alive by machines. We talked about this decision later on and all expressed how easy it was. It was only our faith and knowing the love of Christ that made the decision easy.

I called our close friends and family to come to the hospital and said the ventilator was going to be stopped after her pastor, Pastor Chris Tomah, read her the last rites. Mom went to Our Savior Evangelical Lutheran Church in Hartland, Michigan, and it was also the church I had gone to as a child. We were all there during the reading of the rites, and she was given to the Lord. All of us were crying. The nurses disconnected the ventilator at 6:25 p.m., but she kept breathing on her own. The nurses told us she could stop breathing then or it could take a few days. Jane, Dad, and I stayed in Mom's hospital room for a while, and after everyone left, Jane and I went back up to Mom and Dad's house. Dad continued to stay by Mom's side at the hospital.

The next morning was my first hearing for the DV charge. With all these events happening at once, I couldn't think straight, wondering what would happen.

The pretrial hearing for the DV charge started at nine on Monday morning. Jess had been talking with Dad the last few days and wanted to be there to tell the judge this had been a mistake and there had been no violence in order to help get this dismissed. She called Dad at eight thirty that morning and told him he had to pick her up and take her to the pretrial because the Focus was not working. Dad was very irritated at this last-minute request and then told her it was too late and there was not enough time to come get her. Jess drove up anyway in the Focus. What the hell was this latest game she was playing? I fully expected and knew she would pull more nonsense, and I had to be prepared to do what it took to protect myself from more damage from her.

When Dad and I were waiting at the courthouse, he told me he hated Jess for everything she had done to our family. He called her evil and said all his neighbors also said Jess was evil. He wanted only to get these false charges dismissed and would not say anything bad to her until after this mess was over. He would just pretend to be nice to her. He also told me to hide any anger I may have toward her, because she would turn in an instant to get revenge. This shows what a caring man my dad is. Even with Mom's death and all the pain and loss he was feeling, he still put me first, ahead of his own feelings. My welfare was the most important thing for him, and he would help to ensure I was cleared of these charges. I'm a blessed man to have him and my mom as parents.

Stan was out of town, so another associate of his, Marsha, served as my attorney. When I first saw Marsha, I didn't get a good feeling about her. She looked like she hadn't washed her hair in weeks, and she was generally unkempt in a wrinkled pantsuit. Her slovenly appearance did not give the look of a competent professional. She met with the prosecutor alone before the hearing in a small room.

During the hearing, Marsha asked the judge to lift the no-contact order due to my mom's condition and the hardship the order was putting on the entire family. The judge asked Jess if she had any objections, and she said no. The judge lifted the no-contact order, and I was free to go home. The pretrial hearing was rescheduled to September 8, when Stan was available to give proper representation. Jess tried to speak to the judge and prosecutor to argue that she hadn't said what was on the police report and the police had lied, but they would not listen to her. Jess even marked up the initial incident report with notes to say what was wrong with it. I hadn't seen the police report yet due to all the issues going on with Mom.

When we left the courtroom, Marsha told me that even though it was clear I was innocent, the prosecutor had offered a deal for me to plead guilty, and Marsha said I should take the plea deal. I would have to pay the county to take classes on anger management and conflict resolution, and then I would be put on probation for two years. The charge would be dropped after the two years. Marsha's reasoning was that going to trial on this would be very stressful and cost a lot of money.

I couldn't believe what she was advising and felt that this woman had no concept of honor. There was no way I would plead guilty to something I hadn't done, especially with the overwhelming amount of evidence I had on Jess's behavior. I knew full well the implications a DV conviction might have on my job, civil rights, firearm ownership, my concealed pistol license, and other issues. This conviction would be on my record forever. I intended to tell Stan that Marsha was to have no part of my defense and that I felt she was a reprehensible human being for not wanting to stand on the truth to save an innocent man.

Jess and I left the courthouse together to go home. When we got home, I asked her what was wrong with the Focus. She told me that nothing was wrong with it and that she had only said that in the hope that the prosecutor would feel more sympathy for our family situation and drop the charges. What the hell? This would not even be an issue for the prosecutor, and I had no idea what she was really thinking. I told her she had to be truthful and not play games, due to how serious this charge was, but she defended her actions and said she would do whatever it took. Not only did I have to defend myself against a prosecutor who wanted to destroy my life; I had to protect myself against Jess, who would unwittingly sabotage my defense with her lies and manipulations.

When we arrived home, it was a mess. The kitchen counters were covered in junk; the sink and dishwasher were full; and the living room was trashed with all sorts of stuff scattered on the floor. Jess left to go shopping, and I spent the entire afternoon cleaning and putting her shit away. I was not happy at this mess, but it was typical behavior of hers. When she got home from shopping, she said she was going to clean it up, but I had heard this excuse too many times. There was no fresh food left in the house, and I didn't see any new food bought.

A few days earlier, Jess had told Dad that the air conditioning in the Focus had stopped working and she'd taken it to a shop to get it repaired. When Jess got back from shopping, I asked where she took the Focus to get it repaired. She would not give me a straight answer and said only that it was a "couple hundred dollars."

I asked, "What did they do? Was it a Freon recharge, or was there a repair?"

She replied that it was only a recharge and cost about $200. I thought she was not telling the truth, so I pressed for more info. I said a recharge should be no more than seventy dollars and asked for the name of the shop that had done it and if she had a receipt. I said I was going to the shop to demand a refund and to pay only a fair price for what they had done. She still would not give me the name of the shop and said there was no receipt.

Later in the evening, I saw a DIY can of Freon in the trunk of the car. It was clear she had lied about taking the car to the shop. Who knew what really had happened? I would never find out. It was more of the same pattern of deceit on her part. When she told Dad about the air conditioning, she also said she was out of cash. That couldn't be right—I had given her $1,000 in cash three weeks earlier, and there had been no major expenses. The money had gone somewhere else, which she wouldn't tell me about. I wondered if Jess had started hoarding cash because she suspected I was going to file for divorce. Anyone would have to realize that getting his or her spouse arrested spelled certain doom for a marriage. In just the few hours since the no-contact order had been lifted, Jess had spun multiple lies and justified them all.

I told Jess about the situation with Elizabeth and that I had arranged and paid for her flight here to see Mom. Jess was glad she came but got very angry with me for paying and demanded Jane pay me back. I told Jess this was a gift to Elizabeth so that she could see her grandmother for the last time while she was still alive; it was the right thing to do, and Jess needed to accept this. Jess would not relent and stayed mad, so, not wanting to argue, I walked away from her. Walking away again and again from her control and freakish behavior was common now.

During the next few days after I got back home, I found out what Jess had done that led to my arrest. On that day when I had gone upstairs to get away from her rage, Jess had gone over to the neighbors' house and spoken to Laura. Jess had recently befriended Laura and frequently spent time with her. Jess now claimed that Laura had told her to call the police. Laura's husband, Travis, was the Washtenaw County deputy who had talked with the cops who arrested me. The facts slowly trickled in, and Jess's actions and manipulations became clear. It began to make sense now why I was arrested.

Jess was apparently telling Laura stories of how horrible and controlling I was just so she could get sympathy. All these false stories of my abuse were her deepening victim mentality and need for sympathy and pity run wild. Her getting pity was usually at my expense.

Jess told me the police had stopped at Laura's house first and talked with both of them. She claimed that Laura lied to the police about what had happened that night. Jess told me that she was afraid to say anything because the police would not contradict another cop's wife and make Travis look bad. Jess also claimed she only wanted the police to talk to me, but because of Laura, I was arrested.

Jess also claimed she never said anything bad about me. She said that Laura made all this up because Laura wants revenge for domestic abuse that had happened to her mother. I didn't believe a word Jess said. Much of what she said was a convoluted mess that contradicted her previous statements.

The next day Jess and I were in the hospital room with Dad and Jane, waiting for Mom's body to stop breathing. I said a prayer to Mom and told her that it was OK to let go and that I would always take care of Dad and Jane. Jess immediately blurted out, "What about me?" That pissed me off, but I didn't say anything. It was another example of her wanting to be the center of attention while completely ignoring the pain others were in. I knew she felt left out and isolated, but at this point, I didn't care.

At 10:35 p.m. on August 12, Mom's body stopped breathing. The doctor officially called the time of death. Dad had stayed by her side all this time.

I went back to work the next day. People were surprised to see me, and even my boss asked if I should be there. I was tired and emotionally drained, but I didn't want to sit around the house and think about everything that had happened. I didn't want to be around Jess in the house all day. I needed to get my mind clear and try to resume my life. It was hard, but I pushed through the day at work. It was a good decision, and not dealing with Jess really helped put my mind at ease.

After I got home from work, I went to make something to eat, and Jess said she would make me something. I asked if we had any more pork loin left. We did, so she asked me how I wanted it. She wanted to make it spicy with Cajun seasoning, but I just wanted simple salt and pepper and not spicy. She really pushed for more spice and stuff, but I had to say multiple times, "Just simple. I only want salt and a little bit of pepper."

She made it spicy anyway with a lot of other crap on it and a heavy dose of pepper. I started eating it without saying anything else. Halfway through eating, she started going off again about Jane. She ranted about the Kansas situation and started in about how Jane prevented her from spending time with Elizabeth while they were here. I got up before finishing eating, left the plate half-full of food, and went upstairs. I could not listen to her self-centered rage anymore.

I couldn't help but think as I walked away that there had been countless times over the years when I'd had to get away from her out-of-control outbursts. I knew I really had to watch what I did or said to her, because she could turn on me anytime and make this DV case far worse.

Jess came upstairs and said she was going out because I had "cut [her] off" and wasn't putting her first. I asked her to please stop and just consider everything that had happened to me between being jailed, all my rights being taken away, and the devastating death of my mother. She immediately said she was closer to Mom than I was and had spent more time with her the last ten years. She kept yapping, claiming I couldn't understand how she felt about Mom's passing and the loss she felt. Jess still had to be the victim without even considering my situation. She now resorted to claiming that my love for my own mother wasn't as great as hers, just to magnify her loss over mine. Her attitude was incredibly pathetic and self-centered.

After Jess arrived back home very late in the evening, she came to bed and started up about Jane again. She demanded that I get Jane to pay for the $200 plane ticket I had bought to get Elizabeth up here to see Mom. I told her again I hadn't done this for Jane; this was a gift to Elizabeth so that she could see her grandma for the last time before she died. Jess was relentless and kept pushing. I thought her obsession about this was truly insane. She then demanded that I not give anything to Jane and ask her first before doing anything for Jane. I ignored her.

A few days later, Jess asked me about what I had said to her at church. She questioned how I could experience the peace and the joy of God after being jailed and my mom dying. She was incapable of understanding how I could forgive, feel joy, and let go of emotional pain. She then asked me to tell her how to do it. I told her she had to ask for help in prayer. She had to let the love of Christ into her heart, give all her troubles to Him, and let go of all hurt and anger she felt. She had to truly forgive herself and others to let go of pain and not be prideful or want revenge for past conflicts.

Jess agreed that she had a hard time letting go of things, but she left the conversation confused, hurt, and angry with me. Later on she asked why I would not help her with getting happy and feeling forgiveness. Jess wanted a do-this, simple answer from me, her fix-it guy, to make everything better, but that couldn't be done. The answer was simple and clear, as I'd told her, but Jess wouldn't accept it and wanted people to change for her. She could not realize that she—not others—was the problem.

The next day, August 14, Jess started repeating again that it was not her fault I had been arrested on these charges. She kept telling me Laura and the police were the ones at fault and they lied on the report. She was telling me all the family was wrong, the neighbors were wrong, and everyone was lying about her. She was in complete denial that she had done anything wrong and tried to convince me that she had not caused this situation or all her other many conflicts with multiple people in the past. She also said that Jane was the cause of all the problems in the family. She claimed "everyone is scared of Jane" and that the family wouldn't stop Jane.

Jess asked me many times what I had said to the family about things that led to my arrest and what Mom had said to them. She was trying to get any information to manipulate the truth and tell everyone she was the victim and had done no wrong. She called multiple people to ask what I'd said to them and tried to get them to reveal what they knew.

After Jess stopped her ranting for the time being, I opened up a letter from the Washtenaw County clerk's office. My concealed pistol license was suspended. I was guilty before being proved innocent again in the eyes of the government.

When we went to bed, Jess started saying again that she wanted to confront Jane about the conflict they'd had more than two months ago, since Jane was here in Michigan. I tried multiple times to explain to her that this was not the time to bring up old conflicts with my sister, as we were all grieving and hurting from the loss of our mother, but Jess refused to stop.

She told me repeatedly that I had to "always" be on her side, no matter what. She was desperately trying to get us all to believe she had done no wrong. She even posted on Facebook that the family was lying about her.

I tried explaining to her that posting personal conflicts on Facebook never solved anything, especially when we were all grieving. These types of posts only caused more problems and should not be made, but she was beyond reason.

TALES OF THE CRAZY - WHY MY EX EMBALMED HER UTERUS

This is her Facebook post from August 14:

Jess Cole
August 14 Edited

I am more angry with the living ones than mom cole left me hanging, and now mom isn't here to give me her wisdom.... Dear Lord, please heal me from my sorrow, pain and anger, and wisdom to deal with the situation... I pray daily in the morning to you, Lord, thank you for God the Father's creations, and that I will not lie and will always tell the truth. The words that come out of my lips will not hurt anyone intentionally or unintentionally, and my actions only full of kindness, caring and loving. Some people in the family had and have been telling the lies about me...(honestly, I would not care, if they tell the truth)...., but when the lies were told and I was not there to defend myself, and no one even want to hear because I am just an in-law. I am praying that anyone, who wants hear to the truth will contact me to give me some peace that I dedicated 13 years of my life to care for the family, didn't go to waste. Especially between Jane and I, (mom was there as well) & Chuck. Please I am asking again stop blaming me..., if you would want my respect and love, and just give me a call at

Like · Comment

 Oh, A, you are hurting. I hope all will be patched up soon.
August 14 at 9:27pm Like 👍 1

 Jess Cole Since Jane and Elizabeth are up here, we all can hear the truth.
August 14 at 9:56pm Like

 I tried to call u ... no one is picking.
August 15 at 12:33am Like

 Jess Cole Many stories were told and twisted every time it was told. And all this happened in Mid of May to the beginning of July. Mom had been sick since returning from the trip, Jane wanted her nasty garage filled of dirt and leaves to be vacuum on Elizabeth... See More

Jess went into verbal-attack mode again on me. I asked her to please stop just this once and let me deal with my mom's death. She blurted out, "Did you block me?" I asked why she would ever think I'd block her on Facebook and said that was a vicious thing to say. I can't describe what restraint it took to beg her to stop. I really wanted to tell her exactly what I thought of her, but I couldn't, due to needing her help on this DV charge. Part of me wanted to start yelling at her, saying exactly what I thought of her and how I was filing for divorce. Dealing with all her shit and constant attacks also made me understand how someone with little self-control *could* hit his or her spouse. To be clear, physical violence is wrong; it can never be justified, but many people are pushed to their limits when someone like Jess is relentless and cruel and will not stop. Jess was damned lucky that I'm not a violent man.

Jess immediately flip-flopped and claimed she had not accused me of blocking her on Facebook, and then she went back into wanting to confront Jane to "get the truth out." She was obsessed with doing anything to prove to people that she had done nothing wrong and was even denying statements she had made minutes ago. Nothing else mattered to her.

My emotions were raging and I finally asked her to please leave the bedroom and sleep somewhere else. She shot back, saying she wanted to leave anyway, and then she went downstairs to sleep on the couch. I was having an extremely hard time maintaining control of my emotions when dealing with her, but I knew anything I said could set her off and get her running to the prosecutor to change her story. It was clear that she would do just about anything to satisfy her sense of pride. Her pride had consumed her.

ELEVEN

Gathering Evidence and My Defense

Stan and I had been preparing my defense against this DV charge for the last few days. I gathered up a lot of old documents about her past problems; her previous involuntary commitment to the Providence Hospital psych ward; and even a video of her from my dash cam as she wove all over the road, crossing lanes when she'd been hopped up on pills four months earlier.

I had to keep all this evidence on my PC without Jess knowing it existed and without raising suspicions that I was hiding things from her. To do this, I installed encryption software that created a hidden password-protected and encrypted file that I buried in the system directory. This file held all my evidence and my diary. I also started notes on the best time to file for divorce. To make sure nothing would show up in any recently used documents, I turned off the recently used function of Windows. I also used another program to make sure that all history was cleared every time I edited documents or searched the Internet.

Putting my impressive nerd skills to use would prevent Jess from seeing or suspecting anything. I also had procedures and techniques for data security I had learned as a Cryptologic Maintenance Technician (CTM2) in the navy. I'd held a top-secret special compartmented information clearance when I served. There was no way she could possibly outmaneuver me in finding out what was on or what I was doing on my PC.

When I showed all the evidence to Stan, he just looked at me and said Jess had a lot of issues and needed help. That statement was not what I had expected. As my attorney, he was supposed to look out for my best interests, not pity Jess. He asked me if she was seeing a therapist, and I told him about her meetings with counselors and psychologists over the years. He asked me what medications she was taking. I knew some of what she was taking, so later on, I went up to the bedroom and made a list of all the pills she had in the cabinet by the bed:

Pill name	Drug use
Vicodin 7.5/325	pain
Hydrocodone 10/325	pain
Morphine Sulfate	pain
Neurontin	pain
Percocet	pain
Ultram	pain
Cyclobenzaprine	muscle relaxant
Lidoderm patch	localized pain
liothyronine sodium	Hormone imbalance
Prozac	depression
Mirtazapine	depression
Amitriptyline	depression
Adderall	ADHD
Ambien	sedative for sleeping
Clonazepam	panic disorders
Xanax	anxiety and panic disorders
Zoloft	depression, panic and anxiety disorders
Trazodone	depression and anxiety disorders
Venlafaxine	major depressive disorder, anxiety, and panic disorder.
Diazepam	anxiety disorders

I'd known she was taking a lot of pills, but the vast numbers and types of pills and opioids I found were shocking. No wonder Jess was acting like a lunatic.

Jess sent me a text on August 15 with part of it saying "nobody has never considered" her as one of the family. Even though we had talked about Mom's death and about how the conflict she'd had with Jane and Mom in Kansas should not be brought up during this time of grieving, she wouldn't stop pushing all of us and trying to bring this old conflict up. Because we refused to talk about the Kansas incident, Jess's latest accusation was that we never had considered her part of the family.

She was completely consumed by trying to get us all to believe her version of what had happened and was beyond any reason at this point. Unless we all agreed to her version of how the many conflicts had happened throughout the years, she would not relent and would continue to tear herself apart, accusing everyone else of not caring for her and lying about her. She wanted to get her way while trying to control and manipulate what everyone thought of her to salvage her pride.

Dad was arranging to take care of Mom's cremation and death certificate all at once the following Monday. I asked if he wanted me to help, but he said no. This was something he wanted to do by himself for Mom, and I understood. He also felt I had been burdened enough already, taking care of everything when Mom was in the hospital. He told me he didn't know how I'd held it together during this time with these charges, Jess, Mom's death, and taking care of the family by getting them all together to see Mom for the last time.

This is the text Jess sent:

> Aug 15, 12:05 PM
>
> I just talked to Jane, and she said that you and Dad are taking care the funeral home, she had idea that I did all the running around with phone calls tRyan to get things done the way he wants. And now Jane said that Dad didn't want you to go pick up the ash... Dad just want go alone. I did mention to Jane that I would like to talk to her about what happened and she refused to talk about it now, because family is grieving... nobody has never considered me as one of the family. Dad is being nice to me, so just to make sure that you won't go to jail... You won't talk to me about mom, and other things... what am I to do!

In the text, Jess claimed that I wouldn't talk to her about Mom, but she only wanted to talk about her conflict with Jane in Kansas. I refused to be drawn into another discussion about this same issue she couldn't let go of. Jess would never stop unless I said she was right and everyone else was wrong. I would *never* talk to her about the Kansas issue again. I'd had enough of it. Jess also couldn't accept that Dad wanted to take care of Mom's ashes by himself. She had to try to force her will on him. When he did not submit to her control, Jess felt she was being pushed out again.

I left work early on Friday so that Jess and I could go to Dad's house. Jane was leaving early Saturday morning to go back home to Kansas, and I wanted to see her before she left. When Jess and I were getting things ready to stay the night at Dad's, Jess demanded I call him and put the call on speakerphone to make sure Dad was OK with her coming over. She then demanded I call Jane to hear the same; she wanted to be sure Jane "would behave and not cause a scene."

I relented and talked to Dad, but I told Jess that Jane had assured me she would behave. Jess still pressed me to call Jane and put her on speakerphone, but I refused. I told Jess I had talked to Jane earlier and that my word was good enough; she needed to believe me. I actually had called Jane earlier to make sure she would be OK with Jess there. Jane and I knew Jess was the cause of all these conflicts and was the troublemaker. We both agreed that Jess was the one we had to worry about going off again.

Jess and I left home and arrived at Dad's around five fifteen that afternoon.

I was helping Jane get her stuff ready and pack her car for her drive back to Kansas, but Jess got very upset. She wanted to go for a walk with only me, so we went down to the lake. Jess was very upset that I was helping Jane and wanted me to stop. I couldn't help but think how far gone she was and what an incredible, hateful control freak she had become. I told Jess that my sister needed my help for the long trip back, and she needed to be OK with that.

During the walk, we saw Mom and Dad's neighbors, Tom and Denise, at the beach. I said hi and spoke to them briefly. It was clear they wanted nothing to do with Jess and would not look at her. I'm sure Jess could sense this, so she remained very distant to them.

When we got back from the walk, Jess was very upset at Tom and Denise. She went to their house, confronted them by herself, and then came back even more enraged and extremely disturbed. Because Dad, Jane, and I were all outside and saw that Jess was about to lose it and go into rage mode again, I turned on the voice recorder on my phone to protect me and everyone else, just in case we needed evidence to defend ourselves against more of her wild rants and false accusations.

Jess told me Denise had accused her of killing Mom. Jess claimed Denise had said, "You killed her; she died because of you." At this point there was no reasoning with Jess; she was livid and out of control, and nothing could be said to try to find out what really had happened or to calm her down.

I went over and spoke to Denise and Tom, and they said they were tired of her manipulations, lies, and control. They both denied that Denise had told Jess, "You killed her," and were shocked at this accusation. They also said they were not putting up with Jess's "shit" and had told her exactly what they thought of her. They told Jess she'd made Mom miserable during the last months of her life. It was brutal and harsh, but they'd had enough of Jess and had spoken their minds.

When I was at their house talking, Jane sent me a text that Jess had called the police, so I left and went to talk to Jess to find out why. What mess had she caused now? I found out that Jess told Dad to give her gun back, but he didn't want to, out of fear that she might hurt herself or someone else because of her wild behavior. He also knew we couldn't have any firearms in our home, since the prosecutor was still pursuing the DV charge.

Jane told me Jess went off, saying Dad just wanted to control her, and then she called the police. After I came over to Jess and asked what was going on, Jess asked me what Denise had said, and I told her both of them had denied accusing Jess of killing Mom. Jess said they were liars, just like everyone else in the family.

Jess went off, saying, "Why didn't Tom and Denise blame it on Jane? Jane started the fight in Kansas." Jess claimed she hadn't started anything;

it was all Jane. She was swearing and said, "You people are so good at blaming somebody else." She also said, "I miss you [meaning Mom]. I'm glad Mom died, so she did not have to suffer through that daughter ever again. She [meaning Jane] caused the fight, and they all blame it on me."

Jess went over and lashed out at Jane, saying she was the cause of the problems, but Jane ignored her and said, "Whatever."

Jess loved Mom and was deeply hurt by her passing, but for her to say she was glad Mom had died revealed how highly disturbed Jess was and how consumed she was by hate for Jane. I thought Jess had been taken over by evil, and I knew anything was possible with her. Later I transcribed Jess's statements from the recording and included it as part of the large amount of evidence showing how messed up she was. If this DV case went to trial and Jess turned on me, I would use all this evidence to destroy any credibility she had.

The Michigan state police arrived, and the officer knew right away that Jess was highly agitated. Even though he did not want to give her the gun, he was bound by law to give her the gun back, since her CPL was not suspended, and there were no mental health orders on her. We tried to have him realize that Jess was not in her right mind, but he said that unless there was a medical order on her, he couldn't withhold her property.

To make it worse, he sympathized with us and understood why Dad didn't want to give Jess the gun. He told us that if Dad didn't give Jess the gun, he would have to place Dad under arrest and charge him with theft. The cop took the ammo out of the magazine and gave the ammo to Dad to prevent Jess from having a loaded gun. He also told us we should go to the gun board and take action to get her CPL revoked. Jess took the gun but refused to tell me whom she was giving it to, since there couldn't be any guns in our home. She left in our pickup without me. Dad said he would drive me home in the morning, since Jess had stranded me there.

With Jess gone, everything was calm and back to normal. It was nice having Jess gone so I could spend time with my sister. While we finished packing Jane's car, Jane told me that immediately after the incident with Jess in Kansas, an anonymous source had notified local police that there was child endangerment and abuse in her home. Jane was sure Jess had called the police on her out of spite, but she couldn't prove it. The police had come over to Jane's house, but as there was nothing going on, they'd left. Jess admitted to me a couple of weeks later that she had called the police, thinking there was real danger at Jane's house. Since Jess's emotional state was so far out of whack, I knew it was possible that Jess really believed Jane was abusing the baby. That was the danger with Jess: she believed her fantasies were real and couldn't see reality.

After Jane left Saturday morning, Dad drove me home. He did not want go in the house, because Jess was still extremely agitated. He wanted to give me $200 to cover the cost of Elizabeth's flight, but I told him I could cover it. He said I was facing major expenses due to the legal problems Jess caused. He insisted I take it, so I did. After Dad left, I told Jess he had given me the $200, but that only ramped up her anger, with her demanding that Jane needed to pay, not Dad. I told Jess this was between Dad and Jane now, and we were out of it. At this point, for my own good, I had to begin withholding even simple facts that might set Jess off. Trying to be open and honest with her only worked against me in her deranged state. I had to carefully watch every word to keep her calm and on my side for now.

During the next couple of days, Jess told me she wanted to go over to Laura's house and talk to her. I tried to stop her, saying nothing good would come of it and that it might hurt the DV case against me due to witness tampering. Jess may have thought she was helping, but she would only cause harm.

Jess gave me a recording of her and Laura on a flash drive a week later. She told me her intention was to secretly record Laura so that her lies could be exposed. Jess told me she tried to get Laura to reveal personal information so that the recording could be used to discredit Laura and force her to say she had lied to the police. I asked Jess what could happen if she was caught secretly recording the wife of a police officer in their own home, but she said Laura would not find out. That made no sense, as Jess intended to use the recording against Laura. Jess knew she had broken the law by recording Laura in the privacy of her home without knowledge or consent, but she did it anyway. Jess couldn't be stopped or reasoned with.

The next day I left work early to meet with Pastor Dannor. We talked about what had happened over the past few months. I told him I had no intention of staying married to Jess. I was worried about what else she would pull, and I told him I would not go to jail again because of her actions. I said, "It's not *if* I will go to jail again because of Jess's deranged state; it's *when* and *how bad* it will be."

He stated that, as a counselor, his training was to help couples work their issues out to stay married, but because I had decided it was over, I should see someone else trained to help with all the stress I was going through and for strategies for dealing with Jess while this court case was in motion. I also asked him not to tell Jess about my intentions for divorce, and he assured me that whatever I said was confidential and wouldn't be repeated.

That evening at home, after I had met with the pastor, Jess wanted to talk, but as with all the times before, she dumped all her issues and hate on me. It was her same tired routine of thinking I never stood up for her and never talked to her. She asked for the old 911 recording from when she was committed, because she said the attorney had told her she could be arrested for filing a false police report (about the DV charge).

I asked, "What attorney?"

She ignored my question about the attorney and instead lashed out, saying I didn't trust her. I wondered what other attorneys she had been talking to. Jess continued her rant, taking a different angle and accusing me of being "in denial that we have problems."

I told her she was putting words in my mouth, but she responded, "You show it from the action."

I told her that when we talked, I would try to tell her something, but she would throw it back and say my feelings were wrong. She said, "We are talking," but I replied, "No, I'm sitting here taking it, and when I try to explain to you how I feel your accusations are wrong, you continue to accuse me. That's why I get frustrated."

She then asked if I was afraid that she would not take my side in court. I said no. This was not true, as I feared she could flip-flop at any moment.

I told Jess we needed to move forward with our lives, but she just brought up all her perceived past hurt and the way I never stood up for her or took her side. I stopped her and said, "This is why we can't communicate and why I get frustrated and leave."

Again I said I just wanted to move on and couldn't take all the constant false accusations, her verbal attacks, and her doing 90 percent of the talking while I just sat there and took it.

Jess shifted direction in her verbal attack and said that Mom didn't want any of the problems with Jane to happen. She said Mom was supposed to stand by the truth and honor God, but hadn't done so. I had not shown Jess the letter Mom had written because I knew it would set Jess off—Mom wrote that the problems with Jane were Jess's fault and that Jess was trying to manipulate people to get her way.

Jess said, "All the things I do is to protect the family, but all I got was a stab in the back."

Jess said she had asked me earlier to see a counselor or pastor, and I told her I had talked with Pastor Dannor the day before and he had given me the number for a Christian counseling service. She was not satisfied that he wanted me to see someone else. I didn't tell her the real reason Pastor Dannor wanted me to see someone else. If Jess knew I intended to file for divorce, it would be devastating to my defense for the DV charge. Jess also said I was not doing anything to help our marriage and was "destroying her soul" by not talking to her. She then blamed her anxiety on me.

Jess continued on for about an hour, reliving the past hurts of her life and her uterus being removed with the hysterectomy, blaming me, claiming I never thanked her for her taking care of past things, and further accusing me of being angry all the time. She said she felt only punishment from me for what had happened with her business.

I told her I was not angry and didn't hold a grudge against her. I told her repeatedly that all was forgiven and I moved on. But she continued talking about how her feelings had been hurt, accused me of not talking to her, and said I never forgave her. I told her I was frustrated with her accusations, and then she said I couldn't use the word *accusation* anymore. What the hell? Now she was trying to control what words I could and couldn't use.

After an hour of taking her verbal attacks, I asked if we could stop now. She left the house, drove off, and came back about two hours later.

The following Saturday I went up to Dad's for the day to help him with Mom's credit cards, her online accounts, and their financials. I had made an encrypted spreadsheet with Mom the year before that held all their account numbers and passwords, so things went very smoothly. It was a very good day, and we talked about the blessings we had in our lives and how all the horrible stuff lately still didn't compare to how bad others had it. I told Dad about a story on the news about a man in the Middle East whose entire family had been murdered. He was forced to watch his wife and children being tortured and then executed by ISIS. They did this only because he was a Christian. When you put things in perspective, we had it pretty good.

A week went by, and then all of a sudden, Jess forwarded me texts between her and Laura.

Message	From
Fwd: I hope this message finds you well. I just wanted to let you know that I forgive you for the lies you have told our neighbors. I still love you and want you to be able to find a way to be at peace and find safety and happiness in your life.	Laura
Fwd: What lies and what neighbors...? You confused me.	Jess
Fwd: The lies that ▇▇▇ and I are getting a divorce and that he hits me, and that I made you say lies to the police. I am sorry if you are still sad.	Laura
Fwd: I don't know any of these accusations ...that you mentioned. But if you're referring to me of being sad, it was because of mom Cole passed away. She has been like a mom/best friend to me for the past 13 years.	Jess

Laura: mom/best friend to me for the past 13 years.

Fwd: I know. I hope you find peace and comfort soon.

Jess: <Subject: Fwd:> - I found peace with the Lord, but I still can't help being sad because I miss her. If she is still alive, I would probably be calling her right now, for what you accused me of. You told me that your dad abused your mom (when we were talking in your living room), you and ▆ helped your mom by letting her to stay at your house. I even asked you, if you reported the abuse to the police...and you said 'no'. You went on about you and ▆ didn't report to the police because he's the police and he would lose his pension funds. So your parents got a legal separation instead, not a divorce.

Jess: The only reason that I have not been visiting you because I was uncomfortable that ▆ advised me that it is okay to break the law. If you recalled the phone conversations when ▆ and you were down in Florida. I asked ▆ if he would know someone that can contact the prosecutor or judge to allow me to visit mom Cole at the same time that Charles would be in the same room. That was the day that the family was going to decide to unplug the life support. That was to follow mom Cole's wish not to be on life support. I, myself wanted to be there, but I didn't, because I didn't want to break any law. I made peace with mom Cole because she knows that I was with her and she is with me in Christ.

Laura was claiming that Jess had been telling the neighbors that she and her husband, Travis, were getting a divorce and that Travis hit her. But Jess claimed Laura was trying to discredit her and save herself by falsely accusing Jess of telling the neighbors that Laura was getting hit. The crazy drama and stories with Jess never stopped. Jess forwarded me the text messages to try to convince me that Laura was the liar. Jess denied telling the neighbors this, but my other neighbor, Libby, told me Jess *had* said to her that Travis hit Laura and that they were getting divorced.

Jess asked me why "all" the neighbors and "all" my family were telling lies about her, but I dared not say she was the issue. She then said she'd heard that evil would attack good people doing the Lord's work and that this was probably why it was happening to her. I didn't respond to this either. There was no way I could truthfully answer without turning her against me.

I asked her again to keep clear of Laura; nothing good would come out of her going back and forth with her, and my troubles had been caused by being caught between the two of them. If Jess continued trying to manipulate facts about Laura, she would probably cause me further harm. Jess knew she could be charged with making a false police report if she admitted she had lied to the police. It was just one lie on top of another that she justified, but there was no stopping her.

I had known for a while that I couldn't believe a word Jess said. Anything she said could be part of a bigger web of her plans of manipulation. I wished she could step back and see everything that had happened and the way people viewed her now.

On Tuesday and Wednesday, I talked with Stan to see what was going on with the DV charge. He was supposed to talk with the prosecutor, Angela King, because he felt Angela was getting an idea about Jess and her issues. Stan also said the charges might be dropped when the truth about Jess was known. Angela was not a real prosecutor; she was an associate attorney at the law firm of McLain and Winters in Ypsilanti and the wife of the deputy chief assistant prosecutor of Washtenaw County. Washtenaw County had hired Angela to prosecute cases. Another tidbit about Angela was that her husband, David, was the deputy chief assistant prosecutor of Washtenaw County.

It sure seemed fishy that Angela got these cases, considering her husband's position with the county. This greatly worried me, knowing that she got paid by the county and that getting charges dropped would not result in financial gain for her or her firm. It appeared to be a huge conflict of interest. Stan and a few other attorneys had also told me earlier that cases like this were now more about money than truth. When the county got more DV convictions, they got more federal and state dollars to fund battered women's shelters.

Wednesday I met with a counselor, Ann, for the first time upon Pastor Dannor's recommendation. We talked for an hour, and afterward she told me I was handling all the stress better than most people could. I was to see her again the following Wednesday. I met with Ann alone at first as part of my plan to keep Jess calm. Jess felt my issues, not her own, were the cause of many of our problems. It would keep Jess pacified a bit to know I was following her recommendation. I have to admit, it was nice hearing a professional tell me I was doing OK, considering all that had happened.

On Friday, I called Stan and found out he had done almost nothing since the pretrial was delayed on August 11. He hadn't followed up with the prosecutor and didn't even know that the new pretrial date was coming up on Monday. I was very pissed off about this incompetence.

This is the e-mail I sent him:

After I called and spoke to you today, I have serious doubts about how you are representing me in this case.

You specifically told me on this past Wednesday, Sept 3, that you felt that Angela King was getting a sense of what really happened with how my wife is acting and that you would get in touch with Ms. King to show her. You also said that this may get dismissed before the pretrial once Ms. King found out the truth, what is really going on with my wife, her psychological issues, and that what she really needs is help. I have provided multiple documents showing my wife's condition and the many verbal and physical conflicts she has had and is currently having with many different people.

I was very disappointed today to hear you say that you didn't even get the chance to call Ms. King. It's been since August 11 that the pretrial was delayed and now I hear there was no effort made on your part. This lack of action on your part is completely unacceptable. You have made no effort to get in touch with me. I had to contact you and ask for you to act and how to proceed. You even said when we met at church on August 24, you would get in touch, but you never did. This is my life and freedom on the line and all you can say you didn't get a chance to call her? This lack of action is deeply troubling.

I'm innocent of these false charges that put me in jail by my wife that has been diagnosed with severe psychological issues. I had my rights taken away by the court and been put through the ringer of the county's legal system. I paid you $1500 for proper legal representation to clear me of this false charge, but there has been virtually no action on your part. From what I see, you have utterly failed through inaction.

All I can do now is pray that things go well at Monday's pretrial knowing that my legal representation did not act properly on my behalf.

If you can't speak to the prosecutor before the pre-trial and if these charges are not dropped Monday, I will seek other legal representation and demand a refund minus a small fee for the little and incomplete work that has been done.

I was really on edge the whole weekend, as I knew things might go very poorly at Monday's hearing. Dealing with Jess only aggravated my tension. On Saturday, I got a flyswatter to kill some flies in the house, but Jess told me I was doing it wrong. I told her I didn't need to be told how to kill flies and could handle it. She accused me of being controlling because I wasn't listening to her.

I couldn't help thinking, *Wow, this woman can't even realize what she does, and people who do not want to be told how to do something are the ones she accuses of being controlling. It's just a damn flyswatter, but she has to control how I use it.* It's unreal.

This Saturday, the flyswatter day, was also Jess's birthday. I asked her what she wanted to do. She didn't give me an answer, instead saying she would get back to me. Later on she wanted to talk, so we both sat on the couch. She showed me a Bible and asked if I believed in it. I asked what type of question that was. I said she knew how deep my faith was. She said she wanted to make sure we were both on the same page regarding our belief in God. The alarm bells went off in my head knowing she was setting up some type of manipulation. We talked about forgiveness, and I assured her again that I forgave her. We both prayed to God for forgiveness and to accept his forgiveness. I really did forgive her, but only a fool would trust her.

The conversation took a turn for the worse with her going into the same mode of bringing up the past, not being able to move on, and expressing her mental anguish. Jess began ranting about her past conflicts with people and the way she felt I did not stand by her. She tried to manipulate me into agreeing that if I didn't accept her version of the truth in regard to all her prior conflicts with others (especially my sister), I was not standing by her and had let evil into my heart, because the Lord knew she was right.

Her attempted manipulation of using my faith against me was clear, but she was angry that I was not agreeing with her. She tried from multiple angles to get me to say she was right and that everyone else and I were wrong. I tried explaining to her no one was perfect and we all saw things a bit differently from the pure truth of God, but she replied that God knew she was right. She then started into the same old verbal-attack mode again, bringing up past incidents of how she was wronged and felt I had not defended her. I told her I was not going to relive all these old issues again and that we both had to move on with our lives, forgive ourselves, forgive everyone, and leave the past behind.

I lost count of how many times I tried to get her to stop reliving her past pain with other people. She did not relent in her verbal attacks to justify all she had done and kept insisting it was others' and my fault. I'd had enough, and I told her I refused to keep reliving the past and would not ever talk again about all her past issues. Out of frustration, I got up and left the house for a few hours. She would never stop and always resorted to the same attack mode while bringing up her past hurts. It was impossible to talk rationally without her trying to control the situation. We didn't speak the rest of the weekend.

I went to church alone on Sunday and talked with a friend, Steve, about getting a different attorney, as Stan had failed to act. He gave me Michael Vincent's contact info. Steve had recommended Michael before, but at that time, Stan had assured me he could take care of it. Going with Stan was a huge mistake on my part. Judy, Steve's sister, told me Michael was very good and was the right guy for the job. Judy laughed and said, "Michael can be kind of an ass, but he will be very aggressive and do everything he can do to help you."

On Monday, September 8, I was at court for the pretrial at nine o'clock. Stan was completely unprepared and didn't bring any of my evidence to court. I came prepared with all the evidence and gave it to him again to show to Angela, the prosecutor. I was very pissed off about this latest act of incompetence, as I had sent him the e-mail Friday expressing my concern about his inaction.

Stan tried showing all the evidence to Angela about Jess's mental condition, pill use, and texts from Laura calling Jess a liar before this pretrial started, but Angela would not look at anything. Just before the pretrial started, Stan said she had offered me a deal to plead guilty, go through classes, attend anger management classes, and go on probation, and then the charge would be dropped after two years. I told him there was no way I would plead guilty to something I had not done. This was the same deal she had offered before. I thought it was very clear Angela was never going to relent, even if she knew there were serious credibility issues with Jess's statements.

During court, the judge asked how I was going to plead. I said, "Not guilty, Your Honor." The judge said this case had to go to trial. I chose a jury trial, and the jury selection was set for Friday, October 3. In my opinion, the prosecutor wasn't concerned with finding truth; she only wanted a conviction to add to her record and to force me to take a plea deal. I'd had hopes this charge would be dismissed, but my hopes were smashed, partly because Stan utterly failed as my attorney. I learned a harsh lesson that a person has to pay a good attorney to get justice.

Before I had left the house for the hearing, Jess and I had planned to leave in separate cars, because I was going to work right after court. Jess started getting ready before me, but she didn't bother to show up on time. I arrived twenty minutes early. When Dad and I were leaving the courthouse at 9:20 a.m., Jess finally showed up, and I told her the hearing was over and I was going to trial. Dad and I left without saying anything else to her, and I wanted nothing to do with her.

Jess stayed and headed into the courtroom. She sent me a text at 10:18 a.m., saying, "You've left by the time I got out. I talked to the prosecutor."

I called her and said, "How dare you tell me I left by the time you got out even though you didn't care enough to show up on time for something so important!"

She started trying to explain that her being late was my fault. I cut her off and said, "I don't even want to talk to you," and then I hung up on her. It was another example of the hundreds of her own failures she tried to blame on me and others.

Also in her text, she wrote, "I love you very much." She called in the afternoon, but I ignored her calls. She then texted me, "I have important message to tell u…call me." I called, but she only wanted to tell me about more squabbles and text messages between her and Laura and that she felt it was important for the DV case to show that Laura had lied and caused this.

I was in a very bad mood the entire day due to the pretrial outcome and Jess's behavior. To add to it, for the last few days, Jess had been talking about putting ads out to sell the store inventory, but like all the times before, she did nothing. Late in the morning, I sent her an e-mail: "I need to see an ad for the inventory in this house tomorrow. No more excuses."

I was very upset with all that had happened that day. Later in the afternoon, Jess said she was sorry for not showing up for the pretrial. She was calling me "sweetheart," but I didn't want to hear it.

I called Michael Vincent's law firm and made an appointment to see them at 5:00 p.m., Thursday, September 11. I also called a few other firms. After I got home from work, Jess wanted to go with me and said we needed to do this together. I said no and told her the prosecutor might see this as me trying to manipulate her testimony. She still argued to go, but I would not listen. I told Jess that some firms said an extended trial could cost up to $15,000.

When I got home after work, Jess started up again about Jane; she said Jane had caused all the issues in Kansas, and Jess felt all my legal problems were the fault of "everyone else lying." With the pretrial's bad outcome, I couldn't stand to look at her anymore or hear more of the same old victim crap she was spewing. Later on, at about 10:00 p.m., she brought up this old crap again. That was it. I told her the best thing that could happen for me was for her to just leave, go home to her family, never come back, and never have any contact with me. I really meant that. I shouldn't have said it, because I didn't want her to turn on me, but I couldn't take her hateful, batshit-crazy behavior any longer.

To make it worse, Jess was still going back and forth with Laura about the same drama. Laura was again accusing Jess of telling the neighbors that Travis had hurt her and was very concerned that Jess was telling this lie to the prosecutor. The psycho never stops.

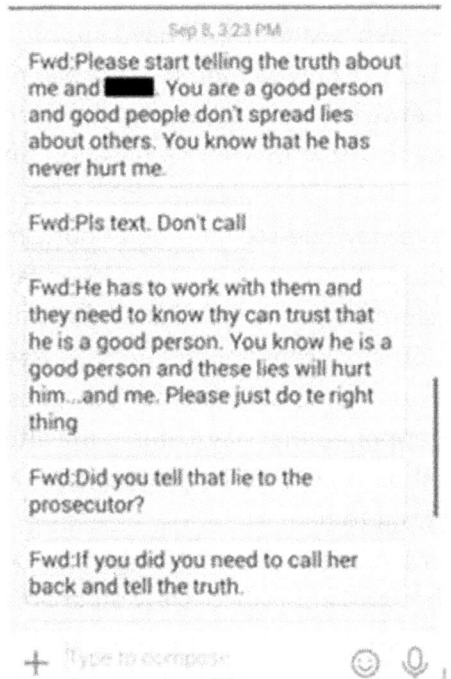

These are all Laura's texts that Jess forwarded to me.

The next day, Tuesday, Jess replied to my e-mail about the inventory ad from the previous day; she ignored the ad and referred to when I was mad with her for being so late and missing the hearing. She wrote, "Again you got angry at me without finding out the truth, you allowed your anger to take over your good heart, which is devilish acts, possessed your heart." She still thought that all these problems were not her fault and was putting the blame on me for getting mad.

After I got back home from work on Tuesday, I met with Steve and Katrina, Jess's close friends, at the Corner Brewery in Ypsilanti. Steve had called me earlier in the day wanting to talk with me. I sure wished I could have one of their good craft beers, with Jack Hammer Old Ale being my favorite, but I couldn't due to the bond conditions banning me from drinking alcohol.

They told me that a couple of months earlier, before the DV charge, they believed much of what Jess said about me to them. Steve said that, from the way Jess described me, I sounded like a horrible, controlling monster. They had told her she should leave me and file for divorce and said she could stay with them. But after a while, they both wondered why Jess would not file for divorce.

Steve said he could not understand why, if I was such a horrible person, Jess was still staying with me. He also said Jess would refer to me as "her better half," and this was very contradictory. They started seeing large cracks and inconsistencies in her stories and began questioning her motives and wondering what the real truth was. Then the DV charge came. They could not understand why I had been arrested, because Jess told them she only wanted the police to talk to me because I wouldn't talk to her that day. To them, it made no sense, and that was why they had reached out to me.

They were very concerned about my health, the way I was handling all the stress, and told me this should have never happened to me. They even said Jess was extremely upset about the whole situation. Jess claimed everything on the police report was a lie. They said Jess told them I had never hit her or been violent to her and that she never felt threatened by my behavior. This also made no sense to them, based on prior statements Jess had made, but they told me that, prior to my arrest, Jess said I had never threatened, hit, or pushed her.

They said Jess had been telling them that "everyone" was lying and she had done no wrong. They both assured me that they now knew this was not the case and that Jess couldn't live in the truth. They said they felt that Jess was feeling the burden of guilt from her own lies and that it was causing her to act in this out-of-control behavior, with her in damage-control mode.

I told them she was doing anything to salvage her pride. Now that she realized how serious this DV charge was and what it would do to my and her life, I thought she would do anything, including telling more lies, to put the blame on others in order to try to get these charges dropped. She still wouldn't tell the truth out of fear that she would get charged with making a false police report.

They felt that Jess purposefully kept me isolated from them so that any truth about my character and who I really was could be hidden and so that she could continue her victim routine to get hugs and pity from them.

I showed them the list of pills in her cabinet by the bed. They were shocked at the vast number and types of pills and said, "No wonder she has been acting this way." I asked if they remembered my mom; they said of course, and then they described how wonderful a Christian woman she had been.

I showed them the letter from my mom describing how Jess had caused all the problems and chaos in Kansas. I went on to describe how Jess had been obsessed with rage ever since Kansas and told them what had really happened the day of my arrest. After seeing the letter from my mom that contradicted everything Jess had told them and knowing my mother would never have lied about this, they knew for sure that all the things Jess had told them about me and the family were lies. They were genuinely disturbed to learn the truth of all these events and felt very sorry for me.

I told them that Jess really felt she was right and everyone else was wrong, due to her controlling nature and pride. She refused to see the reality and consequences of her own actions, and this behavior had gotten far worse in the past few years. They said this made sense, but they also said that made it dangerous for me and harder to deal with. I told them Jess had probably said a lot of what was on the police report, but she wouldn't admit it out of fear she might get arrested for making a false report.

I brought them up to speed on my DV case, Stan's complete failure, and the October 3 date for jury selection for the trial. They were very upset hearing this, as it was just another hit I had to endure. I told them I had fired Stan's "incompetent ass" and contacted Michael Vincent's firm. I said I hoped the new attorney could get this dropped before it went to trial. If it went to trial, I would have to present all this evidence against Jess in court, and it would probably destroy her. I didn't want that to happen. I didn't want to cause her harm, but I wouldn't allow myself to be convicted and go to jail because of her lies.

They both agreed that I had to do whatever it took to clear my name at this point, but they also wanted this case to be dropped so that Jess's mental health could be salvaged. They also agreed that a court case exposing all her lies and manipulations would push her over the edge, and she might never recover from it. Steve and Katrina were both genuinely sorry for believing Jess's lies about me, and I could see the pain Jess's betrayal caused them.

On Wednesday, I met with the counselor, Ann, for the second time. I told her about the bad outcome of the pretrial and showed her the e-mail I had sent to my attorney, Stan. I could tell she was not happy about the poor representation, and she said it was not right. I talked about what I had said to Jess about wanting her to leave, and then I showed her Jess's e-mail stating that I should have not gotten angry. Ann even said that Jess had serious accountability problems and that my anger with everything that had happened on Monday was justified.

During our session, Jess sent me texts to call an attorney she had contacted to handle my DV case. I had already told Jess many times that multiple people had recommended I go with Michael Vincent and that I was meeting with him that Thursday. Jess wouldn't stop telling me what to do. Her texts were for me to call Sam Berstein in Ypsilanti. (He's not to be confused with the 800-call-Sam slip-and-fall personal injury lawyer who advertises in the metro Detroit area. It's a different Sam Berstein.)

I sent Jess a text to "please stop," but she still sent another one. When I got home, she continued badgering me about how I had to call Sam.

She kept going back to the $15,000 that a trial could cost, but I told her I would talk to Michael and find out what the real cost could be. I also told her I would see what he said about the possibility of getting this dropped before trial. She still would not stop demanding I call Sam before Michael.

I told her to stop; I had this taken care of, and we had already discussed it multiple times. Jess was really starting to piss me off. Her reply was that she was only trying to help and that we had to do this together. I told her she was not helping and was only causing me more stress, but she still would not relent. She had a class at church, so she left for the evening but came back early due to a power outage and was very angry—she felt I was not listening to her. I did listen to her up to a point, but there was no way in hell I would consider or follow any of a crazy person's suggestions.

TWELVE

Phase Two of My Defense

Dad called me Thursday to talk about events that had happened at Monday's pretrial hearing. He said Jess had called him after the pretrial to tell him her watch was wrong and that was why she'd been late. He knew she was lying; it was another one of her excuses, and he told me he "saw right through her bullshit." I told Dad I'd left the house to get to the pretrial on time, but she had started doing all sorts of unrelated stuff at the last minute while she should be leaving. This was the same pattern she had followed for years that made her habitually late. She never changed her ways.

Dad said it was like she had two different personalities and couldn't be trusted to tell the truth on anything. He also warned me that even though she'd said she would not testify against me in a trial, she could flip and say anything to make herself look good at my expense.

That evening after work on September 11, I saw Michael Vincent for the first time. It was a vastly more professional and competent experience than I'd had with Stan. He already had the police report and other documents about my case prepared and ready for review. I told him Steve and his sister had told me to get in touch with him about my case, and Michael briefly spoke fondly about them. Michael was a good friend of their dad.

Michael said he wanted to read the report before I spoke about the case. After only a few paragraphs, he said, "Bullshit," loudly. He continued reading and was saying, "This is bullshit," and "Bullshit," multiple times. He looked up at me and asked, "You got arrested over cherries?" He could not believe it and said again, "This is bullshit."

He read more and said multiple times the report was contradicting itself. He said the report stated that the cherries were in the trash in the Ziploc bag, but earlier in the report, it said I'd thrown the cherries at her from across the room and there were food splatters on the wall. He said, "This is bullshit," again and asked sarcastically, "How could cherries be thrown across the room splattering the wall when the police saw the cherries in the trash still in the Ziploc bag?"

He said none of this made sense, and he was genuinely ticked off that this had been done to me. He also said that throughout his career, he had seen multiple times that police had shown extreme bias based on what one person said about an alleged assault. The police then looked for reasons and evidence to support their bias and wrote reports from this viewpoint while making completely wrong assumptions. This is how innocent people get thrown in jail and many times wrongfully convicted.

I gave him a brief rundown of how Jess had descended into a complete victim mentality and how she would not work and did pretty much nothing with her life except for watching TV, surfing the Internet, and shopping. I showed him the list of pills Jess was taking at the time, the letter from Mom detailing how she had caused the problems in Kansas, the letter from the gym when they'd kicked her out, and a few other things documenting her behavior.

Michael just shook his head, said he was very sorry this happened to me, and told me he would take the case. He assured me he would most likely be able to get these charges thrown out, but there still was the possibility it may go to trial. He planned to schedule an evidentiary hearing to review all my documentation with the judge and prosecutor. With all I had on Jess and the conflicting police report, Michael would ask the judge to dismiss the case, hoping the judge would agree. I asked about the cost, and he said there would be a $4,000 retainer. With $1,500 wasted with Stan, now there was an additional $4,000 out of my pocket.

I could see now why people hated cops, hated judges, hated prosecutors, and hated the court system. From my experience of being completely innocent, it was a well-deserved reputation. To top it all off, these people in the judicial process congratulated themselves, saying the system worked when someone was found innocent even though the victim of this legal abuse had his or her life destroyed. These innocents shouldn't have been arrested in the first place.

I'm not anticop, and I know there is a need for law enforcement. I just don't trust them after what I've been through. I'm sure that when Jess and Laura were telling their stories to the police, the two cops were convinced I was a horrible human being and were not looking to see both sides. They were looking for anything to support this contrived drama and justify an arrest. It didn't help that Laura's husband was one of their own. The cops' attitude to me right from the beginning was hostile, and it was very clear that they were not interested in examining facts or evidence that would contradict the women's statements.

Over the next few days, I exchanged calls and e-mails with Michael's office manager, Amanda. She had me sign paperwork releasing Stan as my attorney. Another issue they were taking care of was my CPL suspension. The county gun board scheduled an interview about my suspension. Michael wrote them, stating, "We are requesting an adjournment regarding your request to interview Mr. Cole until this matter has been resolved. Mr. Cole is asserting his Fifth Amendment right to remain silent at this present time."

It was an incredible difference: Michael's firm was proactive and aggressive. Michael was like an aggressive pit bull fighting all-in for his clients, but Stan was a complacent nice guy. I learned a harsh lesson about having a nice guy represent me. Never again. If I ever get falsely charged again, I'll search out the meanest, pit bull-type defense attorney I can find, who will do anything for me. Nice guys lose and get their clients convicted.

The next Friday, September 19, I poked around Jess's laptop, looking for any other evidence I may have to use, and found some of Jess's Facebook messages with her friend Churai from Thailand. Jess sent these messages on August 9, and they showed her contempt for my family.

Jess wrote, "mom cole is now brain dead and this damn family is going to disconnect the life support tomorrow afternoon." She also wrote, "I want to protest, I wish that they give her a few more day to be certain."

The next day, September 20, was Mom's memorial service at her church. I'd spent the past two weeks making all the arrangements. Jess had no part of this, and I had not asked for any of her input. Dad was still an emotional mess from dealing with Mom's death, so I had to be strong for him and take care of everything. Jane and I worded Mom's bio, which was printed on the memorial service pamphlets. I also talked with Jane and suggested that, instead of arranging poster boards of pictures, I would scan a bunch of photos of Mom with family and friends and display the pictures on my HDTV. She thought this was a great idea. I found old photos of Mom as a child and of when Mom and Dad were married. All the pictures were put in a 1080p video file that looped to the beginning when it reached the end.

I left Friday evening to spend the night at Dad's house. Jess did not come. She told me she felt very uncomfortable going. *Good*, I thought. I didn't want her there and was sure nobody else did either, knowing the damage she had done to our family.

Saturday morning I set up my HDTV and laptop in the narthex at church, and started the playback. Everyone loved watching the pictures on a large HDTV, and many said that doing it this way was far more interesting than looking at small pictures on poster board.

After all the greetings were done, everyone went to the sanctuary for the service, which started at 11:00 a.m. The immediate family, including Mom's brothers and sisters, gathered, and we stayed back while everyone else entered the sanctuary. The family was to enter at the beginning of the service with Dad carrying a wooden chest that held Mom's ashes. Just before we were to start walking in, when he was going to pick up the chest, Dad started shaking. I looked at Dad and asked him if he wanted me to carry them. He nodded. Tears streamed down his face, and his voice was choking up. I took the chest, and everyone turned to us as we came in. I set the chest on a small table at the front of the aisle. The pastor said a few words, and then the service started.

It was a traditional LCMS service. Pastor Frank Pies gave the sermon about Mom. He had been the senior pastor until his retirement in 2007, when Pastor Thoma took over as senior pastor. Pastor Thoma led the rest of the service.

There was a lunch at church after the service. Many people from Our Savior came up and told me how much they'd loved and respected Mom. Toward the end of the lunch, Jess walked in. No one greeted her, and her showing up was a surprise to me. As usual she was late. I took her to the table Dad and I were at and got a few things for her to eat. I really didn't want to see her at all, but I had to appear thankful she had arrived.

After the lunch, the family and close friends came over to Mom and Dad's house. Jess went home instead. That was a very good thing, as I'm sure many of the family would have gone off on her once we were out of church. A few of the family from my mom's side said how much they hated Jess for what she had done to our family and me. Mom was very close to her sister, Katherine, and had told her much of what had gone on with Jess. Katherine had told the rest of the family before Mom's death, and they were very upset and angry with Jess.

Many of the friends and family had an incredible amount of contempt toward Jess, and their hate was fueled by the loss of Mom. They did keep many of their comments to me under control, as this was the time to grieve and remember Mom and not to lash out at Jess. I said to them that if I'd told Jess the brutal truth that I didn't want her at Mom's memorial and the way that I really felt about her, Jess would probably turn on me. She would go even more psycho, if that were possible, and make up more false stories out of vengeance. I worried she'd push for the DV conviction and anything else she could charge me with. They told me they would keep quiet until this charge was taken care of.

During a reunion for Mom's side of the family a year later, they didn't hold back and told me how they felt about Jess. One cousin told me that when she saw Jess come in close to the end of the memorial lunch, she'd felt like dragging Jess outside and "slapping the shit out of her."

The next day I was back in the mode of looking for any evidence I could use for my defense. Jess was asleep, so I took her phone and poked around in it. I saw disturbing text messages about divorce sent a few days earlier between her and a mutual friend Alice. It was clear Jess had been plotting and thinking about a divorce and that she was deleting texts after sending them. She probably thought getting me arrested was the last straw and that I would file for divorce. She got one thing right for once. Alice had sent her the name of a divorce lawyer to check out.

Based on her past behavior, I wasn't too worried about Jess filing. She was the queen of procrastination. Plus she had to keep me around to continue to leech off me. If I was gone, her money and lifestyle would be gone also.

A week later Michael Vincent's office manager, Amanda, e-mailed me the police report. This was the first time I had seen it, and reading the report was extremely disturbing and hard to take.

It was unbelievable. The cops wrote that Jess "appeared to be terrified of her spouse and admitted same during my interview." Further down, the cops outright lied about my conduct. Assholes. The one who'd written the report claimed that after I was advised I was under arrest, I tightened my jaw muscles and had my arms folded as I stared at him. The cop wrote, "I advised him again that he was under arrest and he was to place his hands behind his back. Charles did not move and continued to stare at me. So I grabbed his arm and placed it behind his back, and he was arrested without incident."

What a lying, dishonest prick. When I went outside, the cop told me I was being arrested and being handcuffed, and then I put my arms in front of me. The cop grabbed my arm and yelled at me to put my hands behind my back. I sure wish I had a video to prove what really happened. My heart was pounding in my chest, and I felt fear and other emotions as I read this report with the false statements by the police and the completely ridiculous false statements Jess had made.

There were statements from her saying I was pounding walls with my fists and that she feared for her life. Was that what she really thought when she was in the grips of her emotional fits? How could she even feel this when things like that never happened? It was so out of touch with reality, but that was what she'd apparently told the cops. The prosecutor was basing the case on Jess's statements without even considering any other evidence. I felt it was staggering bias and incompetence on the prosecutor's part—she didn't even care about finding the truth so that justice could prevail. After this was over, I intended to pursue a civil case against Washtenaw County for malicious prosecution.

After I read this report, my fear was replaced with anger. I was way past being simply angry; I was in a rage over all the lies she had told about me. This false report spelled serious trouble for me. Going through all this hell with the jail experience and then reading this really put me in a seriously pissed-off mood. After the years of putting up with her crap and bailing her out of trouble again and again, this was the end result of my standing by her.

I yelled, "Fuck the police! Nothing but a bunch of lying assholes." Thinking about Jess, I yelled, "Bitch! Whore! Lying cunt!" There were a lot more choice words about her.

It was way out of character for me to yell like this. I try my best not to use profanity—it's vulgar and low-class. My avoiding the use of profanity was due to a talk my grandfather Cole gave me when I was a kid. I was going through a cussing phase, and he'd set me straight. He told me a very simple truth: "Morons and idiots use profanity to stress their point." They use profanity as a verbal crutch because they can't think of anything else to reasonably articulate what's on their mind. He went into how swearing did nothing to improve a man's character; it only took away from it. He asked me if I'd noticed whether guys swore more when they were with other guys. I said yes, and he said it was because they were followers and were weak. They swore because others were doing it; they wanted to be accepted, to be one of the guys, and were not strong enough to be their own man.

This talk by my grandfather really sank in. I still remember as a kid watching others swear and thinking their behavior was exactly as Grandpa had said. It's even true with adults. Later on in life, I realized great men and women of character do not need to swear. It's beneath them to act that way. People who used the most profanity tended to be those I didn't want to associate with. They were not people I could look up to with respect.

This is also true with many entertainers or comedians today. Instead of developing truly good routines, they substitute f-bombs or other vulgarities in talentless attempts to get laughs. The last comedy club I went to was horrible, and the alleged comedian thought it was funny hurling out f-bombs. I walked out five minutes into his routine.

Whenever I got angry and swore, later on, I realized that instead of using my mind, emotions had grabbed hold, and I had blurted out something stupid. Anger and hostility had clouded my mind and caused me to stop using my brain and instead act like a moron. Grandpa's wisdom has proved itself countless times throughout my life.

Dealing with the stress of my mother's death while reading the police report's sheer level of malice and falseness got me incredibly upset. At that moment I failed to keep composure and use reason. It took a while to calm down, start thinking clearly, and plan the next steps for my defense.

Jess had talked to the prosecutor, trying to convince her that what was on the report hadn't happened, but the prosecutor refused to consider Jess's statements. Jess wouldn't stop accusing the police of lying and saying Laura had fed the police false information. I knew, based on her past behavior, that when she got into these severe emotional states of rage or hopelessness, she would say crazy things but would deny them later on to protect herself.

She had done many things in the past she denied, but this incident was a huge leap from anything else she had done and had completely screwed up my life. She was in complete denial and refused to admit that this was in any way her fault; she wouldn't admit to the smallest of wrongdoing. In her mind, everyone else was lying; she was the victim, and it was my fault for not understanding how she was affected by this.

This was not just my problem; it was an unnecessary burden being put on society. The cost of this prosecution to the taxpayers was very substantial. Adding to this, twelve other people were now going to have their lives disrupted by having to serve on a jury. Many more would have their lives disrupted when they were summoned to go through the jury selection process. I would probably say a few choice words when I saw the next round of ballot proposals with Washtenaw County asking for more taxes to fund their screwed-up legal machine.

Here is a thought: *Never* vote for these types of tax increases. This will force the incompetent fools to streamline the process and only prosecute those who have been fully vetted with evidence and deemed deserving of prosecution. This process of going after someone based only on one crazy person's statements without even wanting to seek the truth is a horrible injustice for both society and the victims of these types of prosecutorial incompetence and misconduct.

I used to think that most people arrested had done something to deserve it, but I know now that's not the case. When I was in jail, I really felt that this matter would be cleared up once the truth got out. What a fool I was to believe that. When I listened to the other prisoners complain about how Washtenaw County abused people's rights and railroaded them, I didn't believe them. The prisoners spoke in very profane and demeaning ways about the prosecutors and how they didn't care about justice, but only increasing conviction rates, extorting money, and getting free labor on work crews. From my recent experience, this reputation about Washtenaw County is very true and well deserved.

My false assumption at the beginning of this mess was that the cops, prosecutor, and legal system actually wanted to seek the truth. That's not completely true either.

I saw a story on the news about a New York man released from prison after serving thirty years on a wrongful murder conviction. I could completely understand how this happened, especially because it was very clear to me that the prosecutor charging me was not interested in finding out the truth; she only wanted a conviction. These types of prosecutors with such a callous disregard for truth or justice have no place putting people behind bars. There needs to be a better system for vetting people who serve in this capacity; we need to see who has the character to do this properly without bias and who wants to uphold truth.

My next hearing was October 20, and during this, Michael Vincent flip-flopped at court, decided not to have an evidentiary hearing, and asked for this to go right to trial with a jury. The jury selection hearing was scheduled for December 5. Maybe taking the chance of not having a hearing to examine evidence and going right to trial was the right course of action. I didn't know at this point. Michael told me he did not want to let the prosecutor know the sheer volume of evidence we had of Jess's screwed-up behavior.

Recently a recruiter called me about a position available in Minnesota. I had a phone interview with their chief engineer, and the company wanted me to travel there for an interview. I didn't want to leave Ford, but this new position was very well suited for me. Who knew—it might be a good opportunity to start my life over with a better job somewhere else without Jess. I had to ask the court permission to travel out of state in Minnesota. The judge granted my travel, but I had to go into the probation office after that morning's hearing to fill out paperwork for the judge to sign. Going into a probation office really sucked, as I knew I hadn't done anything to deserve this or even be convicted of a crime. It was a horrible feeling being treated like a convicted criminal.

Later in the evening, I ordered parts for a new PC so that I could use the old one as a security system that recorded video and audio. I had to protect myself with evidence if Jess went off the rails again. It was a very real possibility that I would get thrown in jail again if she told another wild story to feed her victim mentality. I learned that truth does not matter when you get pulled into the justice system with a prosecutor looking to put another notch in her gun. What matters is whether the prosecutor can get a successful prosecution based solely on one person's statements and emotions, and Jess was a master of emotional manipulation.

If something else were to happen in the future, the only way to prove my innocence was to have hard evidence showing video and audio. For now I was completely screwed with the DV charge; I couldn't prove what Jess told the cops didn't happen. It was very tough to keep taking these hits, knowing that the truth did not matter. If I'd had a recording of what had really happened leading up to my arrest, especially proving the cops had lied about my resisting arrest, all the DV charges could have been thrown out almost immediately. I would have saved thousands in legal fees and eliminated much of the emotional toll. I also would have filed a civil suit against the cops for lying on the police report to justify my arrest.

A month went by, and on November 18, Jess finally destroyed her friendship with Steve and Katrina. They had been willing to forgive her for the lies she had told them about me because they knew she had many issues, but this latest incident made them very angry with her.

Steve and Katrina had been storing about thirty boxes of dresses at their home for close to a year and were trying to help Jess sell the inventory, but Jess would not cooperate and kept coming up with excuses about why she couldn't help. They offered to take all the inventory, saying their father would rent a warehouse and try to sell the dresses. We would get a portion of the profit, if there was any.

Jess was demanding $10,000 up front, but I tried to talk her out of it. She would not listen. I asked her to consider going down to $5,000 and then, out of frustration, told her I was staying out of it. She was too unreasonable and refused to budge. She was causing more problems by trying to control everything, even though all the boxes of dresses had been sitting in our home since 2008, and she had done nothing in six years to sell them. The deal fell apart, due entirely to Jess's crazy behavior, and Steve and Katrina asked me to take the thirty boxes back into my home.

Steve and Katrina were very upset that Jess had acted this way. When I went over to get the boxes, they told me again that they were very sorry for believing her at first. Katrina gave me a big hug. During the start of moving the dresses, Katrina was very cold and distant to Jess and wanted nothing to do with her.

Jess sent them a text accusing them of not being direct with her and was angry they had called me to take care of the dresses. In the text, she accused them of causing marriage issues between us. Jess forwarded the text to me.

Fwd: what sent to
Oh no..., i am so sorry for miss .
I hope that she will feel better. I just talked to my husband and we are on the same page. i asked him to stay out of this and any future contact, he will refer you to talk to me.. and I will be handling all the dresses like i have always been.
I thank you for you taking the dresses when you did. I don't quite understand why can't i have my dresses back. If you want to discuss any offer than what you,   told me the other night, i am all ears. I thought that you were not try to pressure me to do anything, but you turned around and called my husband. What is the deal that you can't tell me....YOU TOLD ME BEFORE THAT ANYTHING I SOLD FROM THE DRESSES, YOU WANTED ME TO HIDE FROM MY HUSBAND, AND THEN YOU TURNED AROUND AND CALLED HIM....? I told him

can't tell me....YOU TOLD ME BEFORE THAT ANYTHING I SOLD FROM THE DRESSES, YOU WANTED ME TO HIDE FROM MY HUSBAND, AND THEN YOU TURNED AROUND AND CALLED HIM....? I told him everything that we discussed the o6her night. I am really hurt, you don't respect my decision. All the dresses are mine and so the DEBTS. I was not aware that you put all of dresses in the garage, the mice probably have got to them. I love you guys, if you want to help me...just be direct with me. You have been telling me to divorce him, because he would never changed......Just you get him involved, just caused us more marriage issues. i am trying to sabe my marriage with conyacted our pastor, but pastor wants my husband to show that he wants to save our marriage, and to reconcile the differences.

On November 25, the last of the boxes from Steve and Katrina's were back in my house. My dining room was full of boxes and unusable. I had lost count of how many times I had shifted these damned boxes around to try to make more room. After we got all of them back, Jess accused Steve and Katrina of stealing dresses even though she didn't make any effort to go through all the boxes. She thought some dresses were missing, but she didn't even look for them. I spoke with Steve about Jess's accusations, and that made them even angrier with her.

When I was at their house loading dresses, I spoke with Steve more about this DV charge, and they asked if there was anything they could do. They were willing to testify on my behalf and to tell the judge about Jess's lies and manipulations. I asked if Steve and Katrina could call the prosecutor and tell her what they knew Jess had done. Later Steve called me and said Katrina would be happy to call the prosecutor. Katrina was still very upset with all the lies Jess had told them and the trouble she had caused everyone.

A few days later, Steve gave me a call and told me the prosecutor would not back down. Katrina informed the prosecutor of the lies Jess had told them, all the problems she had caused, and that I was not capable of the acts Jess had reported to the police. The prosecutor asked if Jess had ever admitted she lied to the police, but Katrina said no. Katrina also informed the prosecutor that Jess had told her shortly after I was arrested that she could be charged with making a false police report. Katrina described to the prosecutor how she had told Jess that, for my sake, she had to start telling the truth to clear this up, but Jess had stayed silent and was scared of being arrested. Katrina also told the prosecutor Jess had told her Laura was the one who'd lied to the police. The prosecutor said that without a direct admission from Jess that she had lied, she would not drop this case.

Now that Jess destroyed her friendship with Steve and Katrina, she had ruined virtually all her long-term friendships with people who knew the whole situation with me. She didn't have anyone close to talk with now. Some of her ex-friends told me she was crazy. Jess had only a few distant or new friends remaining, but I had no contact with them. I was sure she had fed them all sorts of misinformation to make it look like she was the victim in all the trouble she had caused.

On December 4, I had another meeting with Michael to discuss the hearing scheduled for the next day.

In the morning, Jess sent me a text calling this situation an "injustice." I was sure she considered it an injustice because in her mind, everyone else had caused this legal problem, not her.

> Dec 4, 2014, 10:04 AM
> Sweetheart, please forgive me for your injustice, I am so sorry. What will happen to you, if i couldn't stand trial, because of anxiety. Even now, i m having anxiety attack & chest pain, you know that i had to wear a heart monitor for a month. This is because i am feeling your pain and just thinking about what's going through your mind. i love you.
>
> Dec 4, 2014, 1:03 PM
> please call asap

Her text showed how she had to be the center of attention. I was up on serious charges, but she had to shift the focus to her and her feelings. Screw her feelings and her victim mentality. I didn't care how bad she felt. I was like Spock thinking, *It does not compute*, when dealing with her. It was mind blowing to see her try to justify such irrational behavior.

I went to Michael Vincent's office at 3:00 p.m., but I spoke with another attorney there, since Michael was still in court on another case. The other attorney told me that with recent stories in the media about celebrities knocking their girlfriends around, Michael felt that a jury might be biased. They might rule not on evidence but on emotion. He planned to have it changed to a bench trial tomorrow, as a judge would be more objective with facts.

Michael's reasoning was due to events in September's news about a video emerging of NFL player Ray Rice punching his girlfriend in an elevator. It was a vicious attack, and Michael thought the public could be outraged and biased toward anyone accused of violence toward his or her spouse.

To add to the media frenzy during all my DV hearings, the Bob Bashara murder case was all over the news here in the metro Detroit area. Bob had hired his handyman, Joe Gentz, to kill his estranged wife. A jury had convicted them of murder, and they were serving their sentences in prison. They were back in the news because Gentz had recanted his signed affidavit saying he had killed Bob's wife, claiming instead that Bashara had forced him at gunpoint to commit the murder. It's the type of story the media loves with drama and all sorts of plot twists. As they say, if it bleeds, it leads. It was extremely unfortunate timing for my case.

We talked for a while about the procedure of the trial and other legal matters. We went off topic when I said this did not make sense based on facts. The facts I had that would clear my name didn't matter or weren't even being considered. Even the police report contradicted itself. As an engineer, I thought this whole process was horribly unfair. All the justice system wanted was a conviction. I said, "No wonder so many people hate cops, prosecutors, and the trial system."

The attorney said that our system was very emotion based and that this was the unfair reality with cases like mine. He also said that one of the reasons he had become a criminal defense lawyer was to defend the innocent against false charges and injustices and that people like me restored his faith in humanity. He assured me their firm would bend over backward to do their best so that people like me would have their names cleared.

Since the pretrial was the next morning, Jess was supposed to get a subpoena to be at court, but she took off without telling me. She had called another attorney, who advised her to leave the house and stay overnight somewhere else so she could not be found and served with an order to appear in court. The attorney also told Jess not to answer any calls if she did not recognize the number, as these could be from a call service informing her of the subpoena.

Jess called me, but she didn't tell me where she was. I told her it was OK to tell me where she was. If anyone came to the house to find and serve her, I would simply tell the person that if he or she wanted to question me, that person would have to talk to my attorney. They couldn't compel me to say anything. Jess fessed up, saying she was at Dad's and was spending the night there. Later on she did get a call but did not answer it. She Googled the number, and it was from a call service, probably to tell her she had to come to court. Jess stayed the night at Dad's house.

I spoke with Dad later on. Jess had asked him to say that he did not know where she was, but Dad refused to lie for her.

The next day, December 5, 2014, Dad came down to the courthouse for the hearing. The hearing was supposed to be for a jury selection with Michael requesting a bench trial instead. When Jess didn't show up, Michael thought he could use her absence and the weakness of this case in my favor. He unexpectedly asked the judge to dismiss the charges. This turn took me by surprise. Judge Pope asked the prosecutor if she had any objections, and she said no. That surprised me even more, but I was sure the conversation she'd had with Katrina made her realize there was no way she could win this case. The prosecutor also had to know there was no way I was going to back down or take a plea deal.

The judge dismissed the case! This was the best outcome I could have had at this point. It was great news! Sure took long enough, and I was out almost $6,000 and months of stress to fight something I hadn't done. With this ordeal over, I now had to focus on how and when to file for divorce.

There was no doubt that if I filed when Jess was around, she would blow up, go into pure rage mode, and do or say anything to get me arrested on other made-up charges out of pure revenge. So for now, I told her it was time for our marriage to heal, while I secretly planned my next steps.

After this DV ordeal was over, I did a lot of reflection on the current state of the criminal justice system. I wasn't cleared of these charges based on facts and truth; it was based on strategy, guile, and having the means to afford a very good attorney who could game the system. The real facts of my case never entered the equation. Now whenever I hear on the news that someone has been arrested, especially on a domestic violence charge, I am the first one to defend that person's innocence until all evidence is presented.

I've seen both men and women ripping on some poor guy, saying he should be locked up for life for the simple fact that he was arrested on a DV charge. I tell these people exactly how I feel about this situation with them prejudging a person who could be innocent. Most of the time, they will restate their position and try to justify themselves. Sometimes they will say my situation was an isolated incident. They don't realize that innocent lives are destroyed by unjust convictions from juries who automatically assume guilt.

With what I went through, I even have serious doubts about someone's guilt after taking a DV plea deal. I know that if I hadn't had a good income to pay for a great attorney without having a huge amount of evidence to clear me, I probably would have been forced to take the deal to avoid jail time. Innocence does not matter when a biased and malicious prosecutor is going after you.

THIRTEEN

Time to Eject

For the last two months, Jess had been talking about taking a trip to Thailand in late December for her niece's wedding. This would be a great opportunity for me to file for divorce with her gone.

On December 10, Jess sprang an absurd request on me. She asked me to give her sister $500 a month to help support her mom, who was living in Thailand with her sister. I reminded Jess that she owned two vacant properties in Thailand and her mom's house. The house was sitting vacant and should be sold to pay for her mom's care. Jess refused to discuss this and said she didn't want to sell the house in case someone had to move there.

I wondered what she meant by that. I couldn't help but wonder if she was referring to herself. But wow, I couldn't believe what a dreamland she was living in. She wanted to keep all her assets for herself, not help pay off the debts she had caused, *and* have me pay for her mom's care…while she had the means to pay everything. It was incredibly selfish. I told Jess no way and reiterated that she needed to sell some property to pay for her mother's care.

The only other lingering legal issues were getting my CPL restored and having all my firearms returned. On December 17, Amanda sent out letters to get this done.

Jess left for Thailand on December 24. Her niece, Phonphan, was getting married in April 2015, and Jess wanted to help with all the arrangements and spend time with her family. When I saw her go through the TSA checkpoint and disappear, it was an incredible relief. I was very happy as I drove home from the airport, knowing I wouldn't have to deal with her issues for months. Driving back, I did a couple of fist pumps while yelling, "Yes!"

She planned to return on April 17. I was not going to file for divorce right away as she might immediately return. This would give me some peace and quiet until at least March, when I would file, and then I would tell her the news. Dad knew of my plans and said Jess might not come back because I would no longer be supporting her. This would be the best outcome, but I was not going to count on it.

Before Jess left, she trashed the house, pulling out dresses to take to Thailand and not putting anything back. She had the idea that Phonphan could start a dress shop there. During a previous trip, Jess had told me the selection of wedding dresses and formal gowns there was horrible and that starting a business would be a great opportunity for Phonphan. Jess packed six large boxes full of dresses, and it cost $750 in excess baggage charges. This was still cheaper than shipping them. I spent the next couple of days cleaning up her mess after work. I also threw out more of the garage-sale crap she had accumulated. I really was at peace for the next two months and looked forward to a stress-free and happy life without Jess. I hadn't felt this good in years.

The county clerk called on January 21 to tell me the gun board had restored my CPL. That was great news, though I still didn't have the firearms taken the night of my arrest, and the police would not respond to letters or calls from Michael's office. The only option now was going to court. Michael was preparing an order for the court to force the Washtenaw County sheriff's department to return my firearms. This was very frustrating. I had been cleared of all charges, and my property had to be returned. But because they were the police, they thought they were above the law. I, on the other hand, would have been charged with theft if I'd refused to return someone's property. This shows very clearly that people in power will do what they want while ignoring the law. Laws are for peasants, not the authorities or politicians in power.

In February, I joined Powerhouse Gym to get back in the routine of exercising before work, but I was not happy with that gym. It was in a strip-mall space not designed for a gym, so the facilities were very cramped. Lockers were tiny, the place was dingy, and everything was so packed in that people couldn't walk between the exercise equipment. It was on my way to work, so it was very convenient, but it was not very motivating, so I quit.

I looked around a bit for divorce attorneys and decided to go with Ray Waldo. I met him for the first time on February 19, 2015, and gave him a brief history on Jess. He was shocked about all I told him and advised me that, with all her problems, this would be a messy divorce. It would cost far more than most divorce cases, as Jess would surely cause problems. I said, "Let's do this," and we made plans to file the first week of March.

Ray filed the divorce paperwork with the Washtenaw County court the first week of March. I thought of calling Jess and telling her, but I decided against that. I knew she would go off again and accuse me of causing all the problems, and I was done listening to her babbling justifications and constant accusations. I sent her an e-mail. After all the hell she had caused, I felt she deserved no further courtesy.

The e-mail was long, and I vented quite a bit. In part of the e-mail, I wrote this:

> I just don't have any more to give you. I'm too drained by your battles and issues. The long years of dealing with your emotional problems, issues, and false accusations are just too much. I know you try to blame my frustration on other things and my diabetes, but it is from dealing with you. If you followed your doctor's orders to do something with your life and be happy, things would be a lot different between us. Instead, you just sit around the house accomplishing nothing with your life then blame me and others for your issues and problems. I'm not your emotional doormat.
>
> I'm happier when you are not around for the simple fact that I don't have to hear of more misery, excuses, and the same issues you simply refuse to move on from. I've had enough of your self-inflicted problems for multiple lifetimes and will not

listen to them anymore. I remember when you used to say I was the best man you knew, but now you attack me behind my back. All your actions prove you have absolutely no respect for me now and will treat me like dirt.

I really wish and prayed you would get some motivation in your life to help yourself get out of the darkness you are in, but you won't move on. I can't have your self-inflicted misery damaging my life anymore. I don't hate you and I truly want the best for you, but it will not happen in our marriage. I really hope you can find a purpose in your life, to be loved, content, and happy. I really have forgiven you for everything in the past.

Don't bother returning to my home. I and just about everyone else here want nothing more to do with you. You are no longer welcome in my home or life.

I filed for divorce this week. We are officially ended as husband and wife and there is no chance we will ever get back together. I wish I have never met you.

Yes, it was harsh, but I'd had enough with all the years of putting up with her nonsense, hate, and lies.

I went back to the fitness center at Washtenaw Community College and joined up. I was very happy knowing that when Jess got back from her trip, she could not go back there, because the director had kicked her out. I recognized one of the staff there, and we chatted a bit. I told her I filed for divorce from Jess. She remembered Jess and said no one could make her happy. It was very clear from the way she talked about Jess that it was no surprise I had filed for divorce. I got that a lot from people who had known Jess.

I remembered the problems Jess had caused at the gym five years earlier. I sure wished I could have known back then the living hell she would cause for me later. If I had known that, I would have filed for divorce back then. I had stayed married only because of my vows and the promise I had made to her and God. I should have filed for divorce when she had the affair, but we worked that out. Never again. If I ever get married again and the woman cheats, it is over. No more second chances. I learned the hard way what happens if you stay in the marriage.

TALES OF THE CRAZY - WHY MY EX EMBALMED HER UTERUS

On March 9, Jess's Thai friend Preeda had her husband, Jay, drop by the house to deliver some pain-relief gel. Preeda and Jay had visited Thailand a short time earlier, and Jess had asked them to buy ten tubes of Voltaren gel since a prescription was required here but not in Thailand. He told me Jess had asked them to pick her up at the airport. This meant Jess had moved up her flight. I asked him when she was arriving, but he said he did not know. He seemed very troubled and did not want to get involved—Jess had told them about my filing for divorce. He even said they knew Jess had a lot of troubles, including mental disorders. It was very clear that he wanted no part of this situation.

Because Jess was coming back sooner than expected, I needed to get all my sentimental valuables and important documents out of the house before she came. I had no doubt that she would destroy things or take and hide them.

The next day I sent Jess an e-mail asking when she was going to arrive, but there was no response. I wrote that I would clear out the spare bedroom so she could stay in there. I loaded up my F-150 with files, such as school and navy records, plaques, achievement awards, and other documents I didn't want destroyed. I was going to take them to Dad's house after work the next day. I also packed some winter and hunting clothes, books, and other things to clear out the room for her. I removed most of her clothes from my bedroom and put them in the spare bedroom. I left all shared documents at home such as financial and vehicle records.

I also wanted to get my great-grandfather's bedroom set out of the house. This set was over a hundred years old and still had the porcelain chamber pot, washbasin, and water pitcher people had used before indoor plumbing. I didn't want to take any chances of her hacking at or destroying any part of this bedroom set. I planned to move it out that weekend.

My aunt Florence sent me an e-mail at work, and I called her that evening. We talked a bit about all the problems Jess had caused. She told me Jess had made some posts on Facebook claiming I'd told all the family not to speak with her. Aunt Florence knew this was not true and said this was just more of Jess's typical behavior. Jess had blocked me on Facebook; now I couldn't see her posts anymore. I had Aunt Florence take screenshots of her Facebook time line. I had to walk her through doing this with the Windows snipping tool; it took a while, as she told me she was not tech savvy at all. We laughed when I told her my mom was a true tech nerd and could do a lot more on a PC than most people.

On March 11, I went up to Dad's after work and dropped off the stuff I'd packed. I put one of Dad's spare beds in the F-150 to take home for Jess. I wanted to get a chest of drawers, but it was too heavy for just me to carry down by myself. Dad wasn't home—he was still at his Texas ranch during the Michigan winter—and his neighbor Tom was recovering from surgery on his shoulder and couldn't help. I decided I would try to get a friend or one of the kids from church to help move stuff over the weekend.

I talked with Tom and Denise for a while, and they were really happy I was going through with the divorce. They told me they didn't know how I had put up with her for this long. Tom said he had divorced his previous wife for far less than what Jess had done. They both hated Jess, mostly for the pain and trouble she had caused Mom. Denise laughed when she remembered how they had told Jess how they felt about her and that she had made the last months of Mom's life miserable.

While I was driving home, Dad and I talked on the phone a bit. He spoke again about how much Jess had hurt Mom and taken advantage of her. He went into more detail about when he saw Mom crying over Jess's credit card debt. Dad said that because of Mom's good heart, she had thought helping Jess would help me, but Jess had taken advantage of Mom's kindness and manipulated her, causing more damage to everyone. I told him there were a few happy things we could remember Jess for, but the bad far outweighed the good.

He brought up how hard she had worked on altering two of his fleece jackets, adding a large pocket on the inside of each, and how expertly she had done the work. I couldn't help but think how talented she was and how she could have had a bright future and wonderful life, but she'd wasted all her incredible gifts with her victim mentality and pure laziness. It made me sad to know she destroyed so much happiness with friends, family, and especially our marriage. I never thought I would be another divorce statistic.

I arrived home and was shocked. Her luggage was in the dining room. Damn. My heart just dropped, knowing the hell I would have to endure with all the issues she would bring up again and all the new crap she would surely cause. I was very happy with her gone, but now everything had changed. *Shit, shit, shit* was repeating in my mind. Diva and Sasi came running down the stairs to greet me with wagging tails, jumps, and kisses. At least I had them.

I started to bring the bed parts upstairs, and she was sitting in bed and watching TV. The first thing I said to her was that I was setting up a bed in the other bedroom for her. She did not reply. I set up the bed and spent the night in the spare bedroom. Diva jumped off the bed Jess was in and snuggled up with me all night. She's my furry little daddy's girl.

The next day I went online to reactivate Jess's phone. We had suspended the line while she was gone in order to save money on the phone bill. I didn't see the line on the account and couldn't activate it, so after work, I went to Verizon. It turned out that Verizon had deleted her account instead of suspending it. I don't know why this was done, but someone at Verizon had screwed up when I'd changed the plan in January. We were paying $220 a month, and I had to lower this.

The only reason I did this for Jess was that Ray had told me I had to help her and show I was not intentionally trying to cause problems. It was a 100 percent given that she was going to bring on all sorts of false accusations, but the extent and the depths to which she would go were unknown.

At the Verizon store, they tried to get her old number back, but someone else had already taken it. I sent Jess an e-mail saying Verizon couldn't get her number back. I added another line to the plan and got her a new number. They gave me a SIM card for her Galaxy S3 and told me that all she had to do was to put the new SIM in and turn on the phone. Her phone would reset with the new number.

When I got home about six thirty that evening, Jess was in bed watching TV, and I told her what had happened with her phone line. I set the SIM card next to her on the bed with the new phone number written down and told her what to do to get her S3 working with the new number. Jess wouldn't take it and gave me a hard time.

She asked if the plan was under her name. I told her it was under the existing family plan; she had the exact same plan as Dad and me. (Dad's phone was on my account to save him money.) She went on again about wanting a plan under her name and said she wanted unlimited data, but I told her that her old plan was not available and I was not getting her a better plan than I had. She kept complaining about wanting unlimited data, so I told her I was not going to go back and forth with her. I walked out of the bedroom. I came back up late at night. The SIM card was still where I had put it, so I took it. There was no way I was going to engage her or listen to her whining. She could use the same plan I had and was paying for or not; it was her choice.

Because Jess had camped out in the master bedroom and refused to go to the spare bedroom, I couldn't remove the bedroom set until I got a replacement. In the meantime, I took the spare bedroom.

A week went by. Jess started complaining that she was sick, but I wondered if it was only more of her emotions taking her down. I took some containers of soup I had made from the freezer to thaw. I sent her an e-mail early in the morning when I got to work to say I had left them out for her. I had no love for her and didn't like her at all, but I wouldn't be an ass to her. She would use anything against me, and I wouldn't give her any ammo to show I was being cruel or hateful to her.

I told many people that I was getting a divorce, and only a few were surprised. Some were unaware of the severity of Jess's issues and didn't know of her extreme behavior over the years. I had kept all that Jess had done to myself and confided in only a few very close friends. People said I had always treated Jess like a queen, and once they knew the full story or heard about my arrest, they were amazed I hadn't filed for a divorce much earlier. I told them I had taken a vow to honor my spouse and never to speak ill of her in public. After people knew I had filed, they started telling me stories of things Jess had done and said they had never really trusted her.

On March 24, I saw Jess talking on a huge new phone but said nothing at first. A few hours later, I asked her what phone she had. She replied, "A Galaxy Note." I asked if she liked it, and she went into a long-winded explanation about why she had bought it. She falsely accused me of not letting her use the SIM card I had brought home for her but then reversed and said the S3 gave her migraines because she hadn't used reading glasses in a while. She started complaining about the data plan and then went into what would happen when the divorce happened; she didn't want to pay restocking fees on her new phone to go on my family plan but didn't want to pay all that money just for her one line. Blah, blah.

I told her it was her choice what she wanted to do. She could continue to stay on my plan or pay more for her own. I walked out of the room and left the SIM card for her. Two days later I saw the SIM card on my bed. I would go ahead and cancel her line on my plan later. It was unbelievable that a stupid phone had caused all this churn. Nothing was simple with Jess.

A week later Jess asked if I had changed the password for my TCF bank account. Damn straight I had. She asked for the password, but I said no, this was my account. She said it was ours, and she needed to see the balance so she knew how much she could withdraw with my debit card. She also asked if I wanted to hide anything. I told her I was not hiding anything from her; we were separated, and it was my account. I said she could use my ATM card to look at the balance before she took cash. I knew if she had full access to my account, she would probably drain it.

She would not relent and said, "We are not separated. We are still married, and it's our account."

I told her, "No, we are separated and have been since I filed for divorce; we are living separate lives and sleeping in different rooms."

I told her I was tired and walked away from her. When I went to brush my teeth, she asked for copies for the last two years of tax returns, and I told her I would give her a PDF of each. She asked me to e-mail them. I said I would, and I did.

On Easter Sunday, I went over to Aunt Florence's house and had a nice dinner with my family. While I was there, I got the Facebook screenshots my aunt had taken on March 10, before Jess had blocked the entire family.

Jess wrote, "Charles L. Cole gave my niece a wedding present with filing a divorce."

What the hell? Jess was clearly willing to lie and say even the most ridiculous things to get sympathy from others and portray me as an evil, heartless man. It didn't surprise me though; it was her typical victim mentality run amok, and there was surely more to come.

One person replied, "That is so cold blooded! Hang in there."

That person had no idea what Jess was like or how she could manipulate situations to make herself look like the victim.

Jess continued, "Chuck filed a divorce against me while I am away out of the country."

She got that right.

She continued, "He used to demand me not to put private matters on Facebook...My whole family is shocked, especially my mom who has Alzheimer's now so worries, sad and cried with me why didn't Chuck file a divorce when I am there,.....I thought back, he had been wanting to leave the country....Well I am holding on tightly to the Lord and He is also holding me in his arms. Thank you for your support." Jess was really ramping up the emotional blame game to portray me as a horrible person so that she could get sympathy. I knew this was going to happen and that there would be more to come from her.

My cousin Shelia asked how I'd been able to talk her mom through the process of taking a screenshot. Sheila had a surprised look on her face and said she was impressed I'd been able to do it over the phone, with her mom being so computer illiterate. Shelia laughed after I told her the story of how long it had taken to get the screenshot and save it. We laughed again when I tried to explain how to e-mail me the picture. When Aunt Florence had no clue how to attach a picture to an e-mail, I would not even try to describe how to do it over the phone.

The next day Jess left a Post-it note for me on the kitchen counter. It said, "Request for groceries. Raw almonds (no salt)."

I couldn't believe she had the nerve to ask me to pick up her groceries. She did nothing with her pathetic life except lie around watching TV and surfing the Internet, and now she wanted me to buy food for her? I worked a full-time job and had been putting in extended hours lately, plus making all my meals, cleaning around the house, and hitting the gym five days a week, and she couldn't take time to get off her lazy ass, stop watching TV, and go outside to get her own snacks. I felt like telling her to get off her ass and get her own damned food, but I was not doing anything else to increase tensions. I ignored the note.

I showed my coworker Dale the note Jess had left. Dale sat next to me and knew much of what had happened over the last few months with the DV case and the divorce. We both laughed at how absurd it was for her to be too lazy to get her own snacks and to ask me to do it for her. He said that if a woman had done all this to him and they were separated but living in the same house, he would be bringing whores in just to piss her off. We laughed, but I said I couldn't do that. He replied, "You're a better man than me." A part of me would enjoy seeing her in distress after all the hell she'd put me through, but I refused to toss aside my integrity and sink to her level.

Wednesday, April 8, at 10:00 a.m. was the motion hearing at the Washtenaw County 14b court to force the police to return my firearms. It had been four months, and they had ignored every demand from my attorney to return my property since all charges were dismissed on December 5.

At the hearing, Michael Vincent started by telling the judge the "essence" of the DV case, that there had been no "assault at all," and that the case was dismissed. The judge was Charles Pope, the same one who had heard and dismissed the case. The prosecutor, Angela King, was present also. Michael said he had sent two letters to the sheriff and "got no response."

Michael said, "He just wants his guns back, and he has no criminal history. There is no ongoing investigation; nothing is going on, and they're holding his firearms."

The judge asked, "Do you know why they have apprehended them?"

Then Angela King spoke. Michael leaned over to me and said this was the best case!

Angela said, "We don't feel it's appropriate for Your Honor to issue any orders regarding the release of any firearms because you don't have any real information on what, um…whether it's even lawful for Mr. Cole to have these firearms."

It was clear now that Angela was the reason I couldn't get my firearms back. She was grasping and making up anything in court in clumsy and feeble attempts to formulate valid reasons.

She continued, "Are they registered? Are they uh, uh, serial numbered on them, uh, does he have criminal release codes? There is a whole solutions requirements that, um, that uh, I don't believe the court is um, in a position to, to state whether he should be or should not be released so I would submit that he suh, he should sue the sheriff if that's who, you know, has possession of these weapons if they think they're unlawfully uh, being um, um, prevented from having them released to Mr. Cole."

Her bumbling and stammering response showed that she was trying to make up any excuse she could think of to keep me from getting my guns. It was unethical that she falsely claimed that my firearms might not have serials or were not registered and that I might have other criminal actions against me. She was clearly willing to contrive these wild stories in court to stop me from getting my property back. If I lied, that would be perjury. As I've said before, laws are for peasants. Michael was incensed and visibly upset at these allegations she made up trying to smear my character.

The judge asked, "Are they refusing to return them?"

Michael replied, "I have not gotten a reply from two letters. I do know that Mr. Cole has a Second Amendment right. I do know that he has no convictions. I do know, to my best knowledge, there's no ongoing criminal investigations on him. I do know that if these firearms were stolen, like the implication about serial numbers, I'm certain that officers ran these through Link, that protocol."

Michael was an ex-cop and knew all the police procedures, and he was calling her out on her bullshit. Link is a system the cops use to check whether a firearm is stolen. He continued, "There is no reason for him not to get his firearms back. In, in, what's, you know if this was a DV, a real DV, rather than according to the best stated facts, berries against the wall, what my client obviously denies that, but he's perplexed by the criminal justice system. This man is an executive at an automobile uh, company, he's got a spotless criminal record. There's just no reason for this, he is perplexed." Michael went on for a bit, saying what would normally be done and even joking to the judge, "There I go, thinking things would be easy."

The judge said, "I'm going to force a response from the sheriff's department as to why, if they do have a reason."

Michael and Angela went back and forth for a while, with Angela, in a last-ditch, feeble effort, questioning the time line of the letters Michael sent the police. The judge stopped Angela from spouting her nonsense. He said that unless the police could give a legitimate excuse, he was going to sign the motion to get my firearms back. The judge went even further and said he was going to call them today. I thought, *I'm glad I voted for him to be a judge.*

I left the county building, but I had to go back in to get some paperwork I had left and ran into Angela. She told me that only the police should have guns. Right then it was clear to me why she was making things up for the judge. She would not follow the law; she followed her personal agenda in defiance of the law. People like that are dangerous, as they feel it's righteous to violate law and constitutional rights based on their feelings and political leanings. Those types should be disbarred.

Her attitude toward firearms was very revealing, and I realized why she had gone after me with such zeal. I thought that because she knew I had an AR-15, she must have thought I was one of those "evil people" the radical left demonizes. She sure tried to destroy my life with no evidence or proof in the DV case; she'd relied only on emotionally charged statements Jess had made. I had the distinct feeling that she viewed me as a menace to society.

During the time since Jess had come back from Thailand, it had been really tense at home. I avoided her as much as possible and wouldn't talk to her. We were leading completely separate lives in the home when she was there. She was spending less and less time at the house, and sometimes I didn't see her for days. Jess would make snarky comments, but I ignored her and walked off. I ignored any requests she made of me unless they had to do with the divorce.

On April 11, Jess sent me an e-mail. She was looking for a GPS tracker I had used years ago when she was cheating on me.

She wrote, "I was looking for a tracking unit yesterday, but I couldn't find it. This is a question, not an accusation. Did you happen to put the tracking unit in the Focus? Please let me know if you put it in the car. I will remove it myself. It's against the privacy act. Thank you."

This was my response:

There is no tracking devices or spyware being used on you at all. The difference now is we are separated, the marriage is over, so now I don't care what you do now or what happens to you. I only had to use it years ago as a last resort since I still cared about you and wanted to know what was going because I knew you were not telling the truth. The tracking device was thrown out a long time ago.

Since we are separated and I don't give a damn about you now, you are free to be a slut with any dirt bag you want. You did this before and lied about it in our marriage, so it won't be a new thing for you. Just don't bring them to my home.

The tracking device you may think is in the Focus now is just another one of your hundreds of false accusations. I won't listen to any more of them, so do not ever email, text, or call me again. I won't reply and will immediately delete any messages without looking at them.

I'll make sure your mom's pin reset for DFCU works, but after that is taken care of, I'm taking my name off her account to be free of it. It's up to you and your sister to take care of her social security after that.

I thought the only reason she was asking about the tracker was that she was doing something she shouldn't be. Since we were in divorce proceedings, I knew better than to install any tracking devices in the cars or on her laptop. When she was in Thailand visiting her family, I had wiped my PC, installed a SSD, and performed a fresh install of Windows to ensure there were no hidden key loggers she might have put on. There was no chance now she had anything on my PC, and I would not give her any passwords or even enable the guest account.

In the month she'd been home, there had been many times when she had not come home until past midnight, and many times she did not come home at all. I'd guess there was a 90 percent chance, based on her evasive behavior, that she was seeing another man. I was not even going to ask—she would lie about it anyway. This explained her asking about the GPS tracker. Ray and I talked about this, and he said this was a good thing. Seeing someone would make her happier and less prone to fits of rage and bizarre behavior.

On Sunday, April 12, Jess got back home around three in the afternoon. She had been out all night again. I was pretty sure she was staying with a boyfriend, since I'd overheard her talking to a guy on the phone. I could tell by the tone of her voice that it was more than a casual conversation.

I had a very busy Sunday. I did lawn work, replaced the Focus's driver-side mirror, and replaced a liftgate gas strut. I worked on the liftgate latch, but I was going to have to buy a new one; the electric unlatch did not work anymore. I got all fluids topped off in all vehicles, cleaned the garage, worked in the shop a bit, and then finished and e-filed the 2014 taxes. After she got home, Jess stayed in bed, watched TV, and surfed the Internet on her laptop. It was typical behavior for her while I worked.

The next day I had an appointment with Ray. I dropped by his office after work to drop off a $2,000 check for her divorce attorney and to sign our countercomplaint to her attorney's filing. I didn't like having to pay for her attorney, but Ray said either I could do it now and look good or they would take it to court, force me to pay, and win. Because I'd filed first, her attorney responded and asked that "the Court provide for an equitable division of the property between the parties and an equitable distribution of the debt."

The only equitable distribution of the debt I would agree to was that she got all $551,000 of the total debt she had racked up with her store, which included remortgaging my home and an additional home equity loan. Included with this debt was the $73,800 she'd taken from my mom. Our countercomplaint was to state that all the debt was hers. Much of this debt had been discharged with her bankruptcy, but it had cost me $184,000 so far with remortgaging the home, a home equity loan, and interest to fund her store.

I had paid the mortgage off, but there was still $62,000 remaining on balance for the home equity loan. More than $74,000 of her business tax debt remained because she hadn't paid state and federal taxes, so I hoped that this and the $62,000 home equity loan balance would come out of her division of property, since it was for funding her business. This was a best-case scenario for me but not realistic, based on what Ray told me.

I made a spreadsheet totaling her store debt for my attorney. All this came directly off her bankruptcy work sheets:

Citibank	Credit Card	$23,621
Citibank (South Dakota)	Credit Card	$12,682
Bank of America	Checking	$17,147
American Express	Credit Card	$50,932
New Plan reality	Rent for store	$25,344
Pagentry Talent and Entertainment	Magazine advertising	$4,727
DFCU gold MasterCard	Credit Card	$30,515
DFCU Visa	Credit Card	$12,307
LaSalle Bank Midwest N.A.	Checking	$828
LaSalle Bank Midwest N.A.	Line of credit	$17,500
NPC (Merchant acct)	Merchant Account	$300
Cross check	Merchant Account	$180
American express (Merchant acct)	Merchant Account	$50
Discover	Merchant Account	$50
Pronovias	Supplier	$8,811
tiffany	Supplier	$5,000
Ptak's	Supplier	$980
Geno's	Supplier	$200
Pageantry	Advertisement	$4,727
WAMM radio	Advertisement	$600
ann arbor news	Advertisement	$217
Provide Net sunrock store internet	Internet service	$556
The Knot	magazine	$900
DTE	Utilities	$85
Hartford Insurance (store-fire)	Advertisement	$153
University Directories	Advertisement	$262
Jasmine Enterprises, Inc.	Advertisement	$6
Internet Yellow pages	Advertisement	$441
Herbert and Margaret Cole, Charles' parents	Loans and credit cards Charles' mom co-signed for. Initial loan was $30k, the rest is J's credit card debt.	$73,884
	Total declared for her bankruptcy in 2009	**$293,005**
	Federal tax not paid	$48,234
	State of MI tax not paid	$26,100
	Total including unpaid taxes	**$367,339**
	Charles' costs with re-mortgaging the home, a home equity loan and interest to fund her store	$183,905
	Grand total of debt	**$551,244**

Jess's attorney also included in their paperwork that Jess "reserves the right to request a personal protection order or a restraining order" against me. No way would we agree to that, and I was surprised her attorney even put that in, knowing we would object. However, that type of stuff is was what many slimy attorneys do to generate billing hours and line their pockets at their clients' expense. I was sure Jess had given her attorney more outrageous claims of abuse and wild stories about what I had done so that she could get sympathy and appear to be the victim in our marriage. That was OK; her attorney would find out the truth soon enough. The extremely large body of evidence I had collected about her past behavior would discredit just about anything she had to say about me.

I got an e-mail from Michael Vincent's office manager, Amanda, on April 13 concerning the DV charge, stating, "I spoke with the court and you should be all clear to obtain your property back from the arresting agency." The court ordered the police to return my firearms on April 8 or 9, but by April 13, I still didn't have them back. I couldn't ignore or delay a court order without repercussions as the cops were doing.

With all I had been through trying to get them, this e-mail was great news. The only thing was that I had no idea what I had to do. I e-mailed Amanda, "Do I just show up at the front desk at the sheriff's station on Washtenaw, or do I have to call first and tell them what time I'll be there? Or, is there a separate property division I have to go to?"

Ever since the court ordered the police to return my firearms a week and a half ago, the cops had been giving me the runaround and would not return my calls. Who did they think they were? The court ordered the cops to return my property, but they refused to cooperate. When I did speak with them, they gave many lame excuses, including telling me only the arresting officer could release them. When the judge ordered the sheriff's office to give them back, they must lawfully obey. Yet again, laws are for peasants.

I called the sheriff's front desk, asked where to go to get my firearms, and told them Judge Pope had ordered the release of my property. They forwarded me to dispatch, and dispatch told me I had to get in touch with the arresting officer, and he had to tell the property division to release my firearms. I told dispatch again that Judge Pope had ordered the property division to release my firearms, but their reply was that the arresting officer still had to tell the property division to release them. This made no sense, and they were still ignoring the court order.

I was forwarded to the arresting officer's voice mail and left him a message telling him Judge Pope had ordered the release of my firearms and he had to get with property. I also left him my phone number. They were playing more games at my expense, ignoring the order.

On April 22, I sent this e-mail to Amanda, Michael's office manager:

> Amanda,
>
> The police will not respond or call me back. I even called Judge Pope's secretary telling her the police are ignoring the order and what should I do. She said she would call me back, but never did.
>
> Enough is enough. Please speak to Michael about filing a lawsuit against the police/Washtenaw county asking for huge monetary damages.

I got this e-mail back from Amanda:

> I actually spoke with the officer last night, he works midnights so its hard to get ahold of him during the day. The officer stated you would need to go to division 1 to get your property back, but the release has been signed so you can get your things back.

I made some phone calls—and guess what: there is no division 1. What an asshole. My contempt for cops was at an all-time high. From my perspective of dealing with all the problems they had caused by ignoring the law and court order, much of the contempt people have toward them is well deserved.

Finally, on April 27, I was able to get my guns back from property. I sent this e-mail to Michael's firm the next day:

> Great news! I picked all my firearms yesterday at 3:30. Everything was there to my surprise since I was expecting more problems or parts missing.
>
> FYI, there is no Division 1. The proper place to call is the sheriff's property division at 734-973-4651. Even the property people have no idea what "division 1" is. They arranged to have the

firearms up at the service desk at a time of my choosing and unlike everyone else I dealt with, were very helpful and accommodating. The woman I spoke with in Property is Judy, and she was extremely nice and pleasant.

A week and a half earlier, on April 15, Ray had forwarded me a letter from Jess's attorney, Linda, concerning a serious accusation Jess had made about me. The letter stated, "Please be advised that Mr. Cole has retrieved his gun from the police and has been walking around the house with the presumed purpose of displaying it in front of Mrs. Cole. She has felt intimidated and uncomfortable. I have advised her that at any time she feels uncomfortable, she can stay outside of the home for any period she wishes."

This part about my gun was an outright lie—I had not been able to get my guns from the police at that time, and Ray knew this. Jess's attorney also wrote that "Mr. Cole persists in referring to the house as 'his house' and tells Ms. Cole that he and she are 'separated.'" That part was correct: it was my house, and I had bought it before we were married.

Ray sent Jess's attorney this in response:

> I am in receipt of your correspondence dated April 15, 2015. Your client's allegations are pure fiction. Additionally, she has a history of mixing OxyContin, Vicodin and assorted psychotropic meds. I am concerned she has been abusing her medications. Her history of false allegations is well known to local law enforcement.
>
> If your client would like to find independent housing, maybe she should look into the cost of doing so. Please feel free to contact me should you wish to discuss this matter further.

This false accusation of hers was just a small taste of the hell that was to follow.

FOURTEEN

Lies and More Lies

On April 19, I had a really bad day. My neighbor, Libby, was gone for the weekend, and I was taking care of her dog, Tasha. Tasha had known me ever since she was a puppy, and I had taken care of her many times before.

I went to Libby's house before I left for church and let Tasha out to do her business. I was sitting on their deck watching her run around outside, and she was very happy, especially after I gave her some treats. We went back in their house. I bent down to get her toy to play, and then she suddenly turned on me. Without warning she attacked, jumping right at my face and ripping my nose open. She continued attacking and bit my leg. I kicked her back, and she stood there shaking and growling at me. Her attack took me by complete surprise—I'd never witnessed any aggressive behavior from her before the attack that day. I had been her pal for a very long time.

I went home immediately with blood gushing from my nose. I went upstairs, and when Jess saw the blood and heard Tasha had attacked me, she started freaking out.

I told her I was going to the hospital. Jess insisted on taking me, and I let her. That turned out to be a huge mistake, as she went full drama queen at the hospital. She was crying and shaking in the hospital room and then said, "I love you."

I didn't reply. I was thinking, *She does not know what real love is after all the lies and hell she put me through just so that others will give her sympathy.* I didn't say anything else to her. I didn't want her to cause a scene at the hospital.

It was very fortunate that there was a plastic surgeon at the hospital. She put in four stitches, and I went back to see her again in her office a couple of days later.

I was in a bad mood for the rest of the day. After all these burdensome problems in my life, now this. What else was going to happen? I was also worried that soon I would be single and would have a giant, ugly scar on my nose.

The last remaining issue with the DV charge was to get my arrest record expunged. I spoke to Amanda about this, and she started the process to get my fingerprint and arrest card destroyed and all matters related to this arrest removed from the police record.

Jess's mom, Suda, was entitled to social security because her husband had been a US citizen, and I had been taking care of her DFCU account for her social security payments for almost two years. Jess had been responsible for it, but after the Michigan Department of Treasury emptied my checking account by taking $3,300, her name had been taken off her mom's account and my name had been put on.

Jess's sister, Kanya, withdrew money for Suda overseas with the DFCU ATM card. There was an ATM fee, but it was a lot cheaper than wiring her the money. I had told Jess multiple times that because her mom could no longer take care of herself, Kanya needed to have the social security deposits changed to a local bank, where she could manage the money. This had not happened. I had told them both in March when I filed for divorce that I would be taking my name off her mom's account and they needed to get her mom's banking in order. There was no action from them.

On April 15, Jess sent me an e-mail asking me to use my DFCU ATM card to withdraw her mom's social security funds. Jess had told me earlier that she would wire the money to Kanya. In the e-mail, she wrote, "Will you use your card to withdraw the money for my mom and leave." She sure had some nerve to tell me to leave my house.

I had to go to the bank to withdraw $2,100 from Jess's mother's account and then sent an e-mail to Jess and Kanya saying I was giving the money to Jess to wire it over. I didn't trust Jess, so I made sure to let her sister know what was going on. Jess also asked me to reset the PIN, as the card Kanya had no longer worked.

A couple of days later, I went to DFCU to reset the PIN for her mom's ATM card. I sent Jess and her sister an e-mail with the new PIN and asked them to "let me know ASAP if there any problems with it."

Jess was spending more time away from the house. I didn't know where she was staying. She spent more nights away than at home, and recently I had not seen her for a couple of days. I had been taking care of everything at the home, including both dogs. Sasi was an extremely needy little lapdog, following me around the house all the time and whining for constant attention. This little dog was really getting on my nerves. I was very frustrated by the whole situation, and Jess needed to step up and take care of her dog. I would take care of Diva.

I asked her via e-mail on April 23 if the dogs were taken care of. I also asked that she let me know if she wouldn't be at the house so the dogs could get proper care. There was no reply.

On April 26, I sent Jess an e-mail about Sasi:

> I will no longer take care of her. She is your dog and she needs you. Please pick her up and keep her where you are staying. It's unfair to me to be burdened with taking care of both dogs while you are out partying or staying with your new boyfriend.

If I don't hear from you, I'll will give her away to someone this week.

After I sent that, I realized I shouldn't have. My frustration at dealing with Jess was at an all-time high.

Jess replied to this in her typical extreme-drama manner. In part of her reply, she wrote:

Chuck,

    You are frightening me, i am so afraid to read your messages or emails. Why are you, so mean to me, it was not enough of you to abuse me for the past 14 years? You must have to keep me under your foot, please, don't do anything to the girls, you already hurt Diva just for me to reading the message, that you will give away Sasi.

I have no idea what she meant by saying I'd hurt Diva. I replied:

Please stop with your out of control drama and contrived fear. It's just pure fiction at my expense.
    You are fully capable of taking care of Sasi. Do your part, be responsible, show some love for her and take her with you before you leave for over a week without telling me. That's all I'm asking. She needs that love and companionship from you. If you are unwilling to do this, then give her to someone that will care.

But, of course, her reply was devoid of responsibility and consisted only of more contrived drama:

Stop intimidating and name calling me and verbally abusive, please I know that it's hard for you to control. I have asked you to be civilized. ... Then your divorce, that you want will end in a pleasant way. My attorney had confirmed yours, please talk to your attorney.

Dealing with Jess was impossible. She was resorting to claiming I abused and frightened her. I wouldn't have put it past her to forward these types of e-mails to her attorney to demonize me. It was impossible to deal with a pathological liar. The troubling part of this was that I was sure some part of her believed her lies and that this was what she was telling her attorney. I didn't know the extent of how horribly I was being portrayed, but I was sure it was very bad. I was also keeping Ray up to speed on all these events so we could be ready in case Jess and her attorney took legal action against me.

With all the drama Jess was creating, I also had to give her additional money, even though I was paying for all her living expenses. Ray advised me I had to give her $1,000 a month in cash or it might seem I was intentionally being cruel to her. I didn't like giving her cash, but I had to. Jess drained my checking account one day, so I set up a new account for my payroll to go into and kept the old one exclusively for her. That way I could prevent her from draining my account, and I could prove that all withdrawals she made from the old account were hers. She had the only ATM card for the old account.

Jess was now complaining about our Focus. It was old, but it was still a reliable car. She didn't view it this way, though, and wanted me to buy her another vehicle. Jess told me it had stalled on her. I told her she needed to be home so I could work on it. On May 8, I found out the stalling problem was caused by a bad throttle-position sensor and replaced it. I also cleaned the mass air-flow sensor and throttle body.

Five days later, Jess called and demanded that I buy her a car. She wanted me to give her $25,000 for a used Volvo C70 convertible. She said she needed the money right away, as the dealer was holding it for her for only a few days, and that it was a great deal. She also said she did not want another Ford.

I told her she had been in sales and should know the pressure tactics these people used. I said, "You, not the salesperson determine what is a good deal." She still would not relent. I asked her how much insurance would cost, but she would not answer. I also asked what the grand total would be with all the other charges and taxes, but she would not answer.

Our Focus did have a lot of miles, 169,000, but there was no way I was giving her $25,000 for a used car with all the unforeseen costs of the divorce. I didn't have this amount available anyway. At this point I didn't want to give her anything. She even had the nerve to tell me her attorney said this car would be under my name. What a lie that was, as any attorney knew a person couldn't be forced to accept liability for someone else. I told her no way—it would be under her name, and she would pay all the insurance. She didn't like that, but tough. I also had doubts that she wanted the cash for a car. It was possible she only wanted $25,000 for something else.

I knew she could make the car an issue to use against me by falsely claiming I knew the Focus was not safe and was trying to harm her, so I told her $10,000 was all I could do toward the cost of another car. Jess would not relent. I finally hung up on her, stating again that $10,000 was my limit.

On May 13, I sent this e-mail to her:

I'm able to pay $10k for a car. That's all I can afford and it will come out of your part of the divorce settlement. The costs of this divorce are going to be huge.

The rest you will have to come up with. The cost of insurance that you will have to pay for your car will also have to be figured in. How about getting more independent by getting your own income, then figure out what you can afford?

If you get a car now, a lien will be put on it due to your tax debt. There may be a lien on your Focus preventing it from being sold since it's in your name. This vehicle lien can be checked at the Secretary of State. Another bankruptcy for you should be filed this year to clear out your tax debt and clear out all the liens.

The Focus will have to be sold when another car is bought and this will help with the cost of another car. The cost of keeping insurance on the Focus to drive it outweighs the fuel savings I will get vs. driving the truck.

Please check if there are tax liens on your vehicles.

How about selling your motorcycle since you don't ride it? You can get between $2500 and $3000 cash for it that can help with the cost of your car, but there may be a lien on it. This also will have to be checked at the Secretary of State. It's prime riding season right now and bikes are being sold very fast.

Your debts have already cost me hundreds of thousands of dollars and I won't even consider this $25k luxury expense for a Volvo C70 convertible. I've been stuck paying for the remaining $63k of the home equity loan since you won't do anything to help pay your debts, but this equity loan will also come out of your part of the divorce settlement.

Her reply:

> The car will first be under your as my attorney suggested. That's all I can say. It's a safe car....not luxury. It just happens to come in because the prior owner needed a bigger vehicle. I am trying to be civilized on the situation.
> You got the truck that you wanted...the money that came from the business that you and i spent.
> You used the Focus to death, $ 10k.... couldn't get a one year old car of any brand.

The problem with her reply was that her business closed in March 2008, and I'd bought the F-150 in February 2009. These were more contrived lies on her part. She wouldn't even talk about the $551,000 of debt she had racked up with the store. She would lie about anything and ignore reality to get her way.

I sent this reply:

> Your car will not be under my name. I cannot be forced to accept the legal liability of your vehicle under my name.
> Also, I paid entirely for the F-150 partly through the insurance payment when Ranger was totaled, and the rest I took out a loan on my 401k from my salary at Ford. No funds came from your business to pay for it. What little cash came from your business was an extremely small amount and was not enough to even pay basic bills. You accumulated over $500k in debt with your store that put us in a huge financial hole with you doing virtually nothing to help pay off since 2008.
> $10k is all I can afford now. Selling the Focus and your motorcycle will add another $5k. That's $15k total and that will get a very safe and nice used vehicle. This is the reality of the finances.
> You will also need to find out what insurance will cost you per month.

I was not going write the actual dates when her store closed and when I had bought the truck. I was going keep this tidbit of info just in case she should bring it up to the judge. Then I would point out her lie and attempted manipulation of facts.

Her reply:

The accident insurance came from you total Ranger....it was not free money.

Stop controlling me, first was to get a new car, and you said a year old car which I did, even older....selling the Focus or bike, they are different issues. The dealer told me that the brake lights stay on all the time....there is more issue... Please just stop..., get a decent car for my safety and get it over with...they are holding the car for me.

Find the car doesn't have to be under your name. This Focus is almost used by you.

I replied:

$10k is all I can afford. If you want more to pay for a car, then get the money yourself. Selling your Focus and motorcycle is just a suggestion to get more cash for a better car.

You can get whatever you want, but you will have to get the money yourself for anything over $10k, while also figuring in the costs of your own insurance. Some vehicles are a lot more to insure than others. I highly recommend you get an insurance quote for the car you would like to get before you commit to buy.

I will not debate this further. $10k from me for your next car is all I can do.

There were no more e-mails from her about getting this Volvo after this. I was sure she was extremely pissed off that I was not submitting to her demands.

When I got home, she was there and started up on me again about buying the Volvo. She came at me from multiple angles, trying to justify the cost and saying the money was not an issue because it would be part of the divorce settlement. I refused to budge, but she would not give up and started calling me controlling. She said buying this car for her would allow her to be independent. She didn't understand that being independent meant working to get her own stuff, not using manipulations or lies to get it from others. I finally told her that $10,000 was all I could do and that I wouldn't discuss it further. Then I walked away.

There was another issue with Jess's mom's ATM card. The bank deactivated it. Jess was supposed to check and see if the card worked with the new PIN on April 28, but she didn't until May 14. The bank told me they needed her mom to come in or call to get it reactivated. I told Jess this, but all she did was accuse me of trying to control her.

On May 15, I sent her and Kanya an e-mail:

I'll stop in DFCU today and see what happened and try to get your mom's ATM card reactivated.

I asked for you or Kanya to let me know if the new PIN # worked, but got no response. I'll take care of this latest problem, but as I have said multiple times before, I suggest you get her social security deposits transferred to a local bank that Kanya can manage for your mom.

I do not want to be caught up in your mom's finances or bank issues and I will be removing my name from your mom's DFCU account the first week of June.

I'd had enough of this. They had both had ample time and multiple requests from me to take care of their mom's finances. I don't want to be falsely accused of anything, so my name was coming off the account.

Jess replied, "You asked me once. I tried to used it yesterday, and it didn't work."

What? Jess had her mom's ATM card? This was her mom's money, and Jess was supposed to have left it with Kanya to withdraw money in Thailand for her mother's care. This situation was looking very fishy to me. Because I was a joint owner, I had my own ATM card for her mom's account, but I wouldn't give it to Jess. If she made withdrawals with my card and Kanya claimed they never got the money, I would be in trouble, falsely accused of taking her mom's social security money.

I sent Jess this reply:

My card still works. This is your mom's card, she should have it to draw her Social Security money on. That card was supposed to stay with her in Thailand.

Attached is a screenshot of her DFCU balance, $426.50. The last withdrawal was done by me at the bank last month for $2,100.00 and I gave you the money to send to her.

You were supposed to check on the card ASAP with the new PIN#. It was not done. I'll go to DFCU today and see what the problem is, but this is the last time I will do this. I've had enough of this. Get her social security deposits changed ASAP so they can be managed by someone other than me. After I take my name off her account June 1, I'm out of this situation forever.

She e-mailed this reply:

Again, you are so good of accusing / or pointing finger at me, may God bless your heart with his love and kindness, and open your eyes to see who you are hurting!

You lied to me about the divorce? You have been threatening and abusing me through out the marriage and constantly accused me and never let go of the past, for whatever you want to make yourself look good in front of other people or feel superior over me.

Please stop all of them, I am sick of your behaviors, if you don't, our next communication will be through our attorneys which will come out of your pockets, since you can't be civilized in the communication. Through out the years, you've been trying to destroy the house, which makes me wonder why you just don't leave the house. You can stay at your parents' house, so I won't be so be scared to stay home.

You know that I can't do anything with DFCU mom's account.

Enough of your tough guy threats, you ruined Focus and I want a new car that I want...., you just do whatever you have do to make it fair to me, like I have done for you almost 15 years.

Her over-the-top response was classic Jess—she protested too much—when she was caught in something she shouldn't be doing. All she did was make up ridiculous accusations instead of addressing the problem. I wouldn't even reply to this; she wanted to get me to address all these other false accusations in order to deflect the real issue of why her mom did not have her ATM card to draw her social security funds.

Her response was clearly baseless. If I was such a horrible person, why did she still want me in control of her mother's social security? I wouldn't want a soon-to-be ex in control of *my* parents' money. Something else was going on with her, and I wondered if the money I had withdrawn and given her to wire to her mom had been sent. Was Jess giving her sister some excuse to justify keeping her mom's money? The whole situation was very suspicious.

On May 18, Jess called, but I didn't answer. She left a message. I didn't want to hear it, so I deleted it. I wouldn't deal with her craziness. An hour later, she sent this e-mail:

> I talked to Ford dealer sales rep., Chris, he said even 2014 Focus is still about $20,000.00 + up.
>
> You want me to be independent, I need reliable car, this on comes with 100,000 miles warranty, that is a good deal, please they will only hold the car until to tomorrow.

Now she was changing tactics. First, she'd said she didn't want another Ford, especially a Focus, and now she was looking at a Focus? I didn't reply to this, but when I got home from work, she started up again, using all the same manipulations she'd tried when she wanted the Volvo. As usual she tried the same pressure tactics, saying they would hold the car only until the next day. I repeated what I'd said all along: I had $10,000 for the car. She could sell her motorcycle and Focus for another $5,000, and the $15,000 total would buy a really nice used vehicle.

She then changed the subject, saying her attorney had told her she could change the lock on the bedroom so she could feel safe from me at night. What a load of crap that was. I told her that was bullshit; she knew I had never shown violence to her, and she knew she had nothing to fear.

She went back to the car subject again and would not stop, so I walked away.

May 19 was a crazy texting day with Jess. First she asked for me to withdraw her mom's money, claiming her mom had gone into the hospital. I told her I would do it, but I asked her again to get her mother's social security deposits changed to a bank her sister could manage. I didn't believe a word she said now. Her mom might or might not be in the hospital. Jess would do or say anything at this point. I was not convinced she was sending her mom's money to her, but I was not going to get involved between her and her sister. I was thinking about drawing out the money and wiring it directly to Kanya, but that would cause more problems I didn't need.

Then Jess sent me a text asking me to give her $10,000 cash. I laughed when she had the nerve to ask that. No way would I do that. I replied that I would only write a check to the owner of the car. She stopped all talk of a car at that point, and now I was sure she had been trying to manipulate me into giving her the cash all along so she could use it for something other than getting a car. She had wanted large sums of cash for a while, but that hadn't happened. I would give her only what Ray advised. We also had the first mediation meeting coming up on June 12, and I had to pay for that. The first divorce hearing was on June 15.

Jess texted about all the boxes of inventory still in the house. She wanted to take them all and not give me anything for it. That was pure nuts. There was a staggering debt remaining on my house and $74,000 of tax debt from her business. There was no way any reasonable person could expect me to agree to her terms of getting nothing for the inventory. She had done virtually nothing with the dresses during the past seven years since her store had closed. No way was she going to take them all now and give me nothing in return. They had to be included as her part of the divorce settlement. For paperwork submitted to the court as part of her net worth, I estimated the inventory to be worth close to $178,000, with each dress at $200 and each box holding seven dresses. Jess had contacted my attorney saying she was scared I was going to destroy $200,000 of her inventory.

She also asked for an additional $800 that month, but there was no way I was going to do that. I texted back, "You have taken $2,000 the past month and a half. Plus I paid $2,000 to your attorney. This is extremely excessive, and there will be no more deposits in the TCF account for a while. If you want more, get a job and be more independent. I simply can't maintain that amount being taken. It's draining the bank balances."

Jess then texted, "You have been spending a lot of money like crazy with your shopping spree, so just learn to be fair and get this divorce over in peace."

I had to laugh at her accusation of my "shopping spree." I had stopped cable TV and all other nonessential services to save money, and I had trimmed all other costs. I made most of my lunches to save money and rarely went out to eat. When she'd been on her last trip to Thailand, I had kept the house at sixty-three degrees during the day and fifty-five at night during winter to save on heating bills. It was another one of her crazy accusations, and I wouldn't even respond. She threw crap like this out hoping something would stick and deflect attention from the real issues.

When I got home from work, there was a new lockset on the bedroom door, but the door was not locked. She has not been home most nights, and I rarely saw her. So this was just a symbolic act of her control and perceived victimhood at this point. I decided to contact my attorney about how to proceed on this latest act of hers before I removed the lock. At this point I wanted to gather all facts to see what it would take to remove her from the house. She was just too hateful and crazy to deal with.

It was now May 20, and Jess had been spending almost every night somewhere else. I had no idea where, and I didn't care if she was screwing some other guy. If it made her happy, that equaled fewer crazy and conniving threats I had to deal with. I was pretty sure she was telling more wild tales of victimization at my expense and had found some poor sap to believe her. That day she was in the house for only a short time, starting giving me crap, and then left. I didn't even look at or say anything to her.

I sent this to my attorney:

Ray,

She changed the lockset for my bedroom and is telling me her attorney said she could change locks in the home to keep me out of rooms. If she wants to lock a room other than the master bedroom where all my clothes and personal items are, I'm OK with that, but all her stuff must be moved in that room.

She is spending less than half the nights at the home living with someone else, yet has told me in person and in an email, "Throughout the years, you've been trying to destroy the house, which makes me wonder why you just don't leave the house. You can stay at your parents house, so I won't be so be scared to stay home." This woman is bat crap crazy and completely out of control.

What can be done to prevent her from changing locks and stopping this abusive crazy behavior and constant false accusations from her? I'm tired of trying to be civil with her, I just get taken advantage of and am being subjected to her abuse. She needs to be removed from my home, prevented from having any contact with me, and I want to do whatever it takes to remove her. Like I said before, she is living with someone else over half the time.

Eight days later Jess was briefly in the house after I got home from work. I said nothing to her, and she left. This was the first time I had seen her since May 20.

All these issues were incredibly petty and purely driven by Jess's emotions. I talked with her once to attempt to put our differences aside and get this divorce over without arguing, but all she did was accuse me of being the one causing problems. The only people winning were the attorneys racking up billing hours.

Ray called me on June 1, and we talked a bit about how to keep this situation with Jess under control. He talked a bit about game theory and about strategies for dealing with a crazy person. The strategy was to do something even crazier to throw the person off and completely confuse him or her. I told him we could try that, but I was not that personality type—besides, I knew never to underestimate the level of crazy Jess could bring on.

After our conversation, I was thinking that when the divorce was over, if she continued to act in a reprehensible manner, I could really bring on crazy vengeance, but that was not me, and I'd never do that. All I wanted to do was get her out of my life and be happy. Being vindictive only extended emotional pain and prevented people from getting true peace in their lives. Jess had made a choice to be a hateful human being, and I doubted she would ever escape this path in her life. The problem was that right now I was paying the price for her hate. When this was over, I was going to engage in the joys of having a wonderful life, but she would probably continue having a bitter victim mentality.

The next day Jess came into the house around nine at night. I was already in bed half-asleep. I was still staying in the spare bedroom. She knocked on the bedroom door and said, "Charles?"

I ignored her, and she knocked again. "Charles?"

I replied, "Jess, I've had a long day, and I get up at four thirty in the morning and need to sleep."

She asked if I had read her e-mail asking to transfer money. I said no. She said, "I need money to give to people. I have bills to pay."

I replied, "Jess, don't give me that; you don't have any bills."

She pressed on, asking if I was going to transfer money into the TCF account, and I replied, "I'll think about it."

I took two seconds to think about it: no. I couldn't help but think, *She wants to give my money to other people? That's absurd.*

Her excuse sure was a poorly contrived lie on her part. She was a far better liar than that and usually made up more complex story lines. I suspected she was trying to take as much as she could from me to build up cash for herself. The only bills she had were her phone and gas money. I thought she had two mobile phones. Besides, she knew I was giving her $1,000 a month, as my attorney had suggested, but she wanted more.

On June 4, Jess's sister sent me an e-mail notifying me that their mother had died. Jess didn't say anything to me. I called Jess to say I was sorry, but she lashed out, accusing me of not being sorry. Then she started accusing me of "pulling me away from my niece's wedding."

I said, "Forget you, Jess," and then hung up. I could understand her being upset with the death of her mom, but I wouldn't tolerate her abuse. I genuinely felt bad for Jess.

She was so twisted now that she couldn't even accept kindness from me. Her being so hateful and malicious solidified my thought that I had to protect myself from her. I couldn't offer assistance in any way, since it was assured that she would distort anything to demonize me. I would give assistance only if ordered by the court. I was sure she would attempt to take advantage of any kindness I showed her, so there was no more reason to continue. I had tried my best to be civil, but it was impossible dealing with her.

Jess needed money for a flight to Thailand, so I transferred $800 into the bank account for her. An hour later my attorney called, and we discussed the situation. I agreed to transfer another $900 to bring the total up to pay for the entire cost for her flight.

Jess's sister asked me to withdraw the balance in her mom's DFCU account, but Ray said this month's deposit from social security was for the month of June. Because Suda had died, the government would be taking it back. However, Suda had $300 in a separate savings account, and I tried to pull it out with an ATM card. It wouldn't let me.

I sent Jess and her sister this e-mail:

> I couldn't get the $300.00 in her savings account from the ATM. I don't know why. So for now, to make sure you get the money immediately due to the situation, I'll give you $300 in exchange from my checking account and put the money in an envelope on the kitchen counter. I'll go to DFCU tomorrow and see what the problem is. I'll just keep the money from your mom's saving account in exchange for mine.

This brought the total up to $2,000, which I gave Jess that day.

Jess sent me a text early in the morning of June 5: the cremation would cost $3,000, but her sister had only $900, and Jess wanted me to give her an additional $2,500 at the airport. She gave no date or time, but that was typical of her. I did not respond to her text. I didn't have this free cash available, and even if I had, the answer would still have been no. I didn't believe her excuse for needing $2,500, and I was pretty sure she was using her mother's death as a tool of manipulation.

She called twice that morning, but I did not answer. After the hateful rant she'd gone on after I called to offer my condolences, I refused to answer calls from her anymore. I received another call shortly afterward from a local number I didn't recognize, but I did not answer that either, thinking she was using a different phone to call me. She didn't leave any voice messages. However, when I did a reverse number search, it gave a local street for the number. It was a small road, so I might take a drive to see if our Focus was parked there while Jess was in Thailand. This address might be where she was staying.

Jess sent me another text at 10:30 a.m. saying she could withdraw only $500 for the cost of the flight from what I had transferred yesterday and would withdraw the rest when she got to Thailand. She also might borrow the money from Leah for the ticket. That was pure bullshit. The ticket had to be paid in full in advance, not when she got there. Leah was a mutual friend who had worked at Jess's store when she was sixteen. She was the one Suda had accused me of having an affair with. Jess and I never mentioned this accusation to her. Jess also texted that Leah was driving her to the airport right now. I suspected Jess had paid for the ticket using cash or one of the credit and debit cards I had seen during her last trip to Thailand in December.

I texted Jess to tell her to have Leah give me a call so I could get the money back to her. Jess sent a text back: "I need $1,200 for Leah." Jess sent another text: "Call Leah now, please, at once to make it easier for her." Leah was getting married in eight days, and with all the wedding costs, I doubted she had actually given Jess $1,200. Leah was probably being manipulated by Jess to extort money from me. I would play along for now.

Leah sent me a text, and it turned out that the unrecognized number that had called earlier today was hers. She wrote, "Jess said you'd meet me to give me the money. Can we meet tomorrow outside the McDonald's on Whittaker?"

Her text got me thinking. She had known me for more than ten years and had known my mother very well at the store. We'd spent countless hours together. Now she wouldn't come to my home and wanted to meet in an out-of-the-way location? I knew what a master manipulator Jess was and how she had fooled Steve and Katrina about me. There was no doubt in my mind that Jess had been telling Leah wild stories of abuse. I was thinking Jess had most likely told Leah that I gave her no money and that she was broke—this was a way for Jess to get more by manipulating Leah to lie for her. Leah was being her typical nice self; she wanted only to help Jess but had no idea she was being conned.

Leah was young, in her mid-twenties, and was not aware of how Jess's behavior had degenerated and how Jess could expertly manipulate facts to fool people. Jess knew I cared about Leah and would ensure she got her money back, especially with her wedding in eight days. There was no way I was handing over $1,200 without proof that Leah really had paid for Jess's flight. I texted Leah back, saying, "Sure, but I need a receipt as proof as payment to Jess."

Leah replied that she was "uncomfortable about getting in the middle of this." It was clear that Jess's scheme was unraveling. Leah also texted that she would "rather Jess sort things out directly through you when she gets back." Boom—I was right! There was no way Leah would spend $1,200 on this ticket with her wedding only a week away.

I texted back, "I understand. Just want to make sure you get any money back that was given to Jess. I don't know what really happened with the flight ticket and don't want you in the middle of it. Take care."

I meant this—I cared about Leah. I hoped she did not get hurt due to Jess's actions. Jess had destroyed so many relationships, and this might be another innocent whom she harmed.

I sent Leah another text: "Don't know if u have talked with Steve and Katrina about what happened with Jess and I, but let's just say they will tell you a very different reality than the stories Jess told them about me.

If you ever want to talk just let me know. Anyway, have a great marriage ceremony next Saturday!"

This was the last I would say about this to Leah. She had enough on her plate with her upcoming marriage. Hopefully this would get her thinking, and she would approach Steve and Katrina. Leah was very close with them. She trusted them and did a lot of babysitting for their kids.

Three minutes later Leah replied, saying she appreciated my being so understanding. I thought it best not to reply so that she could get on with her life and concentrate on her wedding.

After Leah's wedding, I would give Steve and Katrina a call to see if all of us could get together and have a talk about Jess. I didn't want my reputation trashed and to have Leah and her family thinking I was a horrible human being based on wild stories I was sure Jess had told. I didn't want Leah to be hurt by Jess's future actions either. If we did meet, I would bring a lot of evidence to expose the lies Jess had told Steve, Katrina, and others. I was sure the same evidence would apply to things she'd told Leah also.

Ray called on June 10 and told me the divorce mediation meeting was back on for Friday, because Jess would be back Thursday. It was canceled due to Jess's travel, but she was to be back sooner than expected. We hadn't known she was coming back so soon. I took a half day off work to go home and finalize paperwork for Friday's meeting.

I had mixed feelings on this. I wanted her gone for a longer time to have some peace of mind, but I also wanted this divorce done quickly and not dragged out. Having the mediation on Friday was the best course of action. This mediation was to have us mutually agree on a number of property division items, spousal support, and other financial matters. I felt that not much would be accomplished—Jess would be very difficult and unreasonable during mediation. Mediation would be surely another waste of funds, with more people taking from me, but I had to go through this process.

After I sent all my mediation documents to Ray, I removed the lockset she had put on the bedroom door and put the original doorknob back on using permanent Loctite. I had a big grin on my face as I applied Loctite to the threads of the screws. There was no way she could take it off now.

The only way it was coming off was if she cut the inside doorknob off with a saw, and then she would have to drill out the two screws connecting the outer and inner plates.

Ray called the next day and told me the mediation meeting scheduled for the next morning was canceled due to Jess's claims that domestic violence was involved. I asked why—the domestic violence charge had been dismissed the previous year, but Ray said she was claiming more abuse. Due to a Michigan statute involving domestic abuse cases, mediation was not allowed, and everything had to be done through the court. Damn, this was going to delay the divorce and cost a lot more money.

I had seen Jess only once in the past three weeks, and it had been brief. I was sure her mother's death had put her in another emotional fit of claiming she was the victim, and now she was lashing out again. At this point she was so far gone that I was positive she believed her own fantasies. Now I would have to pay more attorney fees by going back and forth with the court. It was so unfair that she could make up all these lies and never get called out on them, and I constantly had to take huge financial hits defending myself.

I met with Rick, one of the elders from church, after work, and we had a talk about everything. We had met a few times before. I told him I had been considering not going to church for a while because I was always sad after the service. The church was very family centered, and that was a good thing. But with my situation, having my family life destroyed due to Jess, it was a huge emotional hit to hear this family message over and over. It was depressing. I didn't want to hear a constant barrage of happy family life when I had none. Church nowadays was a constant reminder of what I had lost or couldn't have directly, due to all the hell she had put me through.

At this point I wished I had never met Jess. I was very glad we hadn't gone through with adopting a child. I had seen signs of her mental deterioration years ago and hadn't wanted to bring a child into such an environment. Sure dodged that bullet—she could barely take care of herself now.

On June 11 at ten thirty at night, I was in bed trying to get to sleep, and she came into the house for the first time since her Thailand trip. I had moved back into the master bedroom, as Jess was rarely in the house. Someone must have dropped her off, because the Focus had been parked at the house since her trip. I assumed she had gone to wherever she had been staying all this time and then was driven back to the house. She didn't bring any luggage in.

Jess came upstairs and pushed into bed with me with all her clothes on. She was partially on top of my legs, saying, "Excuse me." I asked her to leave and go to the other bedroom, but she said, "Excuse me again," and wouldn't budge.

I had no choice but to leave the room. I knew any other actions on my part would be twisted out of context by her and used against me. When I left the bed, I took my pillow and asked her, "Why do you have to be such a bitch?"

It was clear that she was sending a message that she would do anything she wanted and was purposely trying to push me to do something so the police could haul me away. I was not going to fall for it. I also told her, "Soon you will be out of my life forever."

Her pillow was in the other room, so I got it and tossed it at the foot of the bed for her to use. Jess screamed, "You hit me!"

What a lunatic she had become. The pillow might have grazed her foot, but this was just another one of her drama queen acts. Only an overly dramatic nutcase could think this was an act of aggression. I didn't respond to this silly outburst and instead left the room to go to sleep in the other bed. It was another example of her twisting something I did into a hateful act. I knew better than to try to do something for her. I should have left her pillow on the floor of the hallway so she could get it herself.

The next day I woke up in a bad mood because of her outrageous actions. Before I left for work in the morning, I pulled the cable to the cable modem and disconnected the media server from the network. She wouldn't freeload off me anymore, watching TV or using the Internet at home; she was not home 90 percent of the time anyway. Being civil to her hadn't worked; she twisted any kindness I gave her into something evil. I had to do anything legally possible to assert my rights. I had to be careful though—I didn't want to seem like a jerk to the court. Part of me knew I shouldn't have disconnected the Internet, but I was too pissed off to think straight.

I wrote Ray an e-mail about her climbing into bed with me the night before. I told him her aggressive actions were out of control. I had to get some peace in my home, especially since she was there only one night every two weeks on average.

It was Friday, and I also asked him, "For Monday's divorce hearing in front of the judge, please do everything you can to get her out of my house. Be as ruthless as needed. Could a PPO on her be warranted?" I wanted her prevented from entering my home in order for me to get some peace and protect myself from being set up on more false charges.

A letter from Kay Jewelers arrived, and I opened it. There was a statement of Jess's transactions over the last month. On May 5, she had received a refund of $175. On the same day, there was a "return of merchandise" item for $8,538.90. What the hell! I was shocked and wondered what this woman was doing. How was she buying this stuff? It had to be with her foreign bank accounts. She was complaining about money, and here was a recent return for a large amount of money. This was a great piece of evidence to keep.

On June 13, Jess came into the house all dressed up and smelling of perfume for Leah's wedding. She was looking for the wedding invitation. She had a rushed look on her face, the same look I'd seen hundreds of times before when she was running late. She looked on the fridge, didn't see the invitation, and then asked what I had done with it. That was typical: she lost stuff and then blamed me.

I told her I hadn't done anything with it and that the last time I'd seen the invitation, it was stuck to the fridge with a magnet. She insisted I had done something with it. I walked away and didn't reply. She probably hadn't written down the address or time the wedding started and didn't know where to go. Jess never learned from her mistakes and would always live like this. She left the house for a bit, came back, and then stayed in bed for about three hours. She left again late in the evening. I wondered if she'd even gone to the wedding.

I spoke again with Ray, and he was very concerned about all the crazy stunts Jess was pulling and the malicious acts Jess's attorney claimed I was committing. Ray assured me he knew I had not done what they claimed. Ray wanted to know what was said on the recording Jess had made with

Laura in August last year, so I finally listened to it. It was thirty-five minutes long. Jess's intent had been to get some dirt on Laura to discredit what Laura had said to the police during my arrest. After listening to the recording, I knew there was no dirt on Laura. Laura said her husband, Travis, was not mean and never abused her. Jess even said Travis had a kind and warm face. This proved that Jess had made up the lies that Travis hit Laura and they were getting a divorce. When Jess was unable to get what she wanted from Laura, she made up stories to tell the neighbors.

On the recording, they started the conversation talking about Laura's mother and the way her mom's husband had abused her. He also was a cop. Jess was pressing for details about how Laura's mom had coped with the abuse. Laura said her mom hadn't wanted them to grow up without a dad. Her mom didn't want the kids to know, so she'd hidden it. Laura never saw any of the abuse. Jess spoke briefly about her alleged abuse in her previous marriage in Thailand.

At almost three minutes into the recording, Jess said I was very sweet: "He's kind. It's not as bad." Laura said that didn't mean it was OK. Laura described how her mom had been brainwashed and felt that the abuse was all her fault. Jess talked about her health issues for a while.

At eighteen minutes in, Laura talked for a while about how people in law enforcement and the military have more emotional issues because they see things that cause traumatic and post-traumatic stress syndrome. Even people behind the lines have it. Laura said they have power issues because they tell people what to do and those people have to do it.

At twenty-one minutes in, Jess asked if Travis had the same issue. Laura said he had some post-traumatic stress syndrome, but she had finally convinced him to go to therapy. He was very snippy, very grumpy, but never mean. Jess asked if he had been abusive before. Laura said he was never abusive and didn't get mad at her but was crabby all the time, like a "big ole grumpy man." This was when Jess said Travis had a kind and warm face, but she was intimidated by his height and size—he looked like a big teddy bear. They both laughed at Jess's comments.

At twenty-five minutes into the recording, Jess described feeling threatened by the prosecutor and said the prosecutor was "getting him" and was "out for blood." She was referring to me and the DV case. Jess also said the prosecutor was not listening to her and didn't believe what she said. Jess said, "It's just so unfair." Jess said the prosecutor claimed I had broken her neck on the report, and Jess asked Laura how the prosecutor got that information, because Jess had never said this to Laura. Laura said she wondered if the prosecutor might have pulled medical records, but Jess said, "He never touched me and never broke my neck." Jess said her neck never was broken but she'd had whiplash.

Jess said she really didn't want me to get into trouble. Jess said she cried—I assumed she meant during the talk with the police—and that they (the police) took that as a wrong impression. Jess said she cries a lot with issues and sobbed with Laura before.

"I cry all-out," Jess said and laughed while saying this.

Jess finished the conversation talking about her Yorkie Sasi, who was kissing her on her lap at Laura's.

On June 15, Ray called and told me Jess's divorce attorney, Linda, had quit. The attorney's excuse was that this case was too complicated, but I think the real reason was that she finally realized Jess was a pathological liar. Once her attorney saw our paperwork with the pretrial hearing statements about Jess's mental instability, prescription narcotic usage, and other evidence of her causing problems with others and lying, she bailed on Jess. This complicated case created more fees for an attorney, and the bottom line was that they were all looking at what cash they could get. In this case, there was no way an attorney could properly represent a client who flip-flopped or created wild stories as Jess did. I was sure Jess had driven her to the point of quitting, even though we hadn't even had the first hearing. It was a testament to Jess's ability to create conflict.

The hearing at court for the next day was still on. Claiming she had the flu, Jess asked for a delay, but the judge said no. The judge told Linda she had to represent Jess at this hearing. After that, Jess would have to find another attorney. I had paid a $2,000 retainer for Linda but would not voluntarily pay for Jess's second attorney. I might be forced to pay, but I would put up every roadblock I could. Linda's quitting would only end up costing me more money in the end and delaying the divorce.

When I got back home, Jess's lockset I had removed was back in the bedroom, hanging in a bag from the doorknob. The Phillips heads of the screws in the original lockset I had put back on the door with Loctite were a bit rounded off. Ha! She didn't know I had put thread locker on the screws—they were not coming off! I know this was trivial and petty, but it was funny.

The next day Jess was late for the hearing. It was typical Jess. She called her attorney and said she was stuck in traffic. Of course she was; it was morning, and there was always rush-hour traffic. Any normal person would leave early enough for something as important as this, but not Jess. She had to put the blame elsewhere instead of getting herself ready on time. This caused our hearing to be delayed for almost two hours, as multiple people scheduled to appear after us ended up going before us. Ray said he would probably get a parking ticket for an expired parking meter. I told him it would be funny to send Jess the bill for the ticket. That was the mode I was in with her now.

While we were waiting, Ray and I spoke about Jess's perspective in cases like this, what she thinks she is entitled to, and what the court considers lies. In Jess's case, it was clear she was lying, and if she testified and stuck to her stories, it would be perjury.

When it came to spousal support, her perspective was that I had supported her throughout our marriage and she deserved continued support. However, my perspective was that she had taken enough due to her building up massive debt, ruining our finances, and causing indescribable personal chaos and legal trouble. She was capable of getting a job and getting a paycheck if she put her mind to it. From my viewpoint, enough was enough, and I shouldn't have to continue paying someone who had done so much damage.

Ray asked me how old Jess was. I told him she was fifty-two. He replied that her habits of creating conflicts with people, arguing, and being a victim were so ingrained at this point that she would never change. I agreed and said she was a lost cause. Ray replied that this divorce would take time. But soon she would be out of my life, and things would only get better.

The hearing today in the judge's chambers was to schedule future court appearances. The meeting was with the judge's legal assistant. It looked like the divorce wouldn't be done until November. Linda was there, sitting in the hallway and looking very unhappy, and she did not go into the judge's chambers with Jess. Jess must have really pissed her off. I waited outside while my attorney and Jess were in the chambers with the assistant.

When Ray came out, he was not in a good mood. Jess told him after they left the chambers, "Please tell your client not to hit me." Ray said that he very strongly told her he did not believe her and that the judge's assistant heard him say this to her. Jess waited to say this just outside of the chambers so others could not hear her. I believe Jess did not want anyone else to hear this because it was false. She was very calculating in her actions and false accusations, so this was going to be a very rough couple of months. Ray told me it was very clear that she was a habitual liar and that this case was going to be very difficult.

Part of me wished she would do something so extreme that it got her sent away, and then I could get a PPO on her. That would help me in the divorce when the court realized the extreme lengths she had gone to of falsely accusing me of horrible acts.

For the next few days after work, I completed paperwork required for the court. The court needed a verified personal financial statement showing bank accounts, real estate, vehicles, personal property, retirement plans, spouse's assets, and other assets. This was not too involved, as I already had most of it done for my attorney in a very detailed spreadsheet. The forms provided by the court were really old PDFs. They were not editable digital PDFs with fields that could be filled in on a PC, which showed how far behind the tech curve they were. I scanned them and then used a PDF editor to overlay text on the forms.

It would be interesting to see what Jess submitted. I doubted she would list her properties or bank accounts in Thailand as assets. We also had to list liabilities and judgments. She probably wouldn't mention the 2005 Thai bankruptcy judgment against her and the Thai court warrant ordering her to six months in jail. There was another separate judgment a judge had made against her due to lying on the witness stand in Thailand a few years ago.

The Thai court had ruled in 2011 that she had lied on the stand as a witness for her mother, who sued her niece over stealing a microwave.

This alleged theft occurred almost six years before 2011, and her mom had wanted to sue before the statute of limitations ran out. Suda had been stewing over this all this time and could not let it go. It was incredibly foolish, prideful behavior that never amounted to any good but only caused more problems.

When Jess was going to testify for her mom in 2011, I tried to persuade her to talk to her mother and convince her not to sue family over a $100 microwave theft six years earlier, but they would not listen. Once they felt that their pride had been hurt, there was no stopping them—even over something so trivial. Both Jess and her mom would go into pure vengeance mode and would do or say anything to convince people they had been wronged. The niece countersued Jess for lying on the stand and won the judgment. When Jess traveled to Thailand a few years ago to help her mom with this case, I had known it would be a disaster, just like every other previous time when their pride had been ramped up. They never learned.

I had to redo some of the financials for the court over the next few days. I had made them too detailed, and items with a current value of under $500 could be taken off. Ray also stated that Jess and her attorney said her dresses were worth $190,000, and I had only $175,000 on my estimate. This was very good news—my personal property worth went way down, and hers went way up.

I spoke to Steve about the situation with the flight ticket with Jess and Leah. I asked Steve if he and Katrina had ever talked with Leah about what had really happened with Jess and me, but he said no. I told him what had happened with the flight ticket and how Leah had said she felt uncomfortable getting in the middle of this. I told him I cared about Leah and didn't want to see her get hurt, especially when she was starting her life as a newlywed.

When I told Steve that Jess had claimed Leah had given her $1,200 for the flight but then Leah had balked when I asked for a receipt, he immediately said Leah probably hadn't paid for it but that somehow Jess had convinced her to say this so she could get more money. I told Steve that was exactly what I thought also. He also was concerned that Jess was conning Leah, and he didn't want to see her hurt. When Leah got back from her honeymoon, Steve and Katrina would get with her and share what Jess had done to them and what they had found out about all her lies at my expense.

I also asked Steve if Jess had been at the wedding, and he said no, they hadn't seen her there. My thinking that Jess had not known where to go since she had lost the wedding invitation was probably correct. She had gotten all dressed up for nothing.

On June 19, I discovered that all the bank records, tax documents, vehicle records, my job records, my medical records, and other paperwork in the filing cabinet were gone. Jess took everything. That really pissed me off—I had tried to be civil and keep her able to access all shared financial documents, but she had stolen everything. I sent an e-mail to Ray asking how to get them back, and he said he had started a motion to remove her from the home. He would also request the immediate return of all documents on the same motion. This theft was sure to be another strike against her in the court's opinion.

That day was Father's Day. I didn't go to church—I didn't want to hear about fatherhood. Being denied a family was tough, and I didn't want to hear this message. I did call my dad to wish him a happy Father's Day. I thought about how I would ever have my own son or daughter give me a call on those or other days. My eyes teared up as I thought about this.

I bought a safe that day and decided to wait for the neighbor to get home to help me haul it upstairs. It was not a big one, just a cheap $300 Sentry Safe, but it weighed about two hundred pounds. I needed this to keep all legal and divorce paperwork safe from Jess's prying eyes.

Jess came to the house and stayed the night for the first time I knew of in eight days. It had been ten days since I had seen her. She started complaining about not being able to sleep for a week, having headaches, having a fever, and coughing. I'd had enough of her hypochondria and thinking herself sick over all these past years, but now I had zero sympathy for her and didn't want to hear it. I'd heard enough stories of her misery to last multiple lifetimes. She seemed to thrive on self-pity and craved the attention it brought her. I wouldn't respond to her pity party or give her any sympathy. She even asked if my mom had had any remedies for coughing. I said I didn't know, but Mom probably did.

Later Jess came up to me and said to tell my dad, "Happy Father's Day." She was genuinely glad I still had my father. She asked to give me a hug, but I told her I didn't want a hug from her. I kept about five feet away from her. She also said she was sorry things had turned out the way they had and that she knew I'd had different expectations about our marriage and hadn't wanted this to happen. She told me that I was a good person and that she didn't believe what others said about me. I wondered what she meant about this and thought maybe a part of her felt guilty after hearing people repeat to her all the false stories she'd told about me. She was really nice to me and not falsely accusing me of things for a change.

Her statements about me were a complete 180 degree turn. She was the one who had been making things up to trash me in other people's eyes, but now her guilt had to be getting to her. She still couldn't admit to making up all these horrible lies about me. Her mental state simply prevented her from seeing any fault in her actions. In her mind, it had to be someone else's fault that her new friends who didn't know me thought badly of me. It had to be a hellish existence to make up and believe her own horrible false accusations and then deny them and even believe she had never said them. I couldn't even imagine the mental conflicts going on in her mind. I was not going to have any hope for continued nice behavior—I knew she would flip at any time.

The next day Ray gave me a call about Jess's recent request to pay for her new attorney. He couldn't agree to this because I had already paid for the first one. I reminded him about the Kay Jewelers receipt and that Jess did have money but was hiding it. He exclaimed, "That's right!" He was still in the process of submitting a motion to give me exclusive rights to the home, which would keep her out. I had to put together a list of the crap she had pulled plus the limited days she had spent at the house to show that she already had a place to stay.

Just as I had predicted, Jess flipped from her nice behavior and went into attack and victim mode. On June 22, she sent an e-mail titled "Thank you for our small talks yesterday, please withdraw cash for me." I didn't see it until after I talked with Ray that morning. She wrote:

TALES OF THE CRAZY - WHY MY EX EMBALMED HER UTERUS

I appreciate our small talks yesterday,

Please deposit cash, I still owe the money to a couple of my friends from the trip to my mom funeral for the cost of the airplane ticket and my personal expenses for the trip (this doesn't include the funeral expenses). My mom gave us the money when she was still alive over $17,000.00+ and also bought your flight tickets to Thailand and back.

You transferred the money, and then you withdrew it on the same day, that I was leaving for my mom funeral, it caused additional stress and sorrow to the loss of my mom.

My mom was very sad and upset when you filed the divorce, especially you timed it so cruelly to ruin her joy and happiness for her special moments with her grand daughter, Phonphan's wedding. it was a few days right before her grand daughter's wedding. I had to come back home sooner that I couldn't even attend the wedding. My family has been very kind to you and stood by you.

My mom health deteriorated fast after the news about the divorce. Chuck, when you lost your mom, I was there the whole time to comfort you, your dad, and the rest of the family as much as I was allowed to without being attack either by your families and your mom's neighbor.

Let me get to the point of what seem to be our concern..., I would like you to make a withdraw of cash of for the followings without any further delay:

1. $ 1,671.00, flight ticket
2. $ 800.00..., the money that you promised me on the email
3. $ 2000.00 monthly expense that Ms. Linda Phillips inform your attorney for the month of May
4. $ 2000.00 (subtracts $500.00 of what you transferred to your TCF account yesterday for partial monthly expense for the month of June.
5. 5. Divorce attorneys' fees;
   Linda ******: She asked for $3,500.00 +, (to complete your divorce matters).

Thomas *****: $ 3,000.00 +, (to continue with your divorce procedures).
6. Your attorney makes it impossible for us to have our lives.
7. Your outrage and anger are really my concerns.
8. I asked your attorney at the pretrial hearing to ask you to stop hitting me... and per his own exact words, he said, "He will". I hope that <u>you will stop your violent behaviors, if you feel that you are out of control, please leave the house.</u>
9. Please bring the cash in.
10. At this point, I am still waiting for Mr. Springer to represent me..., but I already paid him $400.00. Again this is another borrowed money.

This was almost all bullshit, and the woman was clearly deluded. When it came to money, she wouldn't even mention the $74,883 she had taken from my mom, which was gone forever. My mom also had spent months at the store sewing and helping her. I thought of coming up with an estimate of the hours she had worked there, setting an hourly wage, and then giving Jess a bill just to be an ass, but I wouldn't.

There was also the almost $200,000 in loan costs from my home that I had paid to fund her store. The vast financial devastation she had brought on my parents and me didn't even matter to her. The $17,000 Jess was quoting came from the sale of one of the properties she owned. It had sold for 2 million baht, about $61,000 in US dollars. I didn't know where the majority of this money had gone.

If she pressed me to pay back "borrowed" money, I would simply ask for receipts from people she had borrowed money from, but I would tell her that these people would be brought to court hearings to testify under oath about money they'd lent her. Ultimately Jess was responsible for paying back money she'd borrowed after I filed for divorce, so this was not an issue for me to be concerned about.

Numbers six and eight on the list were sure to irritate Ray. He had been ticked off at the hearing and had told her he didn't believe her when she told him as they exited the judge's chambers, "Please tell your client not to hit me." Now she was resorting to another lie, claiming Ray had said, "He will."

How could she really think I was hitting her? Who knew? She had descended into such low depths of self-esteem and being a complete victim; it was possible she had convinced herself she was getting hit. The year before, during the hell of fighting the DV charge, she would tell me I was a wonderful, gentle man some days, but on other days, she claimed she was being abused. It was entirely dependent on her state of mind, not on reality. During the few times I had confronted her about her claims of being hit, she would not even discuss it and had run away.

Her claims of being hit might also be a ploy to get me to respond in order to deflect attention away from her. It was one of her habitual strategies to throw out something ridiculous and false to try and get me to respond in order to take the attention off her own lies and issues. In either case, I was not going to respond to this e-mail. If she asked about it, I would say I had to consult with my attorney about the proper thing to do.

When I got back home from work, she was not there as usual, so it was nice and peaceful. Diva greeted me as usual, extremely happy to see me. I got down on the floor with her, and she began jumping, body slamming, and kissing me with happiness. I remembered how Jess used to run to give me a hug and passionate kiss when I came home from work. What a change this had been.

I was going to take an extra three days' vacation before the next week's Fourth of July mandatory shutdown at work. I hoped she would not be in the house. I needed to de-stress and relax for a bit.

On June 30, Jess showed up at the house and stayed the night. She was very hostile and demanded I look through boxes to find her things I had packed when she was in Thailand over Christmas the year before. I had only repacked all the stuff she had left strewn all over the house. I didn't reply. She continued making all sorts of false claims about my boxing away other clothing items she could not find. I hadn't done what she was accusing me of. It was another one of her blame games.

FIFTEEN

SHE'S REMOVED FROM THE HOUSE!

Jess stayed the night in the house on July 1 and left the next morning. I really hoped she wouldn't be here during the Ford shutdown, but that didn't happen. In the evening, she was lying in bed, and I was getting a shirt out of the bedroom for work the next morning. She complained about stuff, and I ignored her. When I looked at her, she was wearing a very revealing nightgown, and her left breast was exposed. The sight of her and her boobs disgusted me.

I thought, *Cover up.*

She complained for a while longer. I said nothing and walked out of the room without saying a word to her. After I left, I realized the amount of contempt I had for Jess. For me to look at a beautiful woman's breasts and be disgusted by them was extremely abnormal. I wondered what her intention was in wearing that revealing lingerie.

After she left the next morning, I did a lot of yard work, mowing, weeding, and working in the garden. When Jess came back to the house around three thirty in the afternoon, she was in a really pissed-off mood and complaining that the Focus was stalling again. She had called me five times earlier, but I hadn't heard the phone—it was inside the house, and I had been working outside.

I had told her the month before that I was not her fix-it guy anymore. I had also told her twice before that Belle Tire also did vehicle diagnostic and repair. She still thought she could call on me anytime to help her out, and she expected me to do whatever she asked.

I told her again that she needed to take the Focus to Belle Tire or another shop to get it fixed, but she replied that Belle Tire was a tire place. Why should she take it there?

I didn't reply to her and then went back to work in the backyard. She came back and said the truck wouldn't start. She had loaded it up with a bunch of her stuff while I was in the backyard. I tried starting it but got the same thing. I couldn't help but think, *What now, and why does all this have to happen?*

I went online to the Ford site to see what diagnostic procedures there were, reviewed a few of them, and then got out my OBDII code reader. There were no faults, so I checked the fuses and relays. I had a spare relay, so I swapped it with some in the fuse box. It turned out to be the starter relay. That was a very lucky and easy fix.

Jess then told me she was taking the truck for four days. I told her she should have asked me about this—I had already made plans and needed the truck the next day and Saturday for the Fourth of July. I also said she couldn't expect me to jump at her last-minute requests and needed to tell me ahead of time. She wouldn't budge and told me she was taking it. She even had the nerve to tell me I had to find alternative ways to haul stuff or have someone else do it for me. I thought she should follow her own advice, but I didn't say it—I didn't want to escalate the situation.

I tried to compromise and said she could use the truck to haul her things, but I needed it back the next day. She refused and went on a rant about how she felt unsafe driving the Focus. It was old and unreliable, blah, blah. She said she had to drive four hours away. This surprised me, and I asked, "Four hours?" I didn't believe her; she would say anything and make up any lie to get her way.

I sternly told her no and that I was through with her nonsense. I popped the hood, and she immediately asked what I was doing. I didn't answer, and she got in the truck and started it up. She started to back out but stopped when I raised the hood. I started pulling relays and fuses in the fuse box, and the truck's engine stopped, as I intended. I put all but two back in and hid the relays downstairs in my shop. One of the relays I left out was the new starter relay I had replaced, so the truck could not be started.

I walked away and started to do more yard work. She stayed in the truck and talked on the phone. About a half hour later, I went inside to make my dinner, and a short time later, there was knocking on the door. I thought it probably was the police. I answered the door, and two deputies were there. They asked if I had any firearms on me, and I said no. I immediately pulled out of my wallet the list of meds she had been taking and told the cops this was what we were dealing with. Since the year before, I had known she would flip out again, so I had made a list of her pills on one side of the paper and, on the other side, had listed proof of her involuntary commitment with a psych hold from a few years earlier.

Having this list really worked in my favor. The cops looked very surprised at all the meds. I asked if they knew Travis. They said yes, so I briefly told them about what Jess had tried to do with Laura by telling our neighbors that Travis beat her. I told them I had Laura's texts and could show them, but they said no. I could tell by the looks on their faces that they now suspected Jess was a nutcase. Her credibility was blown.

I told them the truck was in my name and the Focus was in hers, but I had told her she could use the truck overnight. I explained that Jess was being unreasonable and that I was not letting her take my truck for the next four days when I had already made plans. They went to talk to Jess, came back, and told me that because we were still married, the truck was jointly owned, and she could use it overnight. I told them I had no problem with this. They went over to tell her she could take the truck but must return it by ten the next morning.

She did not respond. She was extremely angry at not getting her way. I overheard them ask her if she had any medical conditions, but I didn't hear her reply. She went back to the truck, and they repeated that she had to bring it back by ten the next morning.

Jess left, and one cop asked me how much longer it would be until the divorce was final. I told him it wouldn't be until November, and he said he had gone through a divorce with something similar, and I should consider living somewhere else so I didn't have to deal with her problems. I told him my attorney was working on a motion to get her out of the house because of her issues. He said that was a good idea.

Afterward I thought, *Why didn't he tell her to consider living somewhere else? Why is it that they ask the man to leave?* It was a huge bias.

About fifteen minutes after Jess left, she called, but I didn't answer. She came back home. One of the same cops also arrived with her. She told me she didn't want any more of "my" conflicts. She started taking things out of the truck and putting them in the car, but she went into the hurt-bird routine in front of the cop, saying she needed help unloading some items because they were heavy. She'd had no problem putting them in the truck, but I helped load her stuff, and then she left in the Focus. What a lunatic.

Jess didn't come back home during the rest of the week I had off work. It was great.

On July 7, I met with Ray to go over the motion to get Jess out of the house and give me sole possession. It also had language stating that she had to return all documents she had taken but would not return, that prevented her from contacting me on my Ford phone and e-mail, and that gave me permission to change the locks. Ray told me her calling the police on me was the last straw, and she had to go. He had been very hesitant to file the motion, but now he realized what a danger Jess was to me.

We were reading some of the e-mails she had sent me, and after reviewing her previous incidents, Ray asked, "How long has she been a pathological liar?"

We both laughed. Ray hadn't seen the e-mail I had forwarded him about what she'd said about him. When I showed Ray the e-mail, he told me, "That's a lie. I never said that."

We prepared all my evidence of her behavior, and Ray submitted the motion to the court on July 8. He also sent a copy to her attorney. The hearing was scheduled for July 16. I was sure their response would be full of more false accusations, but there was no way they could prove anything. Over the last few months, I had known Jess might be recording me at any time, and I had made sure my actions could not be held against me.

I had been very careful around her, knowing she would look for anything to use against me.

One part about getting her out of the house I was not happy about was having to pay her $2,140 per month for interim spousal support. Ray said I couldn't get out of it, but the money I paid would be worth it if I didn't have to deal with her problems at home. This didn't sit well with me, knowing I had to pay her to stop targeting me. It was like bribing a criminal not to harm me. That large sum was really going to hurt me financially, especially since I was still paying all her medical and car insurance.

On July 8, I submitted a Freedom of Information request to the Washtenaw sheriff's department for a copy of the incident report with the police on July 2. I would be able to pick it up in five business days. Ray had asked for it the previous day, hoping it would contain information that showed she had fabricated more lies. This could be used during the motion to get her out of the house.

Jess hadn't stayed the night since July 1, and July 2 was the last time I had seen her. Good. It had been great and stress free without her around causing trouble. Even on the rare occasions when she was pleasant, I knew she could flip in an instant.

When I got home from work, I went into nerd mode. I started redoing my old PC so I could hook up digital video cameras for my network video recorder (NVR) system. I had to prepare to get security video running to protect myself against her false accusations.

I got a call from Ray's secretary on July 10, and she told me the hearing to get Jess out of the home had been rescheduled to July 30 because Jess's attorney would be out of town on July 16. Now I had to wait two more weeks. I was wondering what stunts Jess would pull until then. Knowing I had filed this motion, she was bound to do something malicious. She had to be seething with rage and plotting revenge.

I absolutely had to get the NVR working with the IP video cameras now to protect myself. I started running Ethernet cable throughout the house for four IP video cameras.

I received more texts from Jess about the Focus stalling. She had procrastinated for more than a month about taking it to a repair shop. She wouldn't take care of problems herself; instead, she had a hostile dependency for me to fix issues for her. If I refused, she went into a rage. She needed to grow up, be independent, and realize it was not my responsibility.

Here are the texts:

> Jul 12, 12:29 PM
> Car completely dead while I was driving...please look into getting a new car for me like you said before...this car was 95 % used by you. I am very upset and will not tolerate your going back and forth on your decision... It's not fair to me. You abused this Focus since I got....and it is a junk.... I am asking you to do the right thing.

> I am now stuck on the side of the road and very upset...that you know how to fix the car..., but you rather put me in the danger situation...to drive this piece of crappy car

> Typo....you put me in the danger spot....just do the right...and get it over with..please

> Jul 12, 12:50 PM
> I asked you multiple times for over a month for your own good to take it to a shop. You didn't. Until you do, keep your foot on the accelerator to keep the engine rpm up around 800, and keep the other foot on the brake.

> Jul 12, 12:54 PM
> I'm not your fix it guy anymore. Call your boyfriend. You calling the police on me put an end to any help from me forever. You are on your own. Do not contact me anymore. All communication will go through my attorney.

> Jul 12, 1:03 PM
> This is your responsibility, I called cop because you stopped me from leaving..that was only reason.

On July 12, there were huge problems with Jess again. She came into the house at 11:50 p.m., but this time, I turned on a small audio recorder to make sure I had evidence. This was the first time I had seen her in the house since July 2. When she came in, she was yelling downstairs about "assholes" and having a hard day.

I thought, *How hard can your life be, not working for a living, having no responsibilities, surfing the Internet, watching TV, and shopping?*

She turned on the lights, came into the bedroom, and started throwing and slamming things around. She was extremely hostile and said angrily, "The Focus is fixed." I didn't know and didn't care where she had taken it or what had been done to it. It was not my problem.

She started to get into bed with me. I told her, "Don't even get in bed with me, Jess."

She replied, "I won't get in bed with you. You go to the bed, the bed you bought. Go to your bed."

I told her she was not even living here, but she cut me off, saying, "I live here. This is my house."

I repeated, "Don't even think about getting in bed with me."

Then she grabbed my lower leg. I raised my voice and said, "Jess, don't even touch me."

She said, "I'm not touching you."

It was purely psychotic behavior. She grabbed my leg but immediately denied she was touching me. She pushed against me to move over but denied she was touching me. Then she stopped pushing but stayed in the bed. This was another deliberate attempt to bait me into using physical force so she could call the police on me for assault and get me arrested on another domestic violence charge.

We exchanged more words, with her going off about the car. I told her again to get out of the bed, and she said, "No, this is my bed."

I said again, "You don't even live here."

Then I called her a crazy bitch and told her multiple times to get out of the bed.

She said, "I'm not touching you" over and over and told me to "get into my half." She meant my half of the bed.

She then said, "This is my house, same as yours. You cannot control me."

She rambled on, making more false claims about me hitting her. Two minutes into this, she called me a "fucking asshole." She accused me of lying on "the paper," and I knew she had to be referring to the motion to get her out of the house. The motion to remove her from the house absolutely enraged her.

I got up, left the room, and walked away from her, as I had done countless times in the past. She slammed the door shut and told me not to come in. She constantly contradicted herself by saying it was our bed, our room, and our house but then said I couldn't come in. She made appearances at the house once every week and a half to exercise control and cause trouble. She also only came by so she could claim she was still living there.

This was really getting tiresome. I almost called the police when she was so out of control and throwing things, but I didn't think there was anything they could do—she hadn't thrown anything at me or hit me. They probably would have told me to leave the house, and she would have gotten her way again for being a hateful control freak. Later on I thought that her aggressive behavior could have been a last-ditch effort to get me to do something she could use to combat the motion. It didn't work.

I should have set my phone to record video, not just audio, in order to get a more complete record of her behavior. Next time I would, and if possible, I'd use it to file charges against her so it was not just my word against hers. The only problem I saw was that the prosecutor probably wouldn't go after her, even with evidence. It was clear from my experience the year before that they were not interested in truth and only wanted a conviction of the male.

On July 28, I sent a copy of the July 2 police report to Ray. The lying psycho had told the police I had a gun. In the report she also claimed, "He took some part off her car so it won't run." "Her car"—another lie. The hearing for my motion to remove her from the home was in two days; we couldn't put this latest tidbit in our motion, as Ray had submitted all paperwork to the court already.

The next day Ray gave me a call with great news. Jess had been kicked out, and the court had canceled the hearing for July 30! This was outstanding news and a very surprising and positive outcome.

What had just happened was almost unheard-of in the liberal utopia of Washtenaw County. I made a good salary as an engineer and had family in the area, but she had no family here and was unemployed. The court kicked her out anyway without even considering what she had to say in person. The evidence I had against her was so overwhelming that the court removed her without hearing her testimony. In addition to this, she was required to vacate the house on or before August 8 and could remove only her personal belongings. I could change the locks after 4:00 p.m. on August 8.

All documents she removed from the house were ordered to be returned by noon on July 31, only two days from now. All other items she had taken must also be returned. She had taken inventory from the store, along with sewing machines and other equipment. She did get $2,148 a month in interim spousal support, which I had expected, and I had to pay $2,000 for her second attorney. I had to maintain the status quo in paying for her auto and medical insurance, but she was responsible for her rent, renter's insurance, utilities, and phone. This was a major victory for me.

I called Dad and gave him the good news. He was elated. We talked about this and agreed it was about time she was held accountable for all her malicious behavior. I told Dad that Jess had to be in an absolute rage right now and probably couldn't think straight. On the way home from work, I stopped at Home Depot and bought new locksets for all my exterior doors. They would go on exactly at 4:01 p.m. on August 8. I would also change the garage door code for all the remotes.

The only worry I had now was what her next move would be. She had to be looking for revenge, and it was a given that she would start concocting a whole new series of false accusations out of her lust for vengeance. I had no doubt she was telling people I had lied about everything.

On July 30, I told a couple of people at work that this was the one-year anniversary of my DV arrest. We laughed at that. After I got home from work, I changed the oil in the truck and did some other household chores. Later in the evening, Jess sent a text asking me to give her a Ford A-Plan PIN so she could lease a new Focus. I replied that I would do it the next day. The only reason I agreed to this was that she would be responsible for the car payments. With this new car, I wouldn't have to pay for a new insurance policy, as this was not maintaining the court-ordered status quo.

Jess replied, "I will transfer the insurance over to the lease car."

I called my insurance company and put a lock on the auto policy to prevent any changes.

Jess then texted me, "Do you want me to trade in the car? They will give me $600."

That was a lowball amount, since the Kelley Blue Book value was $2,100. I told her no and said I would give her the $600 trade-in value for the car. That way I could keep cheap transportation as my daily driver to work.

Jess was fighting back on the financial details of this recent court ruling kicking her out of my house. Her attorney scheduled a hearing on

August 6, demanding I give her financial assistance for finding alternate housing. Ray and I replied no, quoting the previous court order stating she was responsible for rent. The judge denied their motion and hearing. This was a futile effort; any attorney must have known the court would deny the motion. The only reason her attorney did this was either extreme pressure from Jess or to get more billing hours.

Jess got four people to help her move her personal stuff out before the August 8 deadline. Due to her history of malicious behavior, Ray told her attorney that a civil standby by the police was required. From now on, Jess could not enter my home unless she arranged a civil standby for a police escort. I had to protect myself. When Jess arrived with people to help her move, she was completely out of character and amazingly nice to me. I had no doubt that she acted this way with others present so she could portray herself as the victim. On August 8 at 4:01 p.m., I began changing the exterior locks, per the court order. I even texted a friend of mine, Alan, at 3:55 p.m. about changing the locks: "T minus 5 minutes."

I got a letter in the mail from my auto insurance stating that a new 2015 Ford Focus had been added to my policy. What the hell? I had put a lock on the account to prevent any changes. I immediately called the insurance company to see what had happened. Jess had somehow gotten through the account lock and added her new Focus to my policy. I immediately canceled the policy on her vehicle. The next day I told Ray what had happened, and he told me I had to put her car back on. I also found out that Jess traded in the old Focus and only got the $600 for it.

His reasoning was that my actions had now caused her to drive illegally in Michigan without insurance, and I would be held liable. The only way this could be stopped was by scheduling a hearing for contempt of court to get her car taken off my policy. The problem with this was that paying him $200 per hour for a half day in court plus all his preparation time would be over $1,100 in legal fees. Ray said that because her only income was interim spousal support, the court would not award me attorney fees—even though her actions were a clear violation of the court order.

The hearing to finalize the divorce was scheduled for November… only three months away. It made financial sense for Ray to talk with her attorney and get this car-insurance mess taken care of between them. The cost of my insurance rose $45 a month when she added her new car, so Ray was able to negotiate that she paid half of the difference. It was better for me financially to pay an additional $22.50 for three months versus $1,100 in legal fees, but it pissed me off to know she could willfully violate a court order with no repercussions. The reality is that people have to pay to get justice, and often they can't afford it in these types of cases.

My NVR security system was up and running with four IP cameras. Some of the cameras also had audio. I could see and hear what was going on at my house using an app on my cell phone. After I showed people the video stream on my phone, some called me paranoid. I simply told them that if they had gone through what I had, they would feel differently. Once they heard the details of what had happened to me, they all agreed it was a good idea. Some were convinced that if someone like me could be arrested and put through all that, it could happen to them, and they went out and got their own NVR systems installed.

With the divorce proceedings moving along, I went to two different law firms to inquire about filing a civil lawsuit against Washtenaw County for malicious prosecution with the DV case. Both firms were surprised at what had been done to me, but they said that for me to win a civil suit, I had to prove the prosecutor had known I was innocent. They told me the prosecutor most likely knew the charges were bogus, but there was no way I could prove she'd known they were false. In addition, the county could use the argument that, because the court had dismissed the charges, the system had worked.

So in the end, the authorities and prosecutors can turn your life upside down based on a lie, and by continuing that lie, they can create huge financial harm to you for their own professional gain. They know that, even if you are probably innocent, you have no recourse. Laws are for peasants.

SIXTEEN

THE EMBALMED UTERUS

When Ray and I filed the motion to get her removed from my house on July 8, I assumed Jess's rage would cause her to go into full-blown psycho mode. I was right.

Jess filed an ex parte personal protection order against me on July 13, 2015. An ex parte motion is a hearing or motion granted on the request of and for the benefit of one party only. With this type of motion, a person doesn't need to be present to get a ruling against him or her, and Jess was hoping to get a ruling without me or my attorney being able to respond. Jess failed to do her legal homework, however. Most jurisdictions require due diligence to contact the other party's attorney if that person has one, and Jess didn't do this. She didn't even tell her own attorney. In addition, the court knew we were already involved in bitter disputes, because I had filed the motion to get her out of my home before her PPO. This PPO raised a huge red flag for the court, and it revealed her vengeful intentions to get back at me.

Even though her claims with this PPO were false, it was a serious legal matter. If the court granted her this PPO just to cover the court's butt, it would have lifelong negative consequences for me because it was a criminal charge. Because Jess did this without her attorney's knowledge, the court sent her attorney the paperwork she had filed. Her attorney faxed the paperwork to Ray on July 30. The crazy never ends with Jess. This was way beyond being malicious; it was pure evil and proved she was willing to make up anything to cause me harm.

The only good news about her latest stunt was that the court immediately denied the ex parte, and there was a hearing scheduled for this PPO on September 3. This month-long delay showed that the court did not take her crazy accusations seriously, but unfortunately, the court was bound by law to follow through on this and schedule future hearings. Ray told me this would significantly delay the final divorce hearing. Damn. It also meant this would cost me thousands more in legal fees.

Ray and I reviewed her two-page PPO statement together. It was pure madness and her claims of abuse were utterly false. I asked Ray what the court would think after reading it. He replied that since it was so far-out and the accusations were incredibly wild with no evidence whatsoever, the court would know something was wrong with her, especially because she had submitted this PPO *after* we'd presented solid evidence of her out-of-control behavior in the motion to get her removed from the home.

The first page of the PPO statement she filed was as follows:

> I, Jess Cole, reside at **** **** Dr. Ypsilanti MI 48197 with Charles Cole and we do not have children in common. I've been married to Charles Cole since November 22, 2000. The abusiveness started as soon as we got married. Controlling me, what to say or do was his major joy. I behaved more less agreeable personality to please Charles, so he doesn't get upset.
>
> The abuse mostly took place at the house, in our store, Formal Diva, with all windows and doors closed or in the car, or sometimes humiliating in the public. There were times that we argued and I wanted to leave the house in the truck (which he claimed to be his vehicle), he would push me very hard, so I couldn't take the truck.
>
> Breaking things, kicking the door down, throwing my clothes from the upstairs to the downstairs and shouting to get out or leave the house has been normal behavior of his.

I lost count of the amount of times, he would throw my personal belongings that had to do with work and personal use that he felt it would hurt me.

Since the divorce procedure started, he became more agitated and sending me threatening email and text messages stating do not come home, it is not your home and threatened to call the police if I returned. He filed a divorce while I was out of the country to take the opportunity to hurt me. He put it on Facebook to humiliate me, I had a serious anxiety attack after my sister saw it on Facebook on March 9, 2015.

In 2014, I called the police because his abusiveness was out of control. After of all of the evidence the police saw in the house, Charles was arrested for Domestic Violence and went to jail for one night. My anxiety level went up thru the roof knowing that Charles would be very angry after he was released. I had been walking on egg shells for the past 14 years trying to keep peace in the house. Due to his arrest of Domestic Violence, Charles guns were taken away and he was very angry expressing his feeling that it was my fault. Charles and his father intimidated me to not show up for the court process. The case was dismissed.

A few weeks ago in June of 2015, he hit me again.

Thursday the 2nd of July, I was trying to go to my girlfriend house, he aggressively approaching me while I was in the truck and he forced his way in to open the hood, and pulled the pieces off the engine and the engine came to stop. The fear of him coming back into the car with his anger, I made a phone to 911. The office told me to stay inside of the car because he has guns.

Two weeks ago, he got his guns back, he started flashing it to make sure that I saw it that he is carrying his gun around the house. As the divorce became more intense his agitations have escalated to the point that I no longer feel safe around him.

He sent message to my phone that if I don't come home, he would give away my dog, a 2.5 lbs Yorkshire Terrier. We have two dogs, but he only mentioned giving away the one he refers to as "mommy's little girl". There were many times that he would break things, and I had to clean up glasses, sometimes I got cut from the little pieces of glass. I was afraid the glasses would cut my dogs paws, he would leave the house after breaking things.

Ray shook his head in bewilderment after reading in her first paragraph that "Controlling me, what to say or do was his major joy." No sane person would believe this level of craziness. Ray even said that this one sentence would cast doubt on her entire PPO statement. Her two-page rambling rants were pure insanity, revealing her complete descent to a delusional victim mentality with a need for vengeance. There was no evidence of her accusations with the PPO, because her wild stories of abuse had never happened. I told Ray I had been extremely careful in what I'd done prior to her being kicked out since I knew she would use anything against me. Ray said he knew I hadn't done anything she claimed on this PPO.

Over the next few days, I spent an incredible amount of time putting together a document for Ray to prove her accusations false. I had nine attachments as exhibits showing evidence for the court that she was a liar. I even included her own text messages and e-mails she had sent me that directly contradicted her statements. I also called Steve and Katrina and told them about Jess's attempted PPO. They were very upset at hearing this and told me they would do anything to help me. Ray prepared subpoenas for them so they could take time off work if needed for the case. I also contacted other people, and they were glad to help.

One woman at church refused, however. She said her husband wouldn't let her. She even had the nerve to ask me a couple of days later in a Facebook chat message, "Please be sure my name is off any records. With my position at St. Paul **** ministry I have to keep confidentiality. Let me know that you have done this."

That really pissed me off. I never replied to her. She had known Jess for years and was fully aware of how many issues Jess had. She knew I was innocent, but she was willing to sit back and let this latest criminal charge ruin my life because of her church position. I thought back to all the times she and her husband had preached about helping others and doing the right thing during their classes, but now all their churchy preaching turned out to be only lip service. Others would stand up for me, regardless of their positions—they knew they had a moral obligation to defend an innocent against false charges.

Jess's second attorney withdrew from her case on August 12. It sure seemed like he'd had enough of her nonsense. I suspect that Jess's filing this PPO behind his back was the last straw for him. There was no way any attorney could ethically defend her statements as true. This was also the one-year anniversary of Mom's passing. It was a very sad day for me, remembering Mom and all the hell I had been going through with the DV charge, and now the psycho was attempting to slap me with a PPO. I talked with Dad about this, and he said the best thing that could happen for all of us would be for Jess to overdose and die. I agreed completely.

During this PPO mess, Ray and I also had to deal with Jess's violation of the court order to return my tax, vehicle, and medical records. She also didn't return all the store equipment she had removed from the house. On August 18, we reviewed and submitted a contempt of court motion Ray had put together ordering Jess to show cause for why she had not complied with the court order.

Jess's third law firm, The Reed Law Group, worked on Jess's case. One of the attorneys there, Jessica, gave a feeble response to Ray, writing, "Since I have not heard from you regarding a mutually agreed upon date/time for a property exchange, I believe my client is planning to drop everything off at our office for your pickup, as you previously suggested."

That was crap. The court had ordered Jess to return everything, not for her to make us go out of our way to get it. Ray replied, "Your client was obligated to return these documents to the house before she left. I would like your runner to bring them to my office since it is your client who did not comply with the court order."

On August 25, a runner dropped off some items at Ray's office, but much was missing. Jess had made copies of my entire medical, job, and vehicle records and returned only the copies. She even copied all my original immunization records from when I was a baby and in the navy. She kept all the originals. I had many color photographs from old projects I had worked on at Ford; now I had only low-quality, black-and-white copies. Jess's motives were very clear: she was going to intentionally cause problems for me.

The contempt of court motion was going to proceed. Jessica then had the nerve to ask on Jess's behalf that she be allowed to keep all the store equipment she had removed from the house. Had Jess followed the court order, not been a vindictive she-devil, and given me back my original documents instead of copies, I would have agreed to let her keep the equipment. Not now. She could go screw herself.

Ray continued working on our response to Jess's PPO for the September 3 hearing. We were looking for anything we could use to show her mental instability. I informed Ray that she'd had her Yorkie Sasi designated as an emotional support and medical assist service dog in September 2010. This was great evidence, and I sent Ray a screenshot of Sasi's entry into the National Service Dog Registry.

The day of the PPO hearing finally arrived. Jessica brought in the rest of my original documents that Jess had taken and asked Ray if our contempt of court motion could be dropped. The hearing for this contempt motion was scheduled for a later date. I was opposed to this—I was pissed off about all the crap Jess was still pulling—but Ray was able to calm me down.

He bluntly told me that Jess would be held in contempt, but I would be out over $1,000 in legal fees for him to be in court for another half day. He also said that because I had all my documents back, if we dropped this contempt motion, I would look even better to the court, as I wouldn't appear to be vindictive. Let Jess be the bad one in the eyes in the court, he suggested. I agreed with his reasoning. This was one of Ray's great qualities: he knew how to present his clients to the court to get favorable rulings and calm down people like me in the middle of emotionally charged events by explaining the reality of how the courts viewed actions.

The PPO hearing was brutal. Jessica spoke first on behalf of Jess and tore into me. She described me as a hateful, controlling person who had ruined Jess's life. It was extremely hard to take all these shots in court. My heart was racing, and I felt nauseated as I listened to all the false accusations being hurled at me. She even accused me of rape.

Jess had a friend from church with her at the hearing, and the friend gave me a look like I was the spawn of Satan. Jess probably had her convinced that I was pure evil. Jessica continued, hurling out more incredibly false accusations, and then claimed that Jess was in such fear for her life that she had stayed in a safe house from July 26 to August 12. Her being in fear for her life was completely false, and we would be requesting proof of my actions to verify their claims. It was possible that she *had* stayed in a safe house as part of a calculated strategy to discredit me.

It's hard to describe the feelings I had during this. This was a court of law, and here was Jess's attorney falsely accusing me of truly horrific felonious acts. As an innocent man, I found it deeply troubling, and I knew much of what she said could not be defended with evidence because it had never happened. I was shaking and felt nauseated by the intensity of the savage accusations. I was extremely worried about how I was going to counter all this.

Ray got up to testify and stumbled with his response a bit at first. The sheer level of craziness and amount of false accusations within Jessica's ranting had thrown him off; however, he recovered and plainly stated the facts. Ray was hoping to get this PPO thrown out today, but I had a bad feeling it was not going to happen.

The judge spoke up. My heart was racing, and I was extremely worried that the PPO was going to be granted based on the horrific accusations Jessica had made. Ray also had a look of concern on his face. Then the judge said he was requiring an evidentiary hearing brief. Jess was required to put together an exhibit list of evidence to prove what was presented in court was true. All parties involved were allowed to conduct discovery and see evidence the other had.

Ray leaned over and told me this showed that the court did not believe her; he said this was a great ruling for me. The burden of proof was now on Jess, and all the evidence I had gathered showing her to be a liar would be considered. It was an incredible relief, but there was still a long road ahead to clear my name. The evidentiary hearing was scheduled for November 6, two months from now. This long time also showed that the court did not take her accusations seriously, but it also further delayed the divorce proceedings. Damn.

On September 10, Jessica sent Ray an amended attachment to the petition for a PPO. Ray sent me an e-mail with this and asked me to review and put together statements refuting the allegations. I read through it, and the amended attachment was six pages of more ranting lunacy with no evidence to support Jess's claims of abuse. I spent the next two weeks putting together another extremely detailed nine-page document with eleven more multipage exhibits of evidence that clearly showed her accusations were complete fabrications.

However, Jess's amendment was brutal to read. We had been married for fifteen years, and Jess knew all my fears, faults, and insecurities. She used all her intimate knowledge of me to fabricate half-truths and vicious false accusations, which she used to portray me as a truly horrible person.

Ray and I met at his office to review what I had put together and go over Jess's latest statements. Paragraph eight on Jess's PPO amendment was one of the more outrageous false accusations: "Starting in 2000, the year the parties were married, Petitioner became pregnant and Respondent was upset with her. Respondent would not take the Petitioner to the hospital when she was spotting, and she ultimately had a miscarriage."

This statement about her getting pregnant was completely false. Jess was never capable of getting pregnant, as she had only one intact fallopian tube, and it was blocked. I also had records of us going through two separate in vitro procedures in an attempt to conceive. Ray looked at me and said, "This is crazy of her, trying to say this."

I replied, "I have something freaky to show you."

I showed Ray a full-page color picture of Jess's uterus in a quart mason jar filled with formaldehyde.

Ray asked, "What's that?"

I said, "The psycho keeps her uterus preserved in a jar of formaldehyde."

His head snapped back, and he had a look of utter bewilderment. Ray told me he had seen some bizarre stuff in more than twenty years of practice as a divorce attorney, but this was the weirdest and most disturbing thing he had ever seen. I told Ray this was my golden ticket to show the court just how crazy Jess was.

This is the uterus.

TALES OF THE CRAZY - WHY MY EX EMBALMED HER UTERUS

When the court had removed her from the home, I had been getting all of Jess's personal belongings together and found the uterus. I knew how valuable this would be just in case she went off the deep end. I hoped she wouldn't look or ask for it. She didn't. Now that I was armed with this freakish evidence, my path to getting the PPO tossed out had just become a whole lot better. Jess and her attorney were clueless about what was going to happen next. I was going nuclear.

Years ago when Jess had her hysterectomy, she convinced her obgyn to give her the uterus. Before she brought it home, the doctor had it sealed in a plastic bag containing formaldehyde, and then at home, Jess took it out of the bag and put it in a mason jar for safekeeping. I saw it and was stunned. Jess said she wanted to keep it as a remembrance of her being a whole woman. She wanted me to build a miniature shrine to display her uterus in the jar. I wasn't about to say no—she was already unhinged from the recent surgery—but I said, "We can discuss what you want later when you are feeling better." Luckily she never brought up the subject of a shrine again, and the uterus had been tucked away in a closet for all these years.

Ray and I spent the next couple of days e-mailing back and forth as we prepared a response to her amendment. Because Jess had cited medical issues on her amendment, we had the right to conduct discovery and ask for all her medical records. I told Ray we needed to see her psych records so we could address her bizarre behavior; however, I knew Jess's pride would not allow her to grant access to all her medical and psych records. She had an extensive psychological treatment history, but she would not allow proof of her issues to be displayed in court for all to see.

I told Ray there was no way she would allow this record access, and Ray told me it was in my best interest for her to block access. If we had no access to her records, Jess couldn't use any medical arguments in the PPO, as we would have no ability to examine evidence of her claims. On September 29, Ray sent a request for a HIPAA medical record release to Jess's attorney, and they denied our request. Good—Jess thought she had won, but her decision would ultimately work against her.

On October 9, Ray sent out our evidentiary hearing brief and exhibit list. Much of my detailed document was not used. Ray kept it simple and to the point, but it was extremely damaging to Jess's statements and showed how ridiculous her false accusations were. Of course, having the picture of Jess's uterus in the mason jar was the most freakish piece of evidence in our reply.

Some of our statements submitted to the court and Jessica were as follows:

I. Procedural Background
Ms. Cole has a long history of mental health problems. If Ms. Cole maintains her position that Mr. Cole is not entitled to her medical records due to privilege, prior to the hearing, Mr. Cole anticipates bringing a Motion in Limine to prevent Ms. Cole presenting any

sort of medical evidence, including evidence of her emotional upset at the time she made calls to the police.

II. Statement of Facts

In the summer of 2014, petitioner was taking various mixtures of the following medications: Vicodin (pain), Hydrocodone/Noro (pain); Morphine Sufate (Pain); Neurotin (pain); Percocet (pain); Ultram (pain); Cyclobenzaprine (muscle relaxant); Lidoderm patch (localized pain); Liothyronine sodium (hormone imbalance); Prozac (depression); Mirtazapine (depression); Adderal (ADHD); Ambien (sleep); Clonazepam (panic disorder); Xanax (anxiety); Zoloft (depression); Diazepam (muscle relaxant); Progynova (hormone replacement).

Some of these medications were prescribed, others were brought to Ms. Cole by her mother when she visited from Thailand, and the source of others is unknown. Mr. Cole will prove this through his testimony, having seen these medications in his wife's possession at this time. Mr. Cole will also prove some, but not all, of the medications by way of Mr. Cole's health insurance records.

Ms. Cole has a significant history of mental health and emotional issues. Mr. Cole will testify that made a 911 call after Ms. Cole threatened suicide, the result of which was a short commitment to mental health facility. Mr. Cole will also offer documentary evidence that Ms. Cole requested and received "service animal" status for her dog based upon emotional and anxiety disorders.

Mr. Cole was charged with domestic violence on or about July 30, 2014. The case was ultimately dismissed after Ms. Cole failed to appear for the trial. After the incident, Ms. Cole told her friends and family that the domestic violence incident did not occur and that the police and prosecutor lied about the allegations she made against Mr. Cole. Mr. Cole anticipates calling the following witnesses.

Katrina - was Ms. Cole's close friend- Katrina is expected to testify that Ms. Cole told her and her husband that the domestic violence criminal complaint did not occur and that both the prosecutor and police officer lied about what Ms. Cole told them.

Steve- was Ms. Cole's close friend- he is also expected to testify that Ms. Cole told him and his wife that the domestic violence criminal complaint did not occur and that both the prosecutor and police officer lied about what Ms. Cole told them.

Herbert Cole- is Mr. Charles Cole's father- he is expected to testify that he refused Jess Cole's request to lie about her whereabouts the day before the domestic violence case in an effort to avoid service of process."

Mr. Cole will also produce text messages, which in the divorce proceedings, Ms. Cole admitted sending. Ms. Cole texted her husband the following text after the criminal case was dismissed. "Sweetheart, please forgive me for your injustice, I am so sorry. What will happen to you, if I couldn't stand trial, because of anxiety. Even now, im having anxiety attack & chest pain, you know that i had to wear a heart monitor for a month. This is because i am feeling your pain and just thinking about what's going through your mind, i love you." "please call asap"

Testimony will show that Ms. Cole told many people that Mr. Cole was wrongfully charged with domestic violence and that the event she complained of did not exist. Mr. Cole unequivocally denies the allegations that he abused Ms. Cole. Rather, Mr. Cole spent years supporting, caring for, encouraging, his wife. However, her mental health issues result in her fabricating grandiose stories and paranoid fantasies involving just about every person with whom she becomes emotionally close. Her grandiose pride prevents her from ever acknowledging she is wrong, and instead, she creates even greater lies to keep her stories alive.

III. Issues and Law

The court must find there is "reasonable cause" to believe that the person to be restrained or enjoined may commit one or more of acts prohibited by the PPO statute MCL 600.2950(1). The court must consider (a) Testimony, documents, or other evidence offered in support of the request for a PPO, and (b) whether the individual to be restrained or enjoined has previously committed or threatened to commit one or more of the prohibited acts. MCL 600.2950(4). The petitioner bears the burden of proof.

Kampf v. Kampf, 237 Mich App 377, 385 (1999).

In this case, Mr. Cole did not commit any acts that would cause a *reasonable person* to be in fear. Rather, the timing of the request in this case -- after Mr. Cole initiated divorce proceeds and sought court assistance in the return of his property and the right to live at his home unmolested- would cause a reasonable person to believe the request for the PPO is solely the result of gamesmanship by Ms. Cole to gain a tactical advantage in the underlying divorce action. Testimony from credible witnesses will prove that Ms. Cole said that the allegations she now makes in her PPO did not occur.

Ms. Cole's own text messages contradict her allegations in this case.

IV. Evidentiary Issues

Ms. Cole should be prevented from offering testimony as to her emotional and physical state.

Ms. Cole has asserted doctor-patient privilege in connection with her medical records in this case. These records would be important in supporting Mr. Cole's defense. For example, records of Ms. Cole's medications, especially if it can be shown that she was obtaining prescription drugs by "doctor shopping" would support Mr. Cole's assertion that Ms. Cole has mental health problems such that her testimony is not credible. These records would also show that Ms. Cole's anxiety concerning Mr. Cole, if it exists at all, is not reasonable. Medical records would flatly contradict certain allegations in her petition. For example, Ms. Cole now claims that during the marriage, Mr. Cole ignored her medical concerns when she was pregnant. In fact, Ms. Cole has not been able to become pregnant since the parties married. Rather, she had a hysterectomy and inexplicably she keeps her surgically removed uterus preserved in a jar. Thus, her allegations of miscarriage are pure fantasy, and medical records would prove this.

Medical records would prove that Ms. Cole suffers an anxiety disorder. This disorder requires multiple medications and a service dog. Thus, if testimony from, for example, police officers suggested that Ms. Cole seemed emotionally upset with or fearful of Mr. Cole, this testimony would not be subject to cross examination with records that would prove her anxiety was the result of her medical condition and not the result of Mr. Cole's conduct. Unfortunately, Mr. Cole has been denied access to these records that support his defense.

A few days after we sent our response, Ray got a call from Jessica. They wanted to drop the PPO. I thought of a scene in the movie *Mortal Combat*. Flawless victory! I was elated and called my dad to tell him the good news.

Of course they wanted to drop this. Jessica had to know that if we went into court and presented all the freaky evidence I had, Jess would be completely discredited. We would prove her to be a liar, and none of her further testimony in the divorce could be held as true. Contempt of court for submitting false testimony would have been a sure outcome. I would happily pay attorney costs to get this ruling. They had no choice but to ask us to agree to drop it.

At first I didn't want to drop this PPO. I wanted to see this through just to prove I was innocent and Jess was a pathological liar. I really wanted to humiliate her in court for all the hell she had put me through with her web of lies. I thought, *The liar must pay.* Ray calmed me down again, stating that the goal here was to get her out of my life as quickly as possible and not to delay this divorce any further. Ray could have made a lot more money off me. But he genuinely felt bad for me, and he wanted me to start my life over free of Jess.

What Jessica proposed was that we agree to a mutual civil restraining order. I did some research on this, and it was not a court ordered restraining order. It was simply a written agreement between parties that there would be no contact. It was a civil, not criminal, matter, and police had no authority if terms were broken. If one person broke the agreement and contacted the other, the other had to petition a judge and schedule a hearing to determine if the agreement had been broken. Ray also said that once the divorce was finalized, the mutual civil restraining order and any other orders were terminated.

I agreed to this, so on November 2, both Ray and Jessica signed an order that dismissed the PPO. The PPO evidentiary hearing scheduled for November 6 was canceled. Now it was time to focus on the real issue: getting this divorce done and removing the psycho from my life for good. Ray and I talked about this PPO and the implications it had for Jess.

I asked him if the court now realized that she was nuts. Ray replied, "No doubt."

I imagined the court staff calling one another about the embalmed uterus picture and saying, "You have got to come and see this!" Truth really *can* be stranger than fiction.

I also spoke with Ray a bit about Jessica's actions. I was very troubled that she would give statements in court she had to know were false or greatly exaggerated. It was clear from this amended PPO that Jessica was willing to do almost anything without a shred of evidence. Ray said she was a good attorney and was only representing her client's best interests.

This statement was very revealing about how attorneys work. Truth does not matter with many of them—only attempting to destroy the other party by any means possible matters. I told Ray I thought Jessica was a reprehensible human being and devoid of ethics. I told him that if I entered data I knew or suspected to be false in engineering reports, I would be fired. But Jess and her attorney had no legal repercussions from committing perjury.

The harsh reality in today's divorce and criminal court system is that honesty and integrity are for chumps. Liars and their attorneys or prosecutors are in full attack mode, and decent and honest people have to spend all their time in pure defense mode. I have no plans to ever allow myself to be put in this position in marriage again, knowing I'd have to make things up in court to get the upper hand. I'd also have to find a sleazy attorney to support me. The thought of tossing aside your values and resorting to this behavior is unacceptable to any decent human being with a sense of integrity.

The problem is that when you are dealing with a spouse and attorney who will make up anything to destroy you, the financial and emotional burden will be huge. Even though I was innocent of Jess's bizarre accusations, the court still effectively punished me through exorbitant legal fees to defend myself. If there is no solid evidence for your defense, as I had, be prepared for a PPO or other criminal charges to be granted; the court will certainly err on the side of the weeping spouse playing the victim card. The judges will cover their behinds, as none of them want to be known as the judge who let off someone who later harmed the spouse. Now someone who is innocent has a criminal charge on his or her record for life only because that person can't definitively prove that the false accusations are bogus.

In my case, the things that saved me were my own guile and ability to gather and interpret data that proved Jess's crazy accusations false. An attorney can't do all this for you—an attorney handles multiple cases, and there is no way attorneys can keep all the sordid details straight. Keeping an extremely detailed diary after I was arrested turned out to be a lifesaver for me, because I had an accurate time line of events I could reference. Someone else without my abilities would be in a much worse situation even if he or she were innocent. The truth doesn't matter unless you have evidence to prove it.

When I talk to people about this divorce and all the hell I've been through with the DV charge and the PPO, the subject of the uterus preserved in a jar of formaldehyde always comes up. The expressions on people's faces are pure shock. No one has ever heard of something so bizarre. Men will say something like, "Glad you are still alive and not in jail from doing something to her." Women will typically say, "Hope she gets some help," or ask if I know how she is doing or where she is living.

Some of the more colorful comments I've heard after people saw the uterus picture are the following:

- "Holy shit!"
- "That's divide-by-zero level of batshit crazy."
- "Damn, dude. Glad that you got out alive."
  - "No kidding. The uterus in a jar is just freaky."
    - "No, that's weapons grade fucking nuts."

TALES OF THE CRAZY - WHY MY EX EMBALMED HER UTERUS

- "Holy shit balls. A uterus in a fucking jar. OK, now I've seen it all."
- "Wow, I am a female and never thought to do such a thing. That is just plain weird and nasty."
- "That's just nuts. How does a person hide that level of bonkers?"
- "She's nuttier than squirrel shit."
- "Holy crap! You're in first place in the horror-stories race."
- "Hope I never see my uterus."
- "Did you get to keep the uterus in a jar? Based on no-fault law, I'm guessing half."

SEVENTEEN

FINALIZING THE DIVORCE

Jess and her attorney had the gall to submit another motion to the court asking for attorney fees related to the PPO they'd filed. In response, Ray and I asked for my attorney fees based on the frivolous nature of this PPO. The judge quickly squashed her request and also denied mine. Once again I was being punished for Jess's actions by my wallet being drained with attorney fees.

Because Jess withdrew all the PPO claims, the next step in the divorce was mediation to attempt to negotiate the terms of the divorce judgment. We had to determine how much spousal support she would get and divide personal and shared property, equity in the home, and all other financial matters in the estate. We scheduled mediation for December 4, 2015. I knew this would not go well. Jess wanted to take me for all she could get, and it was a sure thing that she would be very difficult in negotiations.

Prior to mediation, both attorneys submitted interrogatory requests for all assets we held. Jessica even sent a subpoena to Ford asking for my employment records. I gathered all my assets together, along with my 401(k) balance at the beginning of the marriage. Jess was entitled to get half of the marital portion of my 401(k), pension, and all other assets that had increased during our marriage. We had been married close to 60 percent of the time I'd been employed at Ford, so she would take half of the marital portion. This worked out to be 30 percent of my gains while we were married.

I asked Ray if all the massive financial devastation she'd caused would lower the total value of what she got, but he said no. This was incredibly unfair, and she could continue to profit from her lies and take more from me. Jess had about $5,000 in net worth when we were married, and all the gains we'd made were because of my hard work. The huge losses were due to her. I should have been a lot farther ahead financially, and I was still paying off my starter home because of Jess. Her low net worth when we met and the amount she could take now did not sit well with me. I now understood why so many men use the c-word when describing their ex-wives. It's crude and not right, but I understood how they felt.

On November 14, Jessica sent Ray an e-mail to ask if Jess could come to my house and get some more personal items and pick up Sasi. Jess needed her winter clothes, coats, blankets, and a computer monitor. This was sent on a Saturday, but Ray didn't work on Saturdays. What was Jessica thinking with this last-minute request? She should have known better than to do this. Ray forwarded me the e-mail on Monday morning, and I replied that I was available on Tuesday or Wednesday after 5:00 p.m. Jess didn't show up.

Jessica and Ray also agreed to have the divorce settlement conference delayed to until after the mediation meeting. The settlement conference was set for February 25, 2016, with a trial date set in March if we couldn't agree to mutual terms of the divorce.

At the mediation meeting on December 4 at The Reed Law Group office, Ray and I were in one room, and Jess and Jessica were in another. The mediator, Craig, first met with us for about fifteen minutes, and then he met with Jess. He came back with a dismayed look on his face. Craig told us that within thirty seconds of talking with Jess, he knew she had major issues and was unemployable. This was not good, as he also was supposed to give suggestions as to how much spousal support she would get. Luckily his opinions were mere suggestions and were not enforceable. Jess and I had to agree on everything.

I had Craig ask Jess if she could come over to my house and take Sasi with her. Sasi was not doing well without Jess, and my concern for Sasi's welfare was genuine. Craig went and talked with Jess, and then he came back with another look of dismay. Jess demanded that I pay her $10,000 to take Sasi. She was trying to extort me, claiming she needed the money to get a new place that allowed dogs. I didn't believe this latest con. She had planned to pick up Sasi two weeks ago, but now she was using her dog as a bargaining chip to get cash. Jess knew Sasi wasn't doing well without her, but instead of doing what was best for Sasi, Jess was using her to get money. That was very coldhearted to the dog Jess claimed to love. My opinion now was that Jess didn't know what love was anymore.

All of us finally met in one room together and attempted to work out division of the assets. It did not go well, with Jess refusing to be reasonable and wanting far more than what she was entitled to. Everyone in the room had frustrated looks on their faces when Jess was trying to get me to agree to wildly unreasonable demands. Mediation ended with barely anything accomplished, and Craig was going to send us his final recommendations.

I expected a detailed report of Craig's recommendations for property division and spousal support, but he sent only a poorly worded and incomplete e-mail. This was extremely unprofessional by my standards. Craig was asking for full payment for the services he had provided, but I told Ray that his failure to give a reasonable report on mediation suggestions didn't warrant full payment. When Craig finished his job as a professional, I would pay him—not before.

On December 17, Jessica's law firm sent a Request, Consent, and Order for Withdrawal of Attorney for Defendant. It appeared either they'd had enough of Jess's nonsense or Jess didn't want them to represent her anymore. That was the third law firm Jess had blown through, and it was very telling of Jess's behavior and her inability to be reasonable and work with others. However, Jessica was starting her own firm, and she was willing to file an appearance for this case and still represent Jess.

I had no idea what actually happened between Jess and the law firm. It was possible that with Jessica leaving the firm, Jess wanted to stay with her. After all, Jessica had been incredibly vicious to me during the PPO mess, and I was sure Jess was impressed with that. I suspected there was also the fact that Jessica knew how much my 401(k) was worth and that she could continue to rack up billing hours for all Jess's unreasonable requests. Jessica knew she would be paid by placing a lien on Jess's portion of the 401(k). Many attorneys love cash cows like Jess who constantly rack up billing hours.

Two days later Jessica sent Ray an e-mail stating that Jess "would really like to come and get Sasi, especially with the upcoming holidays." This was unreal. First Jess failed to pick her up, and then she tried to extort me for $10,000. Now two weeks later, she wanted to get Sasi without my paying. Oh well—I expected crazy behavior from Jess. We agreed that Jess would come over on December 21 to get Sasi with a civil standby.

Jess was an emotional wreck when she came over. A cop was present when she was at my home. I sent an e-mail to Ray the next day describing what had happened:

> It did not go well. She was crying and a wreck when she first came in the house.
>
> She showed up demanding all sorts of things and had a long list of items she wanted to take. Attached is the list. She did take Sasi though. Giving me a long list of demands right when she shows up is unacceptable and I won't allow it next time. She must send a list of things she wants beforehand so I can get them ready. She was ranting to the cop I was throwing her things away because I could not find them fast enough. She also lied to the cop saying I had been hitting her and don't give her any money. I tried to accommodate her, but all I got was more false accusations and abuse. I won't put up with this behavior.
>
> The cop was getting very irritated at her due to her behavior. He had to stop her multiple times when she started going off on me. He even told her to leave the room we were in a few times due to her extreme behavior. She left angry, highly agitated and left before getting all her winter clothes and other items. I wouldn't let her take the TV in the living room and coffee maker that I use every day and that really set her off.
>
> She was very upset that her motorcycle was outside. I bought a cover for it, so it's covered and locked with a chain to the driveway

with a concrete anchor. Told her she can come anytime and put it in storage somewhere because that's what I had to do with mine to fit my vehicle in the garage. Attached is a picture of it outside.

Jess was supposed to take her motorcycle when she was kicked out of the house, but she didn't. She'd had four months to get it, but as usual, she wouldn't act. I couldn't fit my pickup in the garage with her motorcycle in it, so I'd put the motorcycle outside. Jess was very angry and demanded I put her motorcycle in the garage. I told her she could take her bike anytime, but my truck was staying in the garage during the winter so I didn't have to scrape frost off the windshield every day and clear off the snow. This only enraged her more. Too bad. I gave Jess a bunch of items on her list, but much of it still had to be mutually agreed on with future negotiations. Jess wanted to take the entire Pfaltzgraff twelve-setting dinnerware set my mom got us as a wedding gift, but I said no way; that would be determined in the property settlement. That pissed her off also.

Jess was also very upset about being recorded on my NVR system. One camera on the porch was very obvious to anyone coming in the home, and the other inside camera stood out in the hallway to see when people came inside the front door.

Jess told the cop, "He can't record me without my permission."

The cop told her it was my house and I had every right to record what was going on. She went on a couple more rants expressing her outrage, but he ignored her. When Jess went back outside, I showed the cop how I could see all my cameras on my smartphone anywhere in the world where I had Internet access. He was really impressed with the quality of the video feed and said he wished more people had systems with this great resolution. It would make their jobs a lot easier in terms of identifying and arresting criminals. I didn't tell him these cameras were also to protect myself against cops who lie to justify an arrest.

Jess went off on me again, claiming I should pay her back $12,000 from the sale of her property in 2011. She claimed it had been her mother's money and that I'd used it to buy a motorcycle. This was clearly delusional; my motorcycle had cost only $4,400, and we'd both used the cash to pay for household expenses and her motorcycle. I asked her, "How about you paying back the almost seventy-four thousand dollars you took from my mom?"

She immediately shot back, saying that was a "business investment." It was typical Jess. She refused to see the reality of the damage she had caused and wanted only to take more from others.

At the end of December, I discovered that Jess had misused my pretax health savings account. She had drained the account of all funds. She went to an out-of-network dentist to get a new crown; this was a violation of the status quo court order. She also used the rest of the funds to buy an expensive teeth-whitening kit and an electric toothbrush from the dentist, which was double the cost she would have paid in a store. Buying cosmetic items is prohibited with health savings account funds per IRS rules, and Jess knew this. She did it anyway. I could have taken her to court for contempt on this with a sure win, but once again my attorney fees would exceed the amount I would get back.

The next few months consisted of typical divorce settlement issues, with us going back and forth as we tried to agree on terms. One big issue was Jess's existing tax debt with the IRS and the state of Michigan. It was huge—more than $70,000. I was stuck with half of it. The only reason I had to pay was because, early in Jess's business, our accountant had suggested we file a joint return so that losses from her business would be subtracted from my income. We would get a larger return that way. It had seemed like a good idea way back then, but now this was coming full circle as another financial hit I had to endure. Because I had profited from the business loss, I also was expected to pay any taxes that had not been paid. Damn. We also tried to work out property division with all the items in the house along with spousal support amounts, but Jess was being completely unreasonable.

We attempted to work with a so-called tax expert, but in my opinion, he was of little assistance and billed more than $300 an hour. So far every high-priced expert referred to me by attorneys had utterly failed. The tax guy's only decent recommendation was to delay the divorce until a compromise offer could be reached with the IRS. The divorce settlement conference was delayed to May 19 with a trial in June if we could not agree on terms.

On March 1, Jessica was supposed to attend a meeting with a different tax consultant since the first expert hadn't done much, but Jess flip-flopped again. Jessica sent this in an e-mail to Ray: "That will not work; I no longer have my client's approval to attend the meeting." Jessica also wrote that she was withdrawing from Jess's case as her attorney. Jess had now blown through *four* law firms. In Jessica's motion to the court to withdraw, she wrote:

MRPC 1.16(b) (3) through (6) apply in this situation.
(3) the client insists upon pursuing an objective that the lawyer considers repugnant or imprudent;
(4) the client fails substantially to fulfill an obligation to the lawyer regarding the lawyer's services and has been given reasonable warning that the lawyer will withdraw unless the obligation is fulfilled;
(5) the representation will result in an unreasonable financial burden on the lawyer or has been rendered unreasonably difficult by the client; or
(6) other good cause for withdrawal exists.

I was not surprised. It was typical behavior for Jess, and Jessica couldn't deal with her anymore. The money must not have been worth it. I didn't feel sorry for Jessica at all in her claim that "the representation will result in an unreasonable financial burden on the lawyer or has been rendered unreasonably difficult by the client." After the pure bullshit she had gone after me with during the PPO hearing trying to destroy my life, too damned bad for her. Boo-freaking-hoo. Any intelligent attorney had to suspect that Jess had severe issues and was full of crap.

I noticed in the title Jessica had given herself at her own firm, she included mediation and claimed she was a "Problem Solver." That was laughable. From my perspective, her actions had only inflamed the situation, causing thousands more dollars in legal fees, emotional turmoil, and problems. A mediator was supposed to calm issues, not ramp them up. Based on my experience with her, I would never, ever consider having or recommending her to mediate any issue. The previous law firm that had employed her, The Reed Law Group, seemed to have it together and engaged in fair representation.

Reflecting on all that had happened to me, I could see that women had caused all my recent problems. It seemed like most of them had utterly failed to seek any truth and had run wild with emotions to attack me. My contempt toward women in general was at an all-time high. I didn't want any of their raging emotional shit or justification to lie in my life.

There were only a little more than two months left to get all the tax issues cleared up and both of us to consent to a divorce settlement. On March 15, Ray got an e-mail from Jess's fifth law firm that was working on the divorce settlement. I wondered if Ray had talked with the new guy and informed him of all the crap Jess had pulled and what to expect when dealing with Jess. To put an end to this madness, we started on the settlement talks immediately.

In the meantime, at the end of March, Jess and I were dropped from the enhanced health insurance plan I had from Ford. The insurance provider put us on a plan with fewer benefits and doubled the copay amounts. Many services were more costly, and we had no out-of-network coverage. For the past few years, Jess and I had done an online assessment, and our primary-care doctors had sent in a qualification form. This year Jess had failed to have her doctor send in her form. Because we were on the same policy, our health insurance provider had dropped us both from the existing plan.

Prior to our being dropped, Ray had sent multiple notices to Jess's attorney stating that she absolutely had to get this done before the end of March. Jess claimed she had, but obviously she hadn't. I called our insurer and was told I would have to appeal to their board to get just myself put back on the enhanced plan. Jess had struck again, and once again I was harmed by her actions. In previous years, Jess had procrastinated until the very last day to get this done, even though I had tried my best to get her to do it earlier.

With Jess's new attorney, we worked out the issue with her tax debt. Before Jess received any distribution from my 401(k), pension, or equity in my house, she had to get an offer in compromise with the IRS and the Michigan Department of Treasury. That way she could prove that she had no savings and that there was no way she could pay this large tax bill. Her inability to pay was to be used to get a better offer from the IRS. The reduced amount of taxes she owed would be split evenly between us. There were also tax liens on my home because of her debt.

Ray and I drafted up a consent judgment of divorce, which we sent back and forth with Jess's attorney, James, and we were finally able to agree on support payments. I was stuck paying her $1,800 a month for four years. Jess wanted more than $2,000 a month for eight years, but James was able to talk sense into her. To my benefit, Jess inadvertently made a huge mistake in denying us her medical records when I was fighting her PPO. With her blocking any medical record access, any inability-to-work claims due to medical issues could not be used to get higher levels of spousal support. Ray pointed this out during the spousal support negotiations.

Michigan spousal support payments are determined by a formula that takes into account the requesting spouse's income potential and schooling, the other spouse's income, the amount of time the couple was married, and other factors. James probably showed her this formula and told her that by law she could get no more. The formula is always the determining factor, and there is no escaping it.

One thing I was surprised Jess agreed to was that we put in a staples bar—this prevents spousal support from being modified. She can't go back to the court later on and ask for more money or to extend my support payments. If this staples bar hadn't been in the divorce judgment and I got a promotion or pay raise, Jess could petition the court that my promotion was because of her support in the marriage, and I would have to pay her more. I also wanted this in because I was sure she would petition the court to extend the support payments when the four years of payments were up.

The downside was that if some poor deluded fool married her, I was still obligated to pay her spousal support. I would take that chance, as only a lovesick idiot would not see how many issues she had developed now. However, Jess's physical beauty was very appealing. It would make many men go stupid by thinking with their peckers instead of their brains. Dad had commented during the DV mess that Jess had lost much of her beauty in the last few years and had a very haggard appearance now. He said the pills she took and stress had taken their toll on her. She was still way above average in looks though and was stunning when she dressed up.

On May 19, 2016, we went in front of the judge with our consent judgment of divorce. While I drove to the courthouse, some evil thoughts entered my head. I still had a $200,000 life insurance policy on her, and we had a $750,000 accidental death policy. The spouse would get only half of the accidental death policy. Still, I thought, if Jess were wiped out on the road that day in an accident, I would get $575,000 with her death. I would keep all my assets with no other payments to her. This $575,000 would allow me to break even, thanks to all the financial losses she had caused. I remembered what countless people had told me before—that they hoped something would happen to her for my family's sake, due to the hell she had put us all through. She was lucky I was a good man and not violent.

I was waiting at the courthouse, and she walked in. Damn.

I saw Michael Vincent at the courthouse while we waited to go into the courtroom. He was with a sleazy-looking guy I assumed was one of his seedier clients. I said hi and told him that today was the final divorce judgment; soon I would be a free man.

Michael was very happy to hear this and said, "Good—that woman is toxic."

I agreed with him. Michael asked me, "Do you have any weights in your pants?"

That comment took me by surprise, and I had a puzzled look; I did not know what he meant by this.

He said, "When you leave with the divorce papers signed, you will be floating and will need weights to keep yourself on the ground."

We both laughed at that and chatted a bit, and then he left.

Prior to this court appearance, I had prepared a long list of all Jess's violations of the court orders. I also had a two-page summary of all the abuses she had committed against me, detailing the more severe false accusations she had made to the court. Based on all she had done, I was ready to submit to the court my "proposal for a judgment of divorce and nullification of the consent judgment of divorce proposal without a trial." I prepared a radical reduction of what she would receive from my 401(k), pension, and equity in the home. I had this ready just in case Jess flipped out again by not agreeing to the judgment we had worked out. I was not sure if it would be considered by the court, but I wanted to be prepared just in case.

While we waited to enter the courtroom, I was very nervous, wondering if Jess would lose it again and reject the consent judgment. Nothing was a given with her out-of-control emotions. Luckily that didn't happen. Jess was sitting in the hallway next to her attorney, James. I hadn't met him yet. A few minutes went by. I looked over, and she smiled and waved at me to come over.

Wow, this was different. Normally she had an evil-incarnate look when she saw me, but other people were present, and she wanted to look good. I walked over to them, and she was extremely pleasant. She asked how Diva was doing, and I said she was mad at me. Jess gave me a puzzled look, and I said she was mad because I had given her a short summer cut.

Jess beamed with a huge smile and talked tenderly about Diva to James. She spoke about the many times we had worked together to cut her fur and the difficulty we had trimming her nails. I told Jess I had taken Diva to a groomer to get her nails trimmed and that she'd sat there calmly while the groomer took her paws and cut her nails. Jess was shocked, and her eyes flew wide-open at hearing how calmly Diva had acted.

Jess described in detail to James how we'd had to wrap Diva in a flannel shirt and hold her tightly because she pulled and jerked so badly when we tried to trim her nails. I told James that I'd been afraid she might get hurt from pulling and jerking her paws away so hard. Jess chimed in, agreeing with me and smiling at the genuinely fond memories of Diva and us together. All during the pleasantries, I knew not to trust her, as I knew she could flip at any minute. I thought about her PPO—one of the statements in it had said she was afraid I would shoot Diva. There was no way I was going to fall for this nice-girl act.

Jess asked if I had a current insurance certificate for her car. She had received a ticket a few days ago and needed to give the certificate to the traffic office within thirty days so she could get the ticket dismissed. I told her I'd look for it. I also reminded her that after today, she would be responsible for her auto insurance. Her attorney chimed in and said she would be responsible for health and all other insurance after today. I immediately realized it had been a mistake to tell her she would be responsible for insurance. Anything could set her off and ruin the consent judgment, but I was lucky nothing happened. When I got back home, I thought, *No way will I help get her the insurance certificate after all the hell she did to me.* She never followed up to ask for the insurance certificate again.

Our time in court was very brief. The judge had reviewed the consent judgment while we waited outside the courtroom. We were the only people in the courtroom besides the judge and his staff. Ray spoke and asked Jess if she understood that the support payments were unmodifiable. She said yes. Her attorney repeated the same thing to her, and she said yes. The judge asked us if we both consented to this judgment and if we agreed to the unmodifiable spousal support and the fact that we would not be going through the friend of the court for her support payments. We both said yes, and the judge approved the divorce. We were in the courtroom for only about fifteen minutes.

It took another fifteen minutes between the attorneys and our signing five copies of the divorce judgment and other documents. One of the documents from the court stated that the court found that no spousal abuse had occurred during the marriage. I was very happy to see this. It was a moral victory but shallow and bittersweet. The court recognized that all the accusations Jess had made were without merit, but she received no punishment or sanctions for her lies. Then I left the courthouse. Driving home, I was elated. It was over. I was now legally a single man, and I was free! I gave my dad and sister a call to tell them the good news.

The next day I removed Jess from my auto and medical insurance. I reviewed my other records and purged her from them. I called human resources and had her removed from all other work benefits. That felt great—purging her from my life. I wondered if she had followed through and signed up for Cobra coverage to continue the existing medical coverage she'd had through my job. If she hadn't...oh well—not my problem anymore.

Finally, after all this hell she had put me through, the divorce was done. Had she acted in a decent manner and not caused all these problems, the divorce would have been over very quickly and with minimal cost. All the lies and malicious stunts she had pulled accomplished nothing positive. They only brought on more pain, misery, and exorbitant legal costs through delaying the divorce with her constant stream of false accusations. The only people who made out were the attorneys.

I was out more than $33,000 in attorney and consultant fees, with fighting the DV charges and all divorce costs. Add in another $10,000 for paying other attorneys for her bankruptcy, DCFU coming after me for her debts, and the state of Michigan garnishing my checking account. Ray told me that Jess's divorce costs would probably be much higher than mine due to her constant badgering of her attorneys and wasting their time. All her legal costs would be subtracted from what she got from her portion of the equity on my home and her marital portion of my 401(k). Any legal funds paid by her from her portion of the 401(k) would also incur a 30 percent penalty from the IRS for early withdrawal. I suspected her attorneys may have hidden this little tidbit from her.

On the way home from the courthouse, I stopped and bought $20 of lottery tickets. It would have been poetic justice if I'd won and Jess couldn't get a cent of it because we were no longer married. As an engineer who is not math challenged, I know the odds of winning, and this was just a fantasy. The next day I checked the lottery numbers; I had won nothing. Oh, if only!

I got back home and, too excited to sit down, started pacing around the house. I texted a few people to spread the good news. After a while, I calmed down and started planning what to do next with my life.

The next day at work was great. People came up very happy for me that this was over. Many of my coworkers knew all that had happened and wished me the best for rebuilding my life. One guy who had gone through two divorces was still very angry at what had been taken from him financially. He told me, "Never forget that if it flies, floats, or fucks, it's cheaper to rent than buy." This was very crude, and I don't agree with the last part. But I understand where he is coming from.

The next big task was to clear out the entire store inventory from my home and get all her personal stuff out. Ray specifically put in the judgment that "the inventory, supplies, and equipment of Formal Diva, LLC, will be sold with the proceeds used to pay the tax obligations of Formal Diva, LLC." Jess's name or approval on how it was done was kept off, because I was sure Ray and her fifth attorney both realized she would only cause problems.

Later in the evening, I went on the computer and saw a post on Facebook by Pastor Sturly, which said, "I am doing research into finding the top 10 best places for Christian singles to meet other Christian singles. Please suggest ideas, and I will compile your answers and share them down the road! This is a church project and not personal (but I may use the findings! LOL)."

I posted this in reply: "The two women I cared about the most, married one and proposed to the other, I met in church. They also lied and screwed me over the worst more than all the other ones I dated outside of church."

Yes, my reply was a bit bitter. At this point, I was very disillusioned about finding a good woman in church. I had little to no trust in women and didn't want any of their emotional issues in my life, but I was sure this would change after I had time to heal all the emotional wounds. Reflecting on all the women I had dated over the years, I realized that the vast majority who had caused the most trouble or wronged me the worst were all churchgoing women. The most beautiful ones were the absolute worst. It sure wasn't supposed to be that way, and I had thought I could find a better class of women to date at church.

Two weeks later at church, my friend Ron came up to me and commented about my Facebook reply. He said, "Sinners go to church, not saints."

I told him, "That's true, but you would think that a woman who has Christ in her heart would at least try to act better and be more honest, but that was not the case in my experience."

So at least for now, I was not even considering dating any women in my church. There were hardly any single women in my age group there anyway.

The issues remaining were the division of property and Jess's tax debt. I knew that the division of our shared property would not go well, as she wanted everything she could take just to be malicious and feed her sense of entitlement. We had prepared separate lists of what we wanted, and her demands were outrageous. She wanted my band saw, drill press, thirty-foot extension ladders, half of my tools, large toolboxes, grinders, framing nailer, scroll saw, half the lumber, and many other items she hadn't used or was not even capable of using.

My band saw was not a normal hobbyist saw. It was a 240VAC, four-hundred-pound beast of a saw and was something only a serious woodworker would ever use. Jess was being spiteful and trying to take anything she could from me.

When I told my coworker Dale about her demands for my band saw and half of my lumber, Dale said I should agree to give her the lumber with the stipulation that she build a coffin for herself within thirty days. We laughed about that remark. Dale then asked me if I had ever heard of the song "Crazy Bitch" by Buckcherry. I Googled the song and saw the video. It was crude but very fitting. I played for Dale the ringtone I had made just for Jess. It was from "Devil Woman" by Cliff Richard. Dale laughed even harder. It was juvenile behavior on my part, but it fit how I felt about her. She hadn't called since I'd set that ringtone, so I had not had the pleasure of hearing it ring.

Ray told me the list I submitted for our proposed property division was very fair. He sent Jess an e-mail about her demands:

> If you are asking for the heavy duty framing nailer, 30 foot yellow extension ladder, drill press and other large tools and toolboxes just to "get back" at Chuck by taking his tools, that is not going to work. Every judge and arbitrator can see this type of behavior from a mile away. Additionally, you have to ask yourself "who is really being disadvantaged by the delay you are causing with these types of requests?" Chuck has the use of the property while all of this is dragging out whereas you have every interest in getting this matter concluded.

Jess still would not relent and refused to be reasonable.

I contacted an auction house, American Eagle Auctions, and spoke with Ken to come get the store inventory. In the meantime, I put a couple of ads on Craigslist to sell the sewing equipment, cloth, and easy-to-sell items. The sales went well, and the $1,500 I received would be split between Jess and me to pay off her tax debt. I wanted to get more for the machines, but they were old with many hours of hard use on them.

In the beginning of June, when I was going through all the store items to get ready for selling, I found a very large stash of her pills she had forgotten. The amount was shocking. One Ziploc bag contained hundreds of Vicodin tablets. Also in the stash were bottles of oxycodone, morphine sulfate, and a bunch of other bottles of pills for pain and mental conditions. No wonder there's an opioid crisis in this country if one person could get all these narcotics.

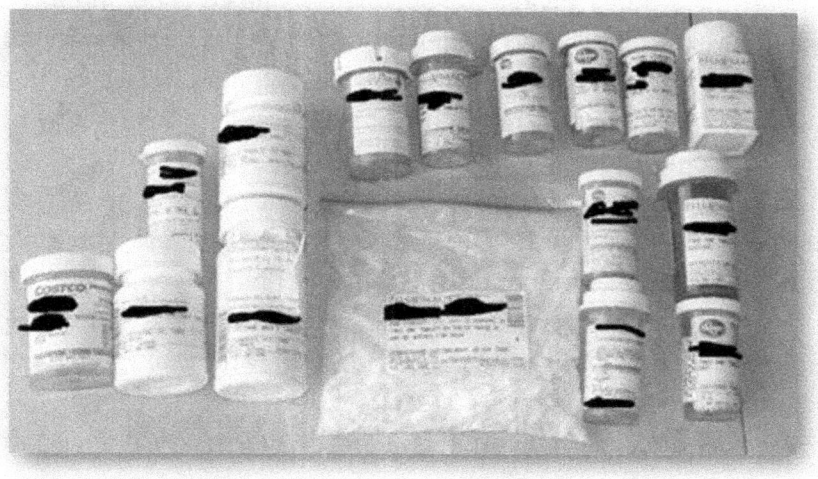

The day before Ken came over to pick up the inventory, I moved a bunch of stuff up from the basement to the garage to make the move go more easily. Halfway through, I was carrying a little twenty-pound box when I went out the door and down one step to the garage, and my ankle just folded over. I hit the ground feeling searing pain in my ankle. Out of all the extreme outdoor activities I did, a little step I had gone on thousands of times before did me in. I immediately hobbled to the kitchen, took a couple of ibuprofens, got a bag of ice, and put my foot up with the ice pack on it to help stop the swelling.

On June 14, Ken and his crew came over and picked up the entire store inventory. It took two trips with his twenty-five-foot enclosed trailer.

Ken was amazed at how much stuff there was. I was able to see my dining room walls for the first time since 2008. It felt great to have my house back again, and now I could start fixing it up. Bruised and swollen, my ankle was really hurting, but when I saw how clear my house was of all her store inventory and clutter that had been there for more than eight years, I thought, *Damn it, spraining my ankle was worth it!*

Ken and I chatted a bit about all that had happened to me, and he told me, "Don't let someone live rent free in your head." That is good advice.

Ray and I had also been trying to get Jess to come over and pick up the rest of her personal items and the shared property we had agreed she could take. We got nothing but inaction from her. I was getting extremely frustrated with Jess refusing to get her stuff. We made multiple requests for her to come get it, but still there was nothing from her. I even told Ray that I was at the point of throwing all her crap away. This was my house, and I wanted her stuff out of my life.

The attorneys went back and forth frequently during the rest of June and July trying to get Jess to pick up her things, but Jess would not act. She broke multiple appointments we made for her to come over. On July 15, Ray sent me an e-mail saying Jess's attorney, James, had withdrawn. That was five legal firms now that had withdrawn from Jess during this divorce. I wondered if that was a record.

After her attorney withdrew, Jess had the nerve to file a motion with the court demanding a walk-through of my home. It was crazy; we had been trying to get her over, but she would not act. Because she tried to do it on her own, she filed it incorrectly. The court would have tossed out her messed-up motion without a response from us, but Ray put together a response anyway, citing the issues we'd had with her, including her breaking appointments to come to the home.

The court smacked her down after seeing evidence of her nonsense. On the ruling given on August 4, 2016, she was ordered to remove all her "not at issue" property by August 31 or it would be forfeited, and I could do whatever I wanted with it. In addition, the court ordered us to attend arbitration to resolve the remaining issue of the "at issue" property, which we could not agree on how to divide. Arbitration had to be completed

TALES OF THE CRAZY - WHY MY EX EMBALMED HER UTERUS

by September 30. The arbitrator would determine the length of time Jess had to remove the at-issue property awarded to her.

Jess came over on August 21 with five people and a fifteen-foot moving van to get her stuff. She had a very large amount of property to move, and the van and other people's vehicles could not hold it all. During this trip, Jess wore a very snug and revealing outfit. I wondered why she had dressed like that. It was not the type of outfit a normal person would wear for a move hauling stuff.

When we were in the basement alone, she gave me a hug, kissed me, and said, "I will always love you."

This was very bizarre, and there was no way I was going to be swayed at all by her display of affection. However, to be civil and try to keep the peace, I gave her four quarts of my homemade canned chicken stew and told her I wanted her to take these just in case she got sick. She really appreciated this. We talked a bit more, and I asked her if she was working. Jess replied that she couldn't work because of all the problems my attorney was causing and all the motions he filed. It was another crazy excuse. Jess could not comprehend that she was the one who had caused all these problems and my motions were in response to all the false accusations she had made.

After Jess and her friends left, a very large amount of her personal items remained. She needed another trip to load a large van with a couple of helpers, but she made only one more trip on the very last day allowed by the court order. She came by herself with only her small Ford Focus to pack things in. A huge amount of her stuff remained after she left. The result of her inaction was that now all her remaining items were forfeited to me, including the large $1,200 kiln she never used, her hobby supplies, garage-sale junk, books, magazines, and many boxes of knickknacks. The next day was trash day, and I maxed out what I could put out for curbside pickup. What I threw out were useless knickknacks; the other stuff I saved to use as a bargaining chip for the property arbitration that would happen later.

I could write another book on all Jess's other bizarre and hateful behavior since September 2016, the mess property arbitration became, the incompetence of the arbitrator, and her multiple filings of more motions, but there's already enough of her craziness to read through. Any more would be overload.

Many unresolved tax and property division issues remain, and it will take months or even years to complete. When dealing with Jess, nothing is easy, and she will always throw a wrench in the works and make simple issues extremely difficult. I'm really looking forward to the day when she is out of my life for good. I've been able to forgive her, but she can never be trusted. The farther she is away with her issues, the better.

I believe Jess continues not facing her own wrongdoing or issues; she functions in a shameless state, thinking she is good and I'm evil. She can't handle the stigma of being viewed as evil, due to her pride and victim mentality, so she marginalizes everyone who does not agree with her version of the truth. If you don't submit to her version of the truth or if you take a position she does not like, the very core of her identity is threatened, and she will react with over-the-top emotion, screaming to the world about how evil you are. She is incapable of thinking any other way or reflecting on the hypocrisy of her own actions.

Another issue with Jess has reared its ugly head, but luckily it is not causing me any problems. On January 19, 2017, I got a call from a Dearborn Federal Credit Union (DFCU) fraud investigator. It turned out Jess never stopped her mother's social security payments after Suda died in June 2015. The government found out, but someone transferred all the money that had accumulated in her mother's DFCU account into a Huntington Bank account in multiple transfers during the first half of January. The amount was close to $4,500. The next day I went to a DFCU branch office and had a chat with them. I told the bank I would cooperate and help any way I could. My name and personal information had been used to access the DFCU account. The only two people who have the account information are Jess and me, so DFCU and the fraud investigators are sure Jess did it. I'm positive Jess did it too; no one else could.

A criminal investigation was started for wire and social security fraud to find out who the Huntington Bank account holder is. I met with a Washtenaw County deputy and gave him all the information I had. The bank investigator told me they would be filing charges when they could prove who it was. The feds were asking questions too—they wanted the social security funds back. The deputy eventually filed a warrant to get the account holder's information from Huntington Bank.

Soon after, I asked the Washtenaw County deputy if Jess was the account holder. Due to this being an active investigation, he couldn't comment. However, he replied, "That being said, I am preparing to interview her as the only suspect in this case."

That sealed it. Jess had done it. In early August 2017, the deputy e-mailed me that his investigation was completed. He was waiting for the prosecutor's office to review the report. I'm sure Jess spun some type of lie to cover her tracks when the deputy interviewed her. The problem is that she is an extremely skilled manipulator of facts and may find a way to spin this in her favor at my expense.

I told my dad what had happened with the social security bank fraud. He said she just might flee the country and go to Thailand, depending on what criminal charges were filed against her. I doubted that would happen, but it would have been great if it had. I'm not a vindictive person and am not seeking vengeance, but it sure would be satisfying to finally see her get something done to her after all the hell and felony-level false accusations she has put me through.

Near the end of August 2017, I learned that the prosecutor was not going to press charges. During the deputy's interview, Jess had contrived a story, claiming she had taken the money because she was safeguarding it from me. She described me as the bad guy in this social security theft she had committed. She also claimed she'd thought she could take the funds to pay for her mother's expenses because she was the executor of her mother's estate.

Jess's next move was to claim she knew the funds had to be returned, so she had contacted the social security office to pay it back. She started a chain of e-mails with the social security office to validate this new story I believe she created. Jess knew she had been caught; now she was doing anything to avoid getting charged with fraud. She eventually started paying the money back. I noticed that her last demands and extortion attempts in July 2017 for me to give her loans were around the same time she was interviewed by the deputy. Now I suspect that the real reason for her demands for money was so she could pay back what she had taken.

I'm sure that because she was paying the money back, the prosecutor didn't want to waste time and resources prosecuting her. It would be a tough case to get a conviction, as Jess is able to expertly manipulate facts.

EIGHTEEN

THE PROBLEM WITH MODERN DIVORCES

It's a bitter pill to swallow that I have to pay to keep someone's vicious and criminal acts out of my life. I view Jess as a disgusting leech who keeps sucking at me. A simple piece of paper that says you were married gives the courts a reason to take from your wallet for years. Even when you can prove the person fraudulently took hundreds of thousands of dollars and ran up huge debts by giving false statements and hiding the truth, the court will not consider this. This is not equitable justice in any way.

I used to be a firm believer in marriage but not anymore. The institution of marriage has been completely perverted by the legal system and attorneys. It did me virtually no good to tell the truth in court, while Jess habitually lied with no consequence. My innocence did not matter financially. When our divorce court system essentially punishes an innocent with huge legal bills for his or her spouse's criminal acts and perjury, the system is broken. Whoever came up with the concept of equal division of assets without considering the spouse's actions should be tarred and feathered. I do believe in the biblical principle of marriage, but the intertwining of this worldly legal system into marriage has corrupted what God intended. My parents used to believe divorce was never an option, but they changed their view after all the damage Jess did.

I can understand paying spousal support if there are children involved and one spouse had to give up a career to stay at home to take care of the kids, but when a spouse makes the conscious choice to stop working and be a lazy bum, that's different. The legal concept of maintaining the person's current lifestyle through spousal support is ridiculous. Any other lazy bum would be homeless, and it's only because the spouse hooked his or her claws into someone that he or she gets paid. No one should be allowed to continue to leech off a person for years. I can understand a very short duration of support, but paying for multiple years is ridiculous.

The main problem I had going through the divorce was the constant barrage of false statements Jess made to the court. I paid more than $33,000 in legal fees through all this. She constantly lied and bent the truth, and I had to defend myself. Nothing fair exists in the divorce court system, which doesn't punish someone like Jess for giving false statements but does punish me with exorbitant legal bills for defending myself. It would cost me more in attorney fees to file contempt motions than I'd get from any damages.

In the end, all Jess's motions and false statements accomplished nothing except lining the attorneys' pockets. Here is some advice: Never try to use the divorce court to get back at your soon-to-be ex. Emotions run high, and each party wants to hurt the other. But everyone loses when the court is used to lash out. The goal of divorce is to get it over with as quickly as possible, to get happiness back in your life, and to keep your money in your own pocket.

I understand the courts simply don't have the time to wade through all the issues someone like Jess creates, but a new system should be started that considers false statements made in court. I'd propose that a simple point system be implemented. When it's found that a person has committed malicious acts, lied, or violated court orders, that person would be assigned demerit points instead of having to go through formal hearings and wasting the court's time. When the divorce is granted, these points would have a monetary value that would be subtracted from the awarded portion of the estate of that person.

If this had happened to Jess and she had seen her portion of the equity of the home and 401(k) dwindling away, I guarantee she would have toned down or stopped her hateful behavior. Divorce courts do not properly examine cases like mine and do not administer justice to those wronged by a malicious spouse. They only split assets in half without considering any other circumstances. Divorce attorneys would surely fight any reform like this, as they all profit greatly off their clients' misery.

I'm not sure if I'll ever get married again, as I know how unfair the legal system is and what can be taken from you. If I do get married, there will be an ironclad prenuptial agreement to protect my assets. I even tell young people who are still single that marriage can be an incredibly fulfilling part of life but that you never know if something will happen to your spouse or if the spouse will go off the deep end. A prenup is an absolute necessity in today's legal system. It must be fair to each person to protect his or her assets. If I had one, I would include that any sexual infidelity would immediately end the marriage and that the cheating spouse would be kicked to the curb with nothing except what he or she brought into the marriage. I'm not sure if that's even possible, but I sure wish I'd had this with Jess.

Bringing up the idea of a prenup to the person you love is very difficult, but it must be done. I'd even take it a step farther and make prenups mandatory for all marriages. This would eliminate many problems in the divorce court system, but attorneys would fight this concept, as it would cut off their revenue stream from bickering clients.

Another issue that reared its ugly head was all the other people who were brought in to settle matters, such as our property distribution and her tax debt. The meeting with the property arbitrator, Gerald, was a disaster. Both Jess and I sent him Excel spreadsheets ahead of time listing what property we wanted, but the guy couldn't open a simple spreadsheet. He was supposed to review all the documents prior to the meeting, but he didn't inform us that he couldn't open our spreadsheets. That was an incredible level of gross incompetence. I had to hook up to his office network with my laptop and print out hard copies of our lists because he was incapable of performing this simple task. He caused many other issues that created a huge mess with distributing the property. He still got paid his full fee. If I had recorded the conversation during property arbitration, I could have proved what was said and saved close to $2,000 in additional legal costs cleaning up the mess.

When meeting with any mediator or arbitrator, always record the conversation for your own protection, just in case the spouse goes nuts and starts claiming things that are not true. Make sure everyone in the room knows you are recording. If people object, too bad. Stand firm and state that the meeting will not continue without being recorded so that everyone has a record of what transpired.

When Jess came over to pick up the last of the property the arbitrator had awarded her, I made the mistake of not setting everything outside and not preventing her from entering my house. I foolishly assumed that the police present at the civil standby would enforce the court order. Jess went into full-blown psycho mode and started taking things she was not awarded or had forfeited per the court order because she hadn't picked them up in time. She was also trying to alter the meaning of the words in her favor. The main word she tried to change the meaning of was *hardware*. She had been awarded half of the hardware, which included nuts, bolts, screws, and other similar items. She was arguing to the cop that *hardware* meant all the tools, woodworking clamps, and other large items.

The cop was getting extremely frustrated when I stood my ground and said no to her unreasonable demands, and then he accused us both of acting like children. Due to his frustration, he wanted me to compromise and give her what she was clearly not entitled to per the court order. He even forced me to give some of it up. It's a clear example of how someone acting crazy gets the upper hand even though it's not lawful, reasonable, or fair. If you divorce an out-of-control spouse, learn from my mistake: get all the property out, and never let the spouse into the house.

Jess didn't have enough room in the vehicles to get everything, so she was coming over again the next morning. After what had happened, I knew better than to let her in the house. I called my friend Alan, and he helped me move the rest of her stuff outside to my driveway. My dad also came over to help. One of Jess's friends helping her move arrived early. I told him that because of what had happened yesterday, no one would be allowed in my house, and I would have no contact with Jess. He nodded in agreement with my reasoning. Jess arrived and was livid at all the stuff outside, but she had no choice. Dad and I were watching the live video from my porch camera, and he burst out laughing at how she was acting. I thought again that I should have moved everything out before to prevent issues with her.

Ray and I discussed the property mess later on. He told me that in negotiations, a crazy person has the advantage over a rational person, because the rational person realizes the consequences of unreasonable requests, and the crazy person does not. The crazy person will list outrageous demands and not realize that those requests make him or her look unreasonable. All these unreasonable demands end up preventing rational discourse and distracting talks from getting to the heart of the issues. Any mediators involved eventually get frustrated and suggest that the rational person make compromises from his or her small but reasonable list of demands to accommodate the crazy person's huge list of demands. This was evident with the cops wanting me to submit to Jess's demands just so they could get out of the situation. You cannot win against a crazy person in a negotiation. The only thing you can do is isolate the person from all talks and thus render the person ineffective in order to minimize the damage the person can cause. Let such people rant and rave all they want and ignore them.

Another mistake I made was agreeing to go with a CPA the attorneys selected. We had to clear up the huge tax mess Jess created. The attorneys said the CPA was a good guy, which was true on a personal level, but he was an utter failure in dealing with the IRS. I give the guy credit for admitting he was not experienced in this, but he still kept my $1,000 retainer for services he failed at. I had to spend another $7,000 for another tax firm to clear up the tax mess.

These excessive costs were due to the wording of the divorce judgment. Our attorneys had written in the judgment that we had to use a tax attorney or CPA. What the attorneys didn't know was that there is another professional certification called an "enrolled agent," which solely deals with IRS tax resolution issues. Jess was being stubborn and demanding that the divorce judgment be followed word for word. That meant we couldn't use a cheaper but more knowledgeable enrolled agent because this was not included in the judgment. She didn't have to pay for the tax attorney, per the divorce judgment, so I was stuck with the cost of a high-priced tax attorney's firm because most CPAs don't deal with these types of IRS issues. Her knowing I would be stuck paying a high-priced tax attorney was the reason I suspected she wouldn't budge.

The problem with all these so-called experts is that even with such poor performance, they still get their money. It's not like having a carpenter mess up with physical evidence of a poorly made bookcase that fell apart. With physical evidence, you can refuse to pay or take the person to court to prove just how screwed-up the work was. With attorneys, arbitrators, or mediators, there is no physical evidence, and it's virtually impossible to prove how bad the representation was in order to get your money back. They always have their hands out demanding payment for their self-proclaimed exalted opinions. There is no measurable metric of quality similar to the work a carpenter can produce. They know this and use it to be paid.

Never, ever go solely on the recommendation of your attorney when a tax professional or any other specialist is required to clear up issues in a divorce. What I experienced is that the professionals I was referred to were friends of attorneys being thrown a bone. Almost all of them failed in some manner or didn't have the expertise required to clear up the issue. I had to investigate the new people's competency by vetting them myself and not relying on attorneys' opinions. You must investigate by using your network of friends to determine who has shown a demonstrated ability to be knowledgeable in their field. Also investigate the people's social media postings to get a feel for their level of professional abilities and sense of their character.

Shortly after the divorce was granted, I did a review of my finances and realized the harsh punishment I am being subjected to due to Jess's profiting from being a habitual liar. I have to delay my retirement an additional five years to make up for the loss of my 401(k), pension, and equity in my home. Evil behavior profits, and an innocent person has to bend over and take it. It makes one want to run out and escape society forever.

I watched a TV show about single people living by themselves out in the middle of nowhere, isolated from society. I understand this now and sympathize with their need to keep the hell away from people and the problems with society. I thought that I could take early retirement, move deep into the woods far away from civilization, and live a minimalistic lifestyle to avoid the pitfalls of relationships. After you go through so much pain, deception, betrayal, and abuse by the legal system, being alone, away from assholes, has a very strong appeal.

The other part of me knows that being alone is not right. We were created by God to give and receive love and need social interactions with others. We must help others with the gifts and talents we have been blessed with to achieve true happiness. Giving people unconditional love is how to achieve a real and fulfilling joy. Keeping away from society has a strong pull to those who have gone through great pain, but it ultimately leaves them lonely, unhappy, and unfulfilled.

One of the other emotional tolls of fighting all these false accusations, especially the PPO, was that I stopped going to church for a while. It was too painful to go. It was not a faith crisis, but when I was going through all this hell, my heart was torn apart, my family life was destroyed, and I found little happiness. When I went to church, I was surrounded by happy families with their children. It was a painful reminder of what had happened to me, and it felt like a knife going through my heart. Church didn't uplift me; it brought me down, so I stopped going.

I even deactivated my Facebook account for a while, after seeing many friends bragging about how wonderful their wives and families were. It cut to my core, and I didn't want to see any of this. I pretty much kept to myself during this time. Christmas and other holidays were especially tough. I didn't want to hear about families gathering together when I don't have a family of my own. I have my dad and sister, but that's not the same as having my own wife and children.

NINETEEN

TIPS FOR SINGLE MEN AND WOMEN
RUN AWAY FROM THE CRAZY

Throughout this ordeal, many people asked if I had noticed any signs of Jess's self-destructive behavior when we were dating or early in our marriage.

The reality is that when a man is deeply in love with a woman, this love blinds him to much that others see in her, especially what other women see in her. Women have same problem with men. I've seen female friends of mine dating a guy, and I can tell right away he's an ass. But she doesn't see it due to the infatuation. The dreaded love fog hides the reality of the other person's true nature.

I had this with Jess. Looking back now, it's hard to believe I didn't see warning signs and how bad she was in many areas, but my deep love for her blinded me to it. My sister commented that she never trusted Jess from the beginning. To my sister, something about Jess seemed off, and Jess tried too hard to make people like her. The affection she showered on others seemed shallow and fake to my sister. Other women said the same thing about not trusting Jess. The problem was that they said this to me only after I filed for divorce.

Jess was an exceptionally beautiful woman. In Jess's case, her beauty was a curse. She did not have the emotional strength or character to handle it. I've met other extremely beautiful women with issues similar to Jess's. Having great physical beauty as a child and into the rest of one's life can be a blessing or a curse.

Very beautiful people, both men and women, are always given more attention. It's not fair to others, but that's just how it is. Women get more attention due to their beauty from both men and women. However, attractive men don't typically get more attention from other men. Women like Jess get used to this extra attention; things are given to them, and they receive many other benefits in life simply due to physical beauty and not their character. With the continuous attention they receive starting as children, they begin to expect it, crave it, and develop a deep desire to be showered with praise throughout their lives.

Jess went out of her way to be syrupy sweet to fulfill this craving for praise. She was showering praise on others with the expectation that she would get it back from everyone. It was an unconscious pattern she had, and she didn't even realize what she was doing. Many times she made people very uncomfortable with this over-the-top behavior. When I met her, I simply thought she was one of the nicest people I had met, but I didn't realize what was really going on.

Women sure saw it though. Close female friends of mine saw it, but they didn't say a word to me. I wish they had, but I'm not sure I would have believed them. From now on, I plan on asking my closest friends, both male and female, for a completely honest opinion about a woman I'm interested in—even if I may not like their answer.

Early on, Jess showered me with this praise, and I gave it back to her. In the beginning of our marriage, it was simply amazing how much we gave to each other. When Jess showered this praise on others but didn't receive it back, she was deeply hurt and felt people didn't like her. She put herself into a depression many times, thinking something was wrong with her for not being praised. Her character was not strong enough for her to stand on her own and not care what others thought.

My thoughts now concerning exceptionally beautiful women like Jess will surely get under their skin and make them think, *Not me*. I've noticed that many beautiful women without strong characters have more issues than average-looking women. Average-looking women don't get showered with praise for shallow physical traits and don't typically develop this unhealthy extreme need for attention, praise, and acceptance.

When I see a beautiful woman now, I can't help but wonder if she has issues. I'm sure this mind-set is due to the horrific experience I went through, and it may subside in time. I'm overly cautious and suspicious for now.

I failed to look at Jess with a very critical eye that wondered about what would happen in the future. You must spend a lot of time dating a person before thinking about marrying him or her—a year minimum. This is to see that person in many different situations and gauge the way the person handles himself or herself emotionally. You have to see the person mad, upset, and unhappy, along with a whole host of other emotions. It's critical to see how the person handles and recovers from the curveballs of life and whether he or she can forgive and move on without holding a grudge due to pride.

From now on, I'll closely examine a woman to see if she exhibits any signs of mental instability or patterns of self-destructive behavior and to see if she can truly forgive others. I won't even consider getting involved with a woman if she is taking Vicodin, Prozac, Adderall, or other similar drugs. If a woman has ongoing depression issues, that's a deal breaker. Been there, done that—never again. I've even joked with friends that I need to train Diva to sniff out Prozac and narcotics. I'll also see if ongoing mental issues run in the woman's family. If her mother has them, there's a chance the daughter will, too. Jess's mother had many control and pride issues similar to Jess's. This overly cautious attitude of mine probably seems extreme, and it may subside in time when I heal from all this emotional turmoil.

One of the great frustrations I had in dealing with Jess's issues was watching her incredibly self-destructive behaviors. Her stubbornness prevented her from following through with doctors' treatment plans. Trying to deal with an adult acting this way is very different from dealing with a child who acts up. When a child acts up, you tell the child what is right, and if he or she doesn't straighten out, the child is punished.

This can't be done with an independent adult. You can't send adults to their room, take their privileges away, or ground them when they habitually lie and refuse to do the right thing. I believe part of Jess knew what she had to do, but her own incredible stubbornness, pride, and refusal to change her ways created all her problems. Jess didn't want to change; she wanted the world changed to accommodate her lifestyle, and her self-destructive problems only ramped up. She was her own worst enemy.

If you see a person with serious unresolved issues that have gone on for a long time, run away—don't even consider getting into a romantic relationship. That person has not taken and will not take the steps required to get his or her life in order. If the person is older, those issues are firmly ingrained, and you have to accept that the issues will not go away. You will not be able to do anything about it or fix the person. There is a very small chance that the person will turn over a new leaf and get his or her life straightened out, but the severe financial, emotional, and legal harm the person can bring upon your family is not worth the slim chance that he or she will change. I really hoped Jess would straighten out, but she didn't. I have heard many other horror stories from people who also had to deal with a spouse with many unresolved issues.

Jess's depression issues added to the problems we had. The love guilt she tried on me was a common theme. I could never do enough to prove my love for her. No matter what I did, in her mind, I didn't outwardly show her enough that I wanted to be with her. This morphed into jealousy, and Jess had a hard time if I interacted with other women at work or social gatherings. This lack of love she accused me of expanded into her trying to control me. If I wanted to try a new hobby or activity, she interpreted this as a way for me to keep away from her. I tried to get her involved in new activities, but because she was so unhappy, all she wanted to do was to sit around the house. I refused to follow her path in life, so she lashed out at me, saying I didn't love her enough to stay with her and be happy at home.

Jess began to view my family as a threat and tried to keep me isolated from them. She did not want to go to family traditions, such as Thanksgiving or Christmas, and then she tried to put a guilt trip on me for abandoning her if I left to be with the family. She justified not wanting to go to family functions by claiming someone had insulted or didn't like her. She claimed I didn't love her if I left to be with my family.

With me being one of the few positive influences in her life, the times we had marital problems sent her into a deep tailspin, spiraling further into sadness and depression. Her reaction was to lash out at me and accuse me of causing all her problems. I spoke to others who have dealt with spouses or girlfriends with depression issues, and their stories are very similar to mine. People with depression issues must make a conscious choice to confront their depression and change how they live their lives to get better. Jess would not confront her issues, because her victim mentality led her to blame others for her problems.

One of the ripple effects this situation with Jess had was a negative effect on my career. Dealing with her issues really took me down at times, and I was not as productive as I should have been. To make matters worse, Jess became friends with the wife of one of our directors at work. She was Thai, like Jess. Jess and I were at their home several times socializing, but as Jess's behavior became more erratic, the director's wife wanted nothing more to do with her. She called Jess crazy.

When I tried to salvage our marriage and help Jess get her issues resolved, I was viewed as weak and indecisive for not stopping her and not taking charge of the situation. The thing is, I couldn't do anything short of divorcing Jess. I was dealing with a grown adult who made all her own decisions, and Jess did what she pleased. She was unstoppable. Jess continued to cause all these problems, destroy friendships, and hurt my career until I had no choice but to get her out of my life before she destroyed it. When I'd had enough and told her to shut the hell up about wanting to sue my sister, I was thrown in jail on bogus charges.

Run away from the crazy. Trust me on this.

TWENTY

What Attracts Us to the Opposite Sex

During all the time with Jess, I learned an incredible amount about social dynamics between the sexes. Men and women both do equally stupid things when dating a person who is wrong for them. Both sexes are led astray by primal, sexual attractions to the types who seem to always cause harm. We have almost all seen a friend constantly hooking up with the wrong type over and over again, and the friend doesn't learn. With men it can be the hot but overly dramatic, needy woman. It's incredible how a woman's beauty can warp a man's mind and have him completely disregard all her destructive personality traits. With women, it's the bad boy who brings drama and problems into her life. I've known a couple of highly intelligent, caring women who habitually went out with assholes. Years ago, when I was single, a couple of my male friends knew one woman in particular who dated jerks, and we just shook our heads in amazement, wondering why. This woman and her consistent bad choices made her undatable to us all.

She did this due to primal reasons. She saw a very sexually desirable masculinity, just as a man sees extreme beauty or femininity that is sexually desirable. Both men and women allow their primal desires to be the first priority, not considering the depth of the other's character.

Years ago I was in a discussion about sexuality and being a Christian. Leo was leading this discussion before he went to seminary. He made a very profound statement that has proved itself over and over again to be true: "Having sex with someone outside of marriage can create a bond that is not meant to be." I've seen this happen many times with people, and it is applicable to everyone. If the man or woman dating an idiot kept his or her pants on and strived to learn about the other's true nature and the couple's compatibility, the man or woman probably would not fall in love and fall into problems.

Dating should not be about getting sex. It should be about finding that person you are compatible with, and it takes getting to know many people, especially when you are young. There is another aspect about dating that is extremely important. Along with finding someone you are compatible with, casually dating many people will also give you an idea of what habits or types of people get on your nerves. It's a process of discovering your own personality traits and learning the traits you can and can't accept in another person. Some may view your personality quirks as cute, but you must be able to discern if these quirks will eventually grate on their nerves also.

What I write next may be very controversial for some, and I'm sure many women will strongly disagree.

While helping my wife in her bridal shop, I noticed certain behaviors of women I wished I had known as a younger man. In my teens and twenties, I'd always had problems with women. I had a very inactive and frustrating dating life, due to my being in the perpetual nice-guy trap.

I saw in Jess's shop that young women, especially teenage girls, are very conscious of where they are in their social circle of other women. In most of their circles, there are the pretty popular ones at the top and the ones who hang around them because association with the top ones elevates their own popularity. Even within the below-average-looking social grouping, there is one woman at the top of the pecking order. All these women want to break into the higher social circles of popularity. There are exceptions to this, but it's rare.

For a guy to be datable and effective with one of these women, he must present himself as a partner who will elevate her status in the social circles. The coolness factor brought by wealth and power is way up there. This is why many physically beautiful women end up with socially popular but physically unattractive men. Rock stars and business titans are great examples of this.

Because most men don't have this extreme wealth and power, they must devise ways to present themselves as popular, fun people women will be glad to show off to their friends. The insecure male or typical nice guy will not be effective with women. Even though the guy could be the best thing for her and treat her like a queen, a woman will view him as wishy-washy and ignore or eventually dump him. This type of guy does absolutely nothing for her social status.

What I noticed in the store is that women do not primarily dress up and put on makeup to look good for men. Sure, they want to look desirable to males, but it is not the driving factor. Women dress up to look fashionable, get the praise of other women, and move higher in their social pecking order. The more popular the designer label and the higher the price tag, the better. The dress could look worse than a lesser label, but that matters little. Many Hollywood female celebrities prance down the red carpet in horrendous looking outfits. They believe it when the popular designer tells them a certain dress would make them look fantastic. In reality, it makes the woman in question look silly, except to other women who want to wear this latest fashion. To be fair, this is only my opinion.

I saw many mothers come into the store to get their daughters extremely revealing prom dresses. It was shocking that a mother would put her sixteen-year-old daughter in a dress that exposed as much skin as possible. The mother was not dressing her daughter to look good to the boys; she was dressing her to look better and more womanly than the other mothers' daughters. A pretty and popular daughter also elevates the mother's social status. Unfortunately the mother is too caught up in improving the daughter's social popularity by making her look like a sexy woman without realizing that in reality she is making her daughter look like a tramp.

On multiple occasions, I witnessed mothers telling their daughters they would not show the chosen dresses to the girls' dads. Sometimes they bought another modest dress for the father's approval, while hiding the real dress the daughter would wear. In their quest to improve their and their daughters' social status and make the girls look womanly, these insecure adult women resorted to lying to their husbands. This was very disturbing and unacceptable behavior to me as a husband.

Another revelation I had when watching the guys' tuxedos being selected is that young and insecure women view a man and his clothes as only an accessory to make them more fashionable and popular to other women. Many of the girls were selecting the style and color of the tuxedos solely to match their dresses. The guys were clueless about what was really going on. They thought the girls were helping to make them look better.

If you are looking for a fulfilling long-term relationship, run away from these types of insecure, self-centered women (or men) with this I-want-to-be-popular mentality. Some grow out of it. But some will never change, and they will make you miserable in the long run. Jess had this wanting-to-be-popular mentality.

A good woman who is secure in her own self-worth does not want a silly boy overly concerned about fashion trends. She wants a secure man; however, don't get in the trap of wearing extremely stupid clothing. No woman wants that. If you are a guy, ditch the pants-hanging-off-the-ass look, trendy tattoos, or over-the-top fashion. All men must realize that women do not view your clothes the way you do. If a man is wearing a *Star Wars* or Dungeons and Dragons costume as his social media profile picture, he is doomed. If you are friends with a woman, ask her to go shopping with you. You are probably clueless as to what women think looks good on you, because you are looking at it from a skewed male perspective. Don't fight her when she wants to put you in something that you think looks kind of weird; however, there is a line that no self-respecting male should cross.

I had a pink shirt that Jess really wanted me to wear when we were out together, but I didn't like the way it looked. Women always complimented me on how it looked, far more when I was with Jess than when I wore it by myself. It was amazing how Jess beamed when other women complimented my clothing. It was another huge ego boost to her when I told others that she had got the shirt for me and knew how to match my clothing to complement hers. This was not a reflection on my fashion sense; it was a reflection on Jess's status with other women.

Constant drama between the girls in the store was another behavior. When I worked in the backroom of the store, I heard girls talk to one another about drama in their lives. It was a very bizarre interaction. They said they wanted stress-free lives and complained about problems, but their own actions repeatedly sabotaged their own contentment. The unconscious need for drama and chaos in their lives ruled over sensible behavior that would bring contentment. The girl with the most dramatic stories in the pack was the center of attention, while the other ones telling stories with little or no drama were ignored. They quickly learned to up the drama to get closer to the center of attention.

Some girls even worked against the others' contentment. When they saw another girl who was really happy with her life, jealousy erupted, and they would cut down that happy girl behind her back. It seemed to me that true contentment wasn't the ultimate goal in their lives; talking about drama seemed to be the real objective with these teenagers.

After seeing this drama unfolding and how it held their interest, I conducted a little devious experiment. Women I met were told stories of happiness and fun, but they were also told stories of drama and conflicts between others. Drama always drew the women to me far more. The raw interest in their eyes as they listened to drama was far more appealing to them…as long as it wasn't my drama. After all, confident men who are attractive to women are above this petty nonsense in their lives. Combining stories of confidence and contentment in my life while describing other people's drama always made for the best conversations. It also got the most interest from women.

I remember one time when Jess and I were talking to an acquaintance of ours, Jake, and listening to him complain how he could not get a date. He had plenty of female friends, but he was always sent down into the friend zone. Jess went into the routine of how Jake had to be nice, be himself, and tell women they look pretty, as well as all the other typical advice a woman will say to a desperate nice guy. All the things Jess and other women told him to do were what he was doing, and these behaviors were the main reason he could not get a date. Women viewed Jake as submissive and weak; they had no attraction to him, and women instantly friend zoned him. I used to be the guy who was instantly friend zoned, so I knew exactly what Jake's problem was: he needed to stop following women's advice about how to act.

I spoke up. I told Jake women didn't view him as desirable. He appeared to be only a nice guy with no confidence, who lacked a take-charge attitude. I looked straight at him and said, "If you see a woman you would like to ask out, you must take charge and be confident. Have the attitude that she must earn the pleasure of being in your company, not the other way around." I also told him to scrub all his social media accounts of role-playing games and remove the profile pictures of him in *Star Wars* costumes. He had to eliminate anything that screamed "immature nerd" and replace it with something women found exciting.

Jess was shocked. She told Jake my advice would never work. I looked at her and thought, *That's how I got you.* Jess spoke again, reinforcing her idea about how Jake should act. Unfortunately for Jake, here was an incredibly beautiful and sexy woman telling him he had to be the ultimate nice and submissive geeky guy, so he was being encouraged to stay in this pattern of utter failure. Jake was clearly desperate, and women seemed to be able to detect this desperation a mile away. They will avoid men displaying this desperation, as it is one of the worst personality traits a man can have.

I sent Jake a message the next day for us to get together, but the damage had already been done. In his eyes, there was no way a short, balding, nerdy-looking guy could give him better advice about how to improve his dating life than a smoking-hot woman could.

Physical attractiveness in a male has some benefit, but it is not the deciding factor. Men are far more visual than women, and that also leads them into picking the wrong woman. Many a man will chase the hot bimbo but overlook a plain woman who could potentially make happy for the rest of his life. The exception to male attractiveness is in online dating. Many women window-shop for the physically attractive guy.

The problem is that many times both men and women are attracted to the wrong type, and that gets them into trouble. Women get tangled up with aggressive bad boys, and men get involved with shallow beautiful girls. They don't learn from previous mistakes, and both sexes continue to make bad choices in their romantic lives, which continuously create problems in their lives. I've seen it over and over again, with men and women being equally foolish about whom they date.

The problem Jess and many other immature or insecure women have is that they are not honest with themselves about what attracts them to a man. They talk among themselves about how they want a nice guy, but they ignore the fact they have a primal sexual attraction to the bad boy. Because women can't admit this, they continually choose the wrong type over a good man. They were raised to want a Prince Charming, but if he's not a confident alpha male swinging a sword and striking down his enemies, he won't be considered desirable as a man.

Many nice men are clueless about this behavior and get frustrated when they see women hanging around and sleeping with dirtbags. Bottom line: Don't listen to women's advice to be attractive to the opposite sex by being a nice guy. It doesn't work. I've heard many female friends complain that they want a nice guy who won't cause issues, but they ultimately ignore and friend zone the nice guy while choosing the jerk instead. It's the do-as-I-say, not-as-I-do behavior that a man must be aware of.

As I wrote this book, I saw an episode of *The Late Late Show with James Corden* on YouTube, and he was doing a skit called "Carpool Karaoke" with a guest, Carrie Underwood. James asked Carrie if she got worried when her husband, a pro hockey player, got into a fight.

Carrie smiled and said, "Have you seen his latest fight? He knocked a guy's tooth out."

James covered his mouth in shock and exclaimed, "Oh my god!"

Carrie smiled again and said, "It was pretty hot."

It was refreshing to see a woman be honest.

When I saw this, I could not help but remember what Jess had told Jake. Jess could not admit that a masculine alpha male dominating another man was sexy to her. There is nothing wrong with being very masculine, but aggressive males without empathy are just assholes. There must be a balance of confidence and aggressiveness while demonstrating the ability to show and give deep kindness and empathy.

TWENTY-ONE

Protecting Your Assets from a Business

Dealing with the financial aftermath of Jess's store has been horrific. Even though she formed Formal Diva as a limited liability corporation, this did not shield my assets from many of her debts. If a spouse wants to start a business, you must protect your family's assets just in case the business goes under. I had no intention of getting divorced when Jess started this business, but I should have done a few things to protect myself even if I had stayed in the marriage.

1. Do not put your name as jointly owning your spouse's LLC. By keeping your name off, you are shielded from potential problems if bankruptcy or frivolous lawsuits happen. You may be sued but can't be held responsible, and your joint personal assets are protected. My name was not on the LLC even though Jess wanted me on it. She tried to persuade me by stating that this was our business, not just hers, but I stood fast and refused.

2. Get the home mortgage in the name of the spouse who is not on the LLC. Joint marital assets are normally not collectible from judgments, but they will try if the spouse's name is on the mortgage. You will waste a lot of time and money fighting this. The IRS and state treasury will put a lien on your home if the spouse's

name is on the deed or mortgage. They may even put a lien on your home if the spouse's name is not on the deed, but this lien is easily removed. The IRS will do as they please and break the law to get their tax revenue. It's up to you to set things up correctly so you can take them to court and force them to obey the law.

3. Consider putting all your personal assets in a trust. This adds another layer of protection from the business for all your family's assets.
4. Never have any company credit cards issued in your name. Have cards issued only in the LLC holder's name, and don't get secondary cards issued in your name. It may be convenient to have a card in the short term, but if something goes wrong, the long-term damage far outweighs the convenience. It does not matter if the spouse declares bankruptcy for the LLC; you may be sued by creditors for any debt if your name is on a card. They probably won't win in court, but it will cost at least $3,000 in legal bills plus all the time and hassle you'll spend to take care of this. It happened to me. The creditors will also put any missed payments or debts on your credit report, and cleaning that up will cause great frustration.
5. Never mix personal spending with the company credit cards. If a creditor can prove you used company funds for personal goods, this opens the door for debt collection on personal assets and court judgments from frivolous lawsuits.
6. The company needs to be set up in all business dealings to demonstrate to the court that you have no involvement. Again, this is to protect your family's personal assets if some lowlife sues. Just remember, people can sue the business for whatever they want, and many scum-sucking attorneys make a sleazy living from doing this. Their claims in the lawsuit may be completely false, but you will still have to pay legal fees to fight it. Separate yourself as much as possible to eliminate potential problems.
7. If the business is having financial problems, take your spouse off any joint bank accounts. The spouse must open accounts in his or her name only. This will be a hassle, but now you and your family's personal assets will be protected from future levies.

8. Do not file joint tax returns combining your personal taxes with business taxes. If something happens with the business falling behind on federal or state taxes, both people on the combined return may be responsible for the tax debt. The government can get a levy on your personal bank accounts and will withdraw everything. Whoever is named on the LLC should file separate business returns.

    CPAs will tell you that, as a couple, losses from the spouse's business will give you a greater joint refund, because they subtract losses from your income, but this sets you up for being responsible for future tax and business debts with a bankruptcy or divorce. It doesn't matter if tax returns are filed individually later. What matters is whether the returns were filed jointly while the business was in operation and whether it can be shown that you profited from the business loss. I was stuck with half of Jess's $74,000 tax debt because I'd filed my returns jointly with our business. I also had liens put on my home. The CPA never told us the future implications of filing jointly.
9. Do not use a CPA for preparing your business taxes. Use an enrolled agent. CPAs don't know all the tax strategies. Enrolled agents do—especially one who is an ex-IRS agent.

TWENTY-TWO

CONCLUSION

I had no plans to write a book about all my experiences with Jess. I didn't decide to do this until a couple of close friends told me this was one of the most freakish and horrific tales of divorce they had ever heard of. They said it would make a great story to tell others to warn them what could happen if they married the wrong person. One person said he would buy multiple copies and give it to all the single people he knew to show that the living hell I experienced could happen to them.

There is also a second reason I wrote this. The repercussions of the financial devastation Jess caused are huge. I was on track to retire at sixty, but that's not an option now. It will be sixty-four at the earliest. Even at sixty-four, I will be worse off than I would have been with my original plan, but at least I can be comfortable. It would be incredible if book sales took off and I could retire as I had planned. Another friend said this story would be well suited for a TV miniseries on the Lifetime network. I laughed at this saying if someone told me fifteen years ago that my life story could be on Lifetime—that would be absurd. Maybe this could be a series or movie on Netflix. Who knows?

As I wrote down all the events from the fifteen years of marriage in this book, I was amazed at how much damage Jess had done over the years, and I felt like a fool for staying with her for so long. There are instances of the words *bitch* and *psycho* in this book, but some were not referring to Jess. The number of these words is not that bad considering all the malicious things Jess did to me.

I only think of her as a "psycho bitch" due to all the horrific and bizarre things she did to me, and I am not implying that as a medical diagnosis or trying to defame her character. It's only my subjective opinion. Her friends may think of her as the sweetest person in the world, but my family and friends, who know the whole story, do not. The same subjective opinion applies to all my other thoughts about her or others mentioned in this book including, but not limited to, mental instability or being a pathological liar.

These instances of *bitch* and *psycho* were a lot more frequent before close friends and family read early manuscripts. Some told me that many of the things I had written were very anti-female. I started writing this book during the divorce, and many times, I was very pissed off when I put the words down. After the divorce was finalized and I had time to get back into a better mood, I saw that they were right. There were some very harsh words aimed at all women in general, due to my bitterness.

One friend told me she would like to read a very early version of this book, from before I had edited out much of the angry and harsh content. She wanted to see what "angry Chuck" was like, because she had never known me that way. I laughed and said all those early manuscripts were destroyed forever, never to be seen again.

With all the hell I went through during our marriage, people will think, *Why would anyone stay with her so long?* There were so many bad times, but in between, there were scattered good times, which renewed my hope for a good marriage. Jess had many highs and lows, but the highs were incredible with her. It was almost like crack to an addict. The passion she showed me when she was happy was mind blowing, but the lows were really, really bad.

Dealing with her issues and mood extremes became a normal but screwed-up way of living, and the good times became less frequent. I was living with hope that our marriage would get better and not with the brutal reality of what she was doing and how she was not going to change.

Her increasingly bizarre behavior also crept up slowly. It wasn't like it happened all at once.

This type of incremental behavior is something I'll keep a close eye on in the future. It reached a point where my friends wanted nothing to do with her. They stopped inviting me over because they did not want to disinvite my wife. All hope for the marriage was extinguished with the Kansas incident, and my resolve to divorce her was solidified when I was jailed because of her wild accusations of domestic violence. I took my marriage vows very seriously. But I had to get out, or she would have destroyed my life. A marriage can't survive if only one spouse is honoring the vows.

Other people told me that writing all this down must have been a cathartic experience for reflection or a way to come to terms with what happened to me. It really wasn't. I had already dealt with all that had happened and had been able to forgive. There was no need to rethink all the events.

Writing this book really took me out of my comfort zone. I'm an engineer, not an artsy author. The types of writing I do are engineering reports, analyses of CAD data, design alternative matrices, PowerPoint presentations, and interpretation of design validation test data. It's a very logical and data-driven form of writing, where I give engineering recommendations based on analysis and facts. Writing a book with a flowing story line full of accurate emotional content was a completely new concept and very difficult for me. I don't have the writing style or artistic flair to paint a detailed emotional picture with words. Good writers have this talent, but not me. In my world, accurate time lines and data are of great importance, but conveying feelings with words are not.

Having a diary I started after my arrest and all the past notes of her behavior was an invaluable resource to get the time line straight as best I could. A friend reviewed my manuscript and made the comment that he could tell an engineer had written it, because it was very detailed and full of facts with a precise time line. He also said that half the facts could be removed and replaced with the filler or fluff that many other books contain in order to make it more readable to the general public. If this book does take off in sales, I expect literary critics to tear me a new one for lack of style. Oh well...their opinion doesn't matter to me. I didn't write this to please those whose lifeblood is ripping on people and complaining.

I originally had a very different opening sentence from "I still remember the day I met Jess. (This is not her real name, which I'm hiding to protect her identity.)" My initial anger at all she had done caused me to put in a very harsh name, but it started the book with a very negative tone.

I went to extreme lengths and took great care to change the names of her family, friends, dog, business, and previous workplaces to ensure her privacy. I also changed other names and family locations to ensure people could not make the connection with her. Jess can go on living her life with new friends and the public not knowing that this is her in my book. If she reads this book, I'm sure she will deny almost everything that casts her in a bad light, and she may accuse me of causing all the issues, just as she has done in the past.

Close to finishing this book, I was talking with Chris Bailey, and we chatted about some of the malicious things Jess had done. Chris said, "Be thankful she didn't cut your dick off!"

We laughed at that, and I replied, "I'd have had to change my nickname to Stubby or Shorty." We had a good laugh over that, too.

Chris also laughed, saying I should send Jess an autographed copy of my book. I laughed, but I would never do that. My intentions and motives for writing this book are not to hurt her or be malicious to her. I have no desire for revenge or shaming and am not trying to defame her character. This is why I'm not using her real name so her identity won't be exposed to the public. I really do want Jess to be happy and I don't want her privacy invaded or the public to think badly of her. People who knew and cared about Jess are still around, and I wonder how they would react if they knew my side of all these events. I'm sure Jess convinced some of them I was an abusive monster.

I've been true to my own emotions and memories as I wrote about these experiences, but also acknowledge that others, including Jess, may remember things differently. I've recalled all these events to the best of my knowledge. This book is not an instrument of revenge and I hope other people that have experienced horrible events may get some hope or shape meaning in their lives by reading this. I also hope that by reading this, people will make better choices with those they date and will think twice before getting married without thoroughly vetting out the other person. Everyone should be aware what can happen in today's screwed-up legal system if they end up with the wrong person.

Some of the statements people made to me when I was dealing with the DV charges and my mother's death all at once were, "What doesn't kill you makes you stronger," "It will get better," and "Time heals all wounds." Some told stories of their own tragedies or other people's problems and the way they'd dealt with these and recovered. Here's a hint: Don't *ever* say these moronic mantras to someone who is hurting. It doesn't help. I cut many people off midsentence and told them I didn't want to hear it. Some wouldn't stop, feeling that their self-proclaimed words of wisdom would help. I sternly told them to tell it to someone else. The last things I wanted to hear were stupid clichés or more stories of tragedy. I had enough problems and didn't want to hear more tales of emotional pain.

The song "Stronger" by Kelly Clarkston has popularized the incredibly shallow statement, "What does not kill you makes you stronger." This has been a plague on society, with thousands of people repeating this statement out of pure foolishness. Many horrific tragedies people have experienced in their lives leave lifelong scars. The pain does subside in time, but it is always there.

I still remember when my mother was in the hospital. During the last day of her life, we all knew Mom was gone and only her body was clinging on. Her body was in pure reflex mode, and she jerked violently with every labored breath she took. My father stayed by her side until the very end. This image of her body jerking with every breath haunted me for a long time. I can't imagine how it affected my father. Horrible events like this don't make you stronger, and people who repeat shallow statements like this have no idea of the pain they add to what someone is going through.

Another statement some made to me when I was in the middle of fighting the DV charge was "The truth shall set you free." They were trying to assure me the charges would be dropped because they were not true. This statement is true in a spiritual sense of freeing up your conscience and eliminating guilt, but it does not work in the legal system. Bad things will happen when you are thrust in the middle of an imperfect legal system and a crazy person is making horrific false accusations about you. If you go into a courtroom expecting that the truth will set you free, you will lose.

In Jess's case, she told all these accusations to the police with incredibly compelling emotion. Jess believed many of her own lies, and that's what made them so compelling. The only thing that matters in the court system is being able to present evidence that proves what the truth is. With no evidence, truth does not matter in the legal system, and the best and most compelling liar will win, unless you have a good attorney who uses guile and tactics to win.

The best thing someone can do is be there for his or her friend. Let the friend vent and express anger and frustration without offering any solutions or trying to fix the problem. Bring your friend some meals, or take the person out to eat so he or she doesn't have to cook. I had a couple of close friends take me out for breakfast or dinner, and that was great.

One of the emotional hang-ups many men, including myself, have is not wanting to appear weak in front of people and ask for help. Don't ask your friend if he or she wants to talk. Tell that person, "Let's go out and get a bite to eat." That way, the friend can open up without having to express the need to talk. Don't offer to go out for a drink. I had to cut out alcohol for a while; it was really having a negative effect on my mood. Even one drink would take my mood down. Throughout this ordeal, I was very blessed to have close friendships with a select group of people I completely trust. Their love and support were a great help in getting me a faster recovery through this.

Having a regular workout routine at the gym and staying physically fit was incredibly helpful with keeping a positive attitude throughout all these troubles. I can't stress enough for others going through tough times the importance of getting off the couch and getting the endorphins flowing with exercise. It's tough at times, and there were many days I didn't want to go, but I forced myself to work out. I did slack off for a short time, and I could tell my attitude took a turn for the worse. Going to a very nice gym like the fitness center at Washtenaw Community College was essential for my well-being, keeping both my physical and mental health in shape that enabled me to emotionally deal with the severe stress.

I'm at the point now where I can joke about much that happened. I regularly meet on Mondays with a group of men from the new church I attend, St. Luke, in Ann Arbor. We call this group "Theologizing." It's just men and some of the pastors getting together and just being guys. We don't focus on only deep theological discussions; we also have fun...and some scotch or bourbon. In late March 2016, close to April Fool's Day, I made an announcement to everyone: "I have some great news! Jess and I have reconciled, and we are getting back together!" The stunned faces were hilarious. I saw pure shock, and the looks they gave me said, "What the hell are you thinking?" They know much of the events and hell Jess put me through. When I told them, "No, just joking," there was a collective sigh and a huge look of relief in the room. It was very funny. Being able to meet with a group of like-minded people who provided counsel and focused on the great blessings we have in life brought out the best in me and kept me from feeling sorry for myself.

During the DV charge and divorce, my good friends stood by me, but those who had latched on to me due to Jess's beauty were the first to leave. The situation was no longer fun for them, and they ran. Even a few people we knew from church bolted. Instead of honor and integrity being a priority, it was no longer in their best social interest to be associated with me. Because I'm an introvert and can have a hard time meeting new people, I enjoyed the popularity Jess brought into my life, but when those new people ran, it stung. I should have known better. I won't make the mistake of letting those types be a part of my life again.

My existing friendships deepened during this ordeal, and I was blessed to develop many new ones. In stark contrast, Jess sent me an e-mail in May 2017, a year after the divorce was finalized, containing the sentence "Because the length of divorce, I lost all my friends just to focus on how to get things done." When I read this, I thought that she hadn't lost her friends because of the divorce; she'd lost them through her own actions. She'd had all the time in the world to work on this divorce. I had a full-time job and got the divorce issues taken care of, wrote this book, and still developed many new, wonderful friendships.

In a way, I feel sorry for her. She can't forgive others or herself, and as Ray said, her victim mentality is so ingrained that she will probably never change. She eventually drives people away from her. There are parts of her personality that are still very beautiful, but based on her past behavior, she can't recognize the blessings and incredible gifts she has and achieve true joy in her life. I hope she finds contentment someday and develops deep and long lasting friendships. Maybe she can find someone to love her and get the type of support she could not get from me.

Her saying she lost all her friends was partly due to the fact she wanted to elicit pity while trying to extort a $15,000 loan from me. Of course I refused to loan her the money, but she was relentless in her attempts and telling tales of woe and misery. She will get no pity from me. Whenever she uses this tactic, I think how weak and pathetic this is, just like all others who desire pity. There is a huge difference between pity and the need for support and love, but it seems that Jess can't distinguish between the two.

She even tried using the fact that I had offered to give her $10,000 to replace her car during May 2015 while the divorce was in process. She was trying to manipulate facts to prove that this old $10,000 offer was still valid, but it was not. In a July 2017 e-mail to me and my attorney about the $10,000, she wrote, "I still need the money to purchase a car. Charles promised to give me $10,000." It's another manipulation of the facts with her trying to fabricate a lie to make it sound as though this is recent, but that deal ended a long time ago. As I stated before, these attempts to get a loan from me occurred at the same time she had to pay back the social security funds she'd taken.

To be fair, her $74,000 tax debt is still not resolved, and she cannot receive any equity in my home or get her marital portion of my 401(k) until this is done. The offer in compromise from the IRS and Michigan treasury probably won't be completed until the middle of 2018. She has to be hurting for cash, but she owns more than $200,000 worth of real estate in Thailand that she refuses to sell. If she sold it, her cash-flow problems would go away, but she tries to take from me instead. This situation with her demanding loans is only one of many other convoluted stories to tell later. Tales of the crazy never end with Jess.

Another weird situation people commented on was how much Jess's niece, Phonphan, looks like her. They said Phonphan looks like she could be Jess's daughter. This really got me thinking. I saw pictures of Jess when she was close to the same age as Phonphan and marveled at how strong the resemblance was. Phonphan's mom, Kanya, didn't look like Phonphan at all.

Then I started thinking about this. I recalled all the unresolved guilt Jess had and wondered if there was any old emotional scarring she had hidden from me that she couldn't come to terms with. I remembered the stretch marks and loose belly skin Jess had. In my opinion, over all the time we were married, Jess never got big enough, even with her twenty- to thirty-pound weight gain to cause these types of marks. Early in our marriage, Jess hid damage to her reproductive system from me, and she never told me what had really happened to cause this. Could Phonphan be Jess's biological daughter? One friend of mine told me he had this suspicion also.

Phonphan had many troubled events throughout the years, and her behavior was remarkably similar to Jess's. I also recalled the extreme pride Jess's mother, Suda, had and thought there was no way Suda would allow one of her daughters to be a single mom in Thailand. That was very frowned on in their culture and would be an insult to their family's reputation. Could Kanya have raised Phonphan as her own, with their family keeping this secret hidden? Could Phonphan know or suspect that Jess is her biological mother?

Early in our marriage, Jess tried to adopt Phonphan and bring her over from Thailand for us to raise as our own, but the government red tape prevented us from getting this done. Jess always wanted Phonphan to call her "Mommy-Aunty." I know that Phonphan being Jess's daughter is pure conjecture on my part, and I may be way off. But all this circumstantial information looked at from one perspective raises many questions, and I may never learn the real answer. There have been so many lies from Jess to hide her past actions and keep her pride intact that I believe this may be possible.

It took a while to get over the hurt and bitterness I experienced during all this time dealing with Jess. The hurt wasn't from not having Jess in my life anymore; I had lost all love for her a long time ago, and it was wonderful to have her gone. The hurt was due to having to defend myself from the onslaught of her false accusations and the abuses the legal system heaped on me. It took more than six months after the divorce before I was able to trust people again and start going to church without a feeling of loss. I finished this book close to a year and a half after the divorce was finalized.

I am single now and have many wonderful blessings in my life, but there is a hole in my heart. I miss having a family life and coming home to a woman to share our lives and love each other.

Before I met Jess, I had a happy and full life, but it didn't feel complete. Even when I was at my happiest and doing what I loved, there was something missing. When I first married Jess, having that deep love and intimate connection only added to the thrill of life. With Jess, I was complete and truly happy. I hope I can find that again with someone who won't go psycho.

When I was younger, there were many eligible single women available. Now that I'm in my fifties, many of the good ones are taken. Some women in my age group are single for very good reasons. They are unhappy and chronic complainers. I'm very thankful for the blessings I have in my life, but many people can't stop having a negative attitude. I also look at many of them close to my age and see women who have completely stopped taking care of their physical health. That's harsh and may offend some, but it's reality. There is no way I would ever get romantically involved with these types. I'm very physically active, and someone who is a sedentary couch potato with destructive personal habits is not compatible with my lifestyle. (And to be fair, many men my age have also let themselves go.)

A few months ago, I went out with a large group of people for dinner, but it wasn't very enjoyable. There were about ten women there, and they had no issues hurling out F-bombs as part of normal conversation. One woman started in on how she was proud of the fact that she'd been able to take her ex for more than she was entitled to. That didn't sit too well with me, but I kept my mouth shut instead of telling her what I felt about her attitude.

Immediately after the divorce, I didn't date much, not wanting to open up and expose my heart to being hurt again. I went out on a few dates only because I was single again, but that was a big mistake, and those dates didn't go well. I couldn't open myself up emotionally and had a lot of suspicions. I was excessively defensive and didn't feel any physical attraction. Deep down, I still had some lingering contempt for women. After I got home from one date, I realized the woman had to think I was an ass due to my conduct. I was open to casual friendships and talking with new people, but my defenses were built up to prevent anyone from getting too close. It was too soon to start dating after the divorce, and it took more than six months to get my head straight.

Once I had accomplished that, I reengaged in the dating world, but doing so made me feel like an aberration in society with my conservative Christian beliefs. These beliefs and values greatly narrowed the field for finding someone I'm compatible with. Most of the women I met did not mesh with my personality. It will take someone really incredible for me to open my heart. There is no way a far-left liberal and I would get along.

To me, the conduct of many women today is shocking, as they have no boundaries in their behavior. I'm not looking for great physical beauty; those types have proved to be nothing but trouble. I need a woman who has similar values, takes care of herself, and has a physically active lifestyle. (Shopping doesn't count as physical activity.) From what I have seen so far, that is a lot to ask for.

One woman even accused me of having sexual problems because I didn't try to take her to bed right away. It's a strange world, and meeting a decent and compatible woman is tough. There were plenty of opportunities if I wanted only shallow, physical hookups and booty calls, but I want more. The physical desire to just go out and get laid can be very strong, but I push those thoughts down and don't act on them.

I didn't go out with a lot of women; my prescreening ruled the vast majority out. I looked at women with a very critical eye—probably way too critical and overly picky. I always found some character flaw with the few women I went out with. I felt these little flaws would cause problems in the future. I never wanted to pursue anything after a second or third date. Then I met Celia.

A mutual friend I knew at the gym, Alice, set us up, so the first time we met was a blind date. The first date was incredible. We talked about many things we hold dear, including our faith. Celia is a very devout Christian woman who takes her faith seriously. That was a huge plus for me. Just two days after we met, she sent me a text stating that God has good plans for me and she was hoping they included her. Wow.

Celia was the only woman in a long time who had been able to get through my defenses and touch my heart. We had many talks about doing things in the future, including deepening our faith walk together. She ran, mountain and road biked, and swam. We went mountain biking, and she kicked my butt. I modified my workout routine to increase my cardiovascular endurance to try and keep up with her. I'd always had a problem finding a woman who could keep up with me, and now I had to push myself to keep up with her. That was another great quality I admired in her.

People I knew said I had that glow of happiness back.

Spending time with Celia made me realize how much financial devastation Jess had caused. Celia lives in a beautiful house, but when I came back to my home, it was a harsh reminder of what had been taken from me. The house I'm in now was only supposed to be my starter home. It needs a lot of work that I can't afford to pay for.

Then disaster struck. We took a road trip, and the next day, she was very distant when we talked on the phone. After the call ended, I had a bad feeling and called her right back. I asked why she'd been so distant, and she said something to the effect that she was scared by how quickly our relationship had become close. I'm not sure exactly what she said due to the turmoil I was experiencing. I asked to meet and get everything out in the open, but she was busy. She told me we could set a day later in the week to meet once she checked her schedule, but she didn't follow up right away.

A couple of days later, she texted me, and we set a time to meet. But then she had to cancel due to a family situation. I wondered if the situation was real or if she didn't want to face me. She called and texted me a couple of times about wanting to talk on the phone. I called her back, and it was a very short conversation.

She claimed that she didn't feel the way I did and wanted to be only friends. I was stunned. After everything she had said before, this was a sharp 180-degree turn. I told her that with everything she had told me about how she felt, this didn't make sense. Why the sudden change? I was dumbfounded. She would not give me a straight answer. She went on about being friends, but I cut her off and said no. I could not be just friends. Her core being and inner beauty were too seductive to me. It was either all or nothing with her; there was no other option.

My voice was trembling and cracking with hurt, and then I told her, "This is good-bye, Celia." When she continued talking, I hung up. I've been around long enough to know that the let's-just-be-friends situation never works.

I spoke with my sister the day after being dumped, and Jane was upset over what had happened. She knew how happy I had been. I spoke openly about being fifty-six years old with no family of my own, no children, and no woman to love. Jane said how unfair it was for all this to happen to me while she saw so many other horrible and undeserving people getting everything I should have had. Jane was coming to Michigan in three weeks to visit the family, and she had been really looking forward to meeting Celia. She was disappointed that was not going to happen.

I did a stupid thing shortly after being dumped. Celia knew I was writing this book, and I added a bunch of rambling about how I felt about her in this last chapter. I mailed it to her. Two weeks later I reread what I had written, and it sounded pathetic and weepy.

Damn, that had been a huge mistake. Here is a hint: Never send any written correspondence to a woman when you are an emotional wreck. Especially after not being able to sleep and writing from eleven at night to four in the morning. The words you write are not really who you are; they're just the heat of the moment, when emotions are raging. I deleted most of what I wrote about her for the final revision of this book.

I went from being elated with life when I was with Celia to feeling sadness mixed with a bit of resentment with her gone. I also was angry at myself for opening up and trusting only to get hurt again; but I kept pushing on and did what it took to get happiness back in my life. No way am I ever going to sit around feeling sorry for myself. I have to remain aware of the blessings I have, not what I don't have. There is so much to live for, and I will take advantage of all life has to offer. It took a while to get over Celia, but I did.

A month after breaking up with Celia, I met a woman, chatted with her a couple of times, and was going to ask her out. She had moved here from

England. I could tell she was interested, but I had some suspicions. Then I asked her, "Are you married?"

She hesitated, looked down, and said yes.

The first thought that entered my mind was, *Cheater*.

She did not have a ring on and had never mentioned anything about having a husband. That confirmed my suspicions, and it sure seems that integrity is lost among many people today. I never spoke with her again and kept clear of any emotional entanglements with women for a while.

In conclusion, when I pay the final spousal support payment to Jess on May 15, 2020, I will cut all ties and communication with her. I'll effectively get an $1,800 per month raise. That sure will be nice. She recently moved to Alabama, so hopefully I won't have the uncomfortable experience of meeting her again here in Michigan. I have forgiven her, but don't trust her and don't want her in any part of my life.

Be very careful whom you marry. I don't want anyone to experience what happened to me. Proverbs 31:10-12 states, "A wife of noble character who can find? She is worth far more than rubies. Her husband has full confidence in her and lacks nothing of value. She brings him good, not harm, all the days of her life."

On the flip side, Proverbs 21:19 states, "Better to live in a desert than with a quarrelsome and nagging wife."

I know the harsh reality of the flip side to be true from firsthand experience.

www.ingramcontent.com/pod-product-compliance
Lightning Source LLC
Chambersburg PA
CBHW070723160426
43192CB00009B/1293